\

Memoirs of a Suburban Medium

Memoirs of a

Suburban Medium

Kerrie Jean Erwin

First published in 2011 in Australia by White Feather Publishing

National Library of Australia Cataloguing-in-Publication entry

Author:	Erwin, Kerrie Jean.
Title:	Memoirs of a suburban medium/ Kerrie Jean Erwin.
ISBN:	9780980715217 (pbk.)
Subjects:	Erwin, Kerrie-Jean. Mediums—Biography. Spiritualists—Biography. Spiritualism—Case studies.

Dewey Number: 133.91092

Distribution in Australia and New Zealand: Dennis Jones & Associates, Unit 1, 10 Melrich Road, Bayswater, Victoria 3153; www.dennisjones.com.au +61 03 9762 9100

Project Management and design Best Legenz www.bestlegenz.com.au
Printed in Australia by McPherson's Printing Group

Disclaimer
Whilst this book is very loosely based on my own experiences, the characters are purely fictitious. Any resemblance to any person, living or dead, is purely coincidental.

This book is dedicated to all my wonderful loving friends and family. It is also a tribute to all the people I have met along the way who have inspired me to believe in following my dreams and living my life to the fullest. I truly believe that now is the time on the planet to really know and love ourselves as souls so we can all move forward with the changing energy Mother Earth is now experiencing. As the energy on the planet moves, towards the new earth, so will we all, as souls through our love to one another and ourselves.

It is also about my life's work and about my experiences to date and the lessons I have learnt. There may be others who have their own experiences, and that is their truth. It is not my intention to think I know it all because that would be incorrect. I "only" see myself as only a student of spirit who is continually growing and learning in the vast consciousness of all that is.

I also thank the Great Spirit for giving me the lessons I needed to learn through people I have met, who taught me about forgiveness and compassion. I would also like to thank my own loving guides and the master Jesus who has always been in my heart ever since I can remember.

I ask for healing and send love, light and peace to every living soul on the planet and to our loved ones who have passed over to the other side and who are still with us eternally in spirit, connected to our love that never dies.

Blessings to one and all …

I would also like to send thanks to my own beloved family, Kathryn Baker for her inspiring artwork with my guides, and all the interesting friends and teachers along the way who have all taught me to believe in myself and my gift and the lesson of love and forgiveness, which is sometimes not easy to learn.

Contents

Introduction

"You need to go back out into the workforce and get a job," said the little spirit woman, standing next to my client in my office one sunny day. "There is nothing you can do for him," she said. "I will help him, don't worry. Go and start your life again. You need to live again and your children need you."

From her chair on the opposite side of the table my client Vanessa just stared at me in silence, not knowing what to say. Tears of grief and sadness started to fill her eyes as she nodded in agreement.

Vanessa was going through one of the worst periods in her life. Her husband and soul mate had just been diagnosed with liver cancer and was given no hope. He was labelled not to be resuscitated; the doctor said there was nothing more he could do so now it was just left up to my client and her children to pick up the pieces.

The lady in spirit, who had once lived in Hong Kong, went on to say what a good wife my client had been to her son and it wasn't her fault that she had not noticed how sick her husband really was until it was far too late.

Vanessa was amazed at how much the spirit woman knew about her life and that of her family. She could not believe her ears, as she had met her husband's mother only once, almost 20 years ago. How was it was possible that her mother-in-law, who had passed over so many years ago, knew so much about her life and what was going on? She seemed to know all about the terrible tragedy that was taking place in the family she had left behind. It was almost as if she was still alive and living in the same house.

I explained to my client that this is often the case with spirit. There are no secrets in the afterlife. Spirit is always around us as our loved ones who have crossed over to the other side always live through our love, which is eternal. Spirit always knows what is going on and they always know what we are up to. They sometimes will leave no stone unturned until they are able to get to us and give us a message.

"Please don't blame yourself," I said. "Your husband loves you very much and is just trying to put on a brave face. I feel he is actually terrified, but his mother has come in now in spirit and will help prepare him for his journey over to the other side," I continued softly, holding her hand and trying to comfort her as tears welled up in my eyes.

Nothing in our lives ever prepares us for death. It is extremely sad to see people who are just about to lose a loved one going through so much pain. When someone we love dies in our life, it is time of reflection about our immortality as souls.

It teaches us to open up our hearts and love and forgive everyone in our life who is around us, and who we have ever loved. This work brings up the spirit of hope, the spirit of strength and the spirit of love.

Even though our souls live on forever, as life is eternal, the sad part is when we lose a loved one in reality we are not going to see them anymore, at least not in this lifetime anyway. That is the part that breaks our hearts.

"Will I ever see him again when he is dead?" she cried, wiping her eyes.

"When it is your turn to pass over, you will return to your soul group and see him again. You have probably lived together in many lives before that is why your love is so strong," I said.

"What will happen to him when he dies?" she asked, crying softly, blowing her nose and staring blankly into mid-air.

"His guide will come and take him over to the other side where he will be joined with all his loved ones, who have already made the journey," I told her. "His mother will join his guide as well. I feel this only because she is here today to make contact with you. It seems he has a lot of spirit people around his energy already, all waiting for him when he returns home to spirit."

Holding her hand I went on. "He will then be taken over to the spirit hospital for healing. All his loved ones will be waiting for him to welcome him home."

"Will I ever see him again?" she repeated.

"You have a long life ahead of you as you are so young," I answered, feeling the energy starting to drop and the session beginning to come to an end.

"I wouldn't be surprised if you are around till well into your 80s. When it is your time your husband will be waiting for you, but in the meantime a bit of counselling will help you as well."

"What if I have another husband after him?" she smiled cheekily, sitting upright and dabbing her wet eyes.

"I am sure then you will all get on really well together and have lots to talk about," I smiled, relieved that she was beginning to come to terms with her husband's impending death. All I could think of was the very painful journey ahead of her. It would be exhausting and she would really have to dig deep for the strength to help her cope. She was lucky she had an understanding daughter who was willing to help her with the process.

"Thank you for everything, I feel stronger now and I know what to do," she said.

"Goodbye and all the best," I smiled as I hugged her farewell, closing the door behind her with a sigh.

Losing a child, loved one or your soul mate, in my opinion, is one of the hardest and saddest things in life to go through. We all, in the end, have to go through it whether we like it or not. It is never easy for anyone, but if you believe in the afterlife it does make it a lot easier.

Psychic mediumship or connecting to the other side for proof of survival is a very humbling experience, and a large part of the work I do. It not only requires a great deal of responsibility but it is also very taxing on the emotional and physical bodies. One needs to be fit to do the work as it can be very draining and the more you do it the more sensitive you become. I always ask to work with love and spirit, but I still get tired as it takes a lot of my energy to make a connection.

It is also extremely important to set up boundaries because some people, if you allow them, will constantly ring you and ask you questions you have already answered in a session. To do this very important work, still frowned upon by some who are essentially sceptical or critical because of ignorance, is incredibly rewarding.

Receiving survival evidence, or what we call "proof of survival", is one of the best type of healings. It allows the client to move on as they understand that in reality there is no death of the soul.

To do this work, the medium requires a vast amount of energy to raise their vibration to receive a link from spirit because they are actually contacting a loved one on the other side, which is in another dimension. The spirit also has to use a lot of energy, and some spirits are easier to contact than others. I can't tell you why this is so, it just is.

Previous publications

*Enjoy the exploits of the energetic and playful
spirits from the kingdom of Fair-Light*

Magical Tales of the Forest is for the young
and the young at heart. The characters
come to life and dance across the page
with joy and delight in the three tales.

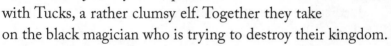

Tale one involves the elemental spirits
of our world and the struggle between
the forces of light and darkness. The
highly spirited Aystanna, the new fairy
princess of the kingdom of Fair-Light,
sets off on a journey of empowerment
with Tucks, a rather clumsy elf. Together they take
on the black magician who is trying to destroy their kingdom.

The Story of Llessur is about the male archetype learning
about boundaries and responsibilities. Llessur, a young and
naughty goblin, whose mischievous spells come to an end when
he is caught red-handed by the guardian of the forest who
happens to be a powerful but beautiful white witch.

The third tale is about an indigo child, Egil Briemmier, who
was born different and doesn't fit in, not unusual in today's
society. Dejected, he decides to run away to find a world in which
he feels he belongs. This takes him on a journey of discovery and
he meets Werdna the Great. The wise wizard helps Egil discover
who he really is.

THE TEN INDIAN COMMANDMENTS

Treat the Earth and all that dwell thereon with respect.
Remain close to the Great Spirit.
Show great respect for your fellow beings.
Work together for the benefit of all mankind.
Give assistance and kindness wherever needed.
Do what you know to be right.
Look after the wellbeing of mind and body.
Dedicate a share of your efforts to the greater good.
Be truthful and honest at all times.
Take full responsibility for your actions.

Author unknown

Part One

The Early Years

Growing up

The wise devotee should be cautious, rather than afraid. He should cultivate a courageous spirit, without rashly exposing himself to conditions that may arouse apprehension.

Paramahansa Yoganandas

Growing up on the south coast was every young person's dream come true. My family was blessed because we were surrounded by nature and everything it had to offer. To live so close to the ocean and all the natural elements is paradise to me. After all, don't they say the best things in life are free?

My family home is by the sea, so growing up as a kid I could hear the waves in the distance pounding on the beach. It was so soothing and relaxing and would help me sleep, especially when I was being woken by spirit people in the dead of the night. On really hot balmy summer evenings, our home was like a hothouse so I would sit with my family on the front porch and wait for the welcome southerly winds to sweep across the ocean and cool everything down, including us.

We were always so relieved and appreciative when the southerly came and we sighed with relief as it quickly took down the temperature a few degrees. We would wait in anticipation and it was always an incredible sight to see it make its way towards us. All the heat from the day would be blown away from where it came, and it would now be possible to have a good night's sleep.

When I finally left the church at the age of 14, my life changed in a dramatic way. Ever since I attended Sunday school, my only real friends were the other children at the church. We were like a small family who met once a week to sing beautiful songs together and listen to wonderful bible stories. However, fate had another path for me because this soon came to an abrupt end when a visiting evangelist came along one day to take the place of our normal minister, who was sick. When I told her about my special gift of seeing spirit, she didn't believe me. Instead, she told me I had the devil in me and I was to leave the small congregation at once and never come back as I was not welcome anymore.

Horrified, my perfect world as I had known it suddenly blew up in my face and everything I had grown to love and knew so well came to an end. To be honest, I found this experience extremely hurtful but it did not surprise me at all, as most people I've ever confided in have behaved the same way.

Over the years as a child I had become quite used to people either laughing at me or calling me horrible names whenever I opened up or told anyone about my experiences. Being called horrible names like "freak" or "freak head" behind my back, or to my face, was common for me. I used to feel a whole range of emotions and it made it hard for me to trust anyone. When you are different and stand out from the crowd it can be a very lonely life. Most people around you have absolutely no understanding of those that are different and in their ignorance can be cruel and judgemental.

Whenever I opened up and told anybody about my world and my experiences, I would often be ridiculed. I soon learnt that it was best for everyone concerned for me to say simply nothing about my ghostly experiences and just carry on like everyone else around me, and try to fit in. I just wanted to be normal and have a life where people liked me so I learnt to keep my paranormal experiences a secret. Even now I worry about this and, in the past, went to great lengths to get people to like me. As I am getting older I am not so insecure because I have learnt to love myself. And I know I cannot please everyone.

I also learnt at an early age to never hold grudges and just go with the flow. It took me a while to learn that but I'm glad I did. My mother always used to say, "Just let it go because holding on to negative emotions makes you bitter and sick." Negative energy or thoughts also block the natural flow of your energy and chakras and I believe it is the root cause of much disease in the body.

Not everyone has my ability to sense things, so who could blame the evangelist for not understanding my perception of the world, as it is like living in two worlds. Most people have absolutely no idea of spirit and what it can teach you or of the afterlife and what goes on there. It is truly a wonderful thing that more and more beautiful souls are coming out and teaching others in society about spirit. Because of this, more and more people are starting to empower themselves and what I call "opening up" and discovering aspects about themselves they could once only dream about. When we learn to open our minds to our spiritual awakening we soon learn that the love of spirit is always with us and we really are immortal souls.

Life in general is about lessons and learning. Another thing to remember is that just because people say they are spiritual does not mean that they are. Action speaks louder than words. Always listen to your own guidance and god-blessed intuition and judge for yourself. Nobody is perfect but you would think that these so-called spiritual people would know better as they are aware of what they are doing, so when they do not practise what they preach it can be very confusing.

Being very open and naive, I had thought this evangelist would give me some clarity and perhaps some advice and guidance on what was going on in my life. I saw this person, because she said she was a minister, as someone I could trust, a teacher who could finally explain things to me about the type of phenomena that I was experiencing. Back then, there was nobody around me who knew anything about the paranormal and what goes on in the spirit life.

It has been one of my life lessons that people are not often who they say they are. As for my own family, I had opened up and told my parents in the past what I was experiencing, but they had no idea what I was going on about. They just put it down to me being over-sensitive as a child who had an incredible imagination and was highly strung.

My parents were also getting sick of me waking them up in the middle of the night and hysterically running into their bedroom and forcing myself into their bed. After constant fights, I was finally allowed to keep a light on in the middle of the night which, funnily enough, acted as a deterrent to unwelcome spirit visitors.

When I was told that I was not welcome at Sunday school anymore, I said goodbye to my old friends, jumped on the donkey with Jesus in my heart and headed to the only place that I loved, the beach.

Beach days

It was a culture shock for me when I arrived at the beach, as most people I met were extremely different from anybody I had ever come across, except for the bikie girls up the road who I was not allowed to have anything to do with. I was a young independent teenager and everyone I met had their own set of rules and just lived in accordance to their own ideologies. My new friends were colourful and had fewer constraints in the way they saw things. They lived their own life, which was simple and carefree.

Nobody ever judged you and you were accepted just the way you were. As long as I didn't say too much, I could just disappear and blend in without too many difficulties. Nobody ever really cared about what you talked about because they were too busy going through their own stuff and just wanted to have fun. It was a good place to just lighten up and just be. When I wasn't riding the waves, I would spend long days going on bush walks in the huge dunes that surrounded the beach. The dunes were a lot of fun and my friends and I would often slide down them on pieces of cardboard I got from my parent's place.

I developed a much-loved hobby of collecting various shells, fossils and rocks, which were all different shapes and colours. I still do this today and have a vast collection from all over the world. As time passed, it didn't take me long to settle in and I was glad that I had moved on and found a new way of life. My perception of the church had changed and I no longer missed my old friends. I was older and wiser, as well, but was becoming increasingly restless and couldn't wait to leave school so I could travel and see the world. But for now, I couldn't wait to get up in the morning before the sun and go surfing.

On the weekends, my friends and I would gather in a small group and spend long lazy days down the beach from dawn till dusk. We would set up a small camp for the day, apply lots of baby oil to our skin and lie in the sun until we cooked, listening to rock music playing on our transistor radios. We would all lie on big fluffy beach towels, munch on fried food all day and drink endless cans of Coke.

The logic behind the sunbaking was that the browner and more tanned you were, the better you would look. Nobody in those days wanted to look white as it was very unfashionable and rather ugly, but I had red hair and freckled skin. No matter how hard I tried, I never really got a tan because the hundreds of freckles I had all over my skin would just blend in all together and become even bigger and darker. Looking back, I realise I must have been looked after by spirit because I was lucky I did not end up with a skin disease or a melanoma.

I spent most of my time sitting under an umbrella, as the sun was too harsh for my skin and it went only one colour, red. Hungry annoying seagulls flew in circles over us for hours, looking for food and dropping dreadful watery bombs. I could never understand why the birds were always so hungry because no matter how much food you gave them they still wanted more.

Everybody I met in those days was so different from my closeted days at the church. All highly spirited individuals, they didn't give a damn what other people might think of them. They taught me not to take life so seriously and just go with the flow. It was a far cry from the church days, where everybody pretended to be really kind and spiritual in the congregation but gossiped rudely about each other the minute they got off their seats and stepped out the doors. I suppose most places where people congregate would be the same. Is it just human nature to talk offensively about people when they can't defend themselves? I wonder.

The beach was different as it was full of young free spirits just enjoying everything the beach had to offer. It was a sub-culture where we could just hang out and do whatever we wanted without judgement or restriction. Most people in those days just kept to themselves and didn't worry about what anybody else was doing. In fact, everyone seemed so detached as if they didn't have a worry in the world.

If you were living in paradise why would you have any problems anyway? I wish I had known what they were on because I was always extremely uptight until I learnt to meditate years later. There were all types of drugs around, which is common in such places. Most people I knew wanted to try them at least once but I quickly learnt, because of my sensitivity to most things, drugs were not good for my energy.

Some of my friends became hooked and all they did then was to wait for their next fix. This was sad to see, but it was a path they chose. I always had plans to go places and do things, so no way was I going to be swept up in a drug-crazed world where people never did anything with their lives. I never had any interest in such things because I had so many plans and dreams I wanted to achieve. The more psychic and sensitive you are, the more open you become to anything toxic. It can really knock you around and take you ages to get over. The only thing I ever got out of these substances was an incredible depression that would last for days. I just preferred to stay straight and get high on nature and the freedom my new life gave me.

Harry the Animal Tamer

There was one particular boy, Harry, who took it upon himself to be in charge of who was allowed to be in the gang. He was known as Harry the Animal Tamer, because everywhere he went a large entourage of stray animals—dogs, cats, and even birds followed. He seemed to understand their language and they obeyed his every command whenever he gave an order. There were always about seven or eight dogs, barking madly at his heels for his attention and making a hell of a racket. Even before he arrived you could hear him coming as the barking was so loud.

Harry was well-respected on the beach, with many holding him in high esteem because he was one of the best surfers on the south coast. He would always be out in the water riding his surfboard. Nobody was ever allowed to cross him or say a bad word as he reigned supreme as the king of the beach. I found out later that he came from a broken home and often slept at the beach when things became really bad there. His situation was so difficult that he never had the chance to finish school but ended up being a keen surfer instead.

His family were always fighting and they often kicked him out and left him to fend for himself. Most nights of his week were spent camped down the beach. Whenever this happened, we all rallied around him and stole food from home and gave it to him, so he never went without. It was just something that we did in those days and never really thought much about afterwards as we were only really kids. We never asked him how he was going, because he was extremely proud and never liked to discuss his private life. Instead of feeling sorry for himself he ended up putting all his energy into his surfing and skills on his board.

Later on in life, he showed the same determination and went back to school and achieved very high marks. So, as well as being a very competent sportsman and winning nearly every competition he went in, he was also an academic and later became a very successful doctor. He was one of my first teachers. He helped me learn about moving on and just getting on with things as he made it a point never to let life's turmoil and frustration get in his way.

Years later I heard he married another doctor and became a Christian to find his peace.

Toby

Toby was a big clumsy Finnish guy and my good mate. He was a very shy, kind boy who giggled and hid behind a large head of wild and woolly brown hair that covered his burnt and reddened round face.

Toby never wanted to look you in the face when he spoke, and always walked around with his head bowed down, staring at the ground. He also was an incredible eater with an enormous appetite who could eat a loaf of bread and a few cans of baked beans within no time. He was always hungry. Whenever we went camping down the coast, I would have to hurry up and eat my share of the food or there would be nothing left in our supplies and we'd end up starving for the rest of the day.

He used to eat so much that I often wondered where he fit it all in. It would take him no time to finish off a loaf of bread and a packet of biscuits. He must have needed the energy for the duration of time he spent out in water and surf. If ever he tried to diet, or simply limit his enormous appetite, he would just end up angry and grumpy and we would all have to duck for cover from his bad moods. It used to amaze me how he often wondered why he was so big. He couldn't see it was because of all the food he consumed. Instead, he just used to put it down to genes. This may have been true on some level, as all the family was big. We are what we eat.

I have never met anyone since who could eat as much as him. Years later, when I was living overseas I heard from an acquaintance that he had moved up to Darwin and married a big, gorgeous local woman, who gave birth to seven of children.

I was told he was happy and content as fatherhood must have agreed with him. The last time anyone saw him, he looked very content and proud of all his snow-haired little ducklings gathered around his feet.

Sophie

A newcomer to my group of beach friends was Sophie, who I met after she had moved to Sydney to study nursing. A few years older than me, she was a delightful girl with long thick red hair that came all the way to her waist. Sophie was originally from the south coast and had grown up a few suburbs away from where I lived with my family.

Once she had moved to Sydney, and got her driving licence at seventeen, she bought a very fast little red sports car and drove it down the coast on her days off from the hospital. She loved the south coast as much as all of us and every spare moment she would visit her family and catch up with all her old friends and new beach friends.

Being a coasty girl at heart, living in Sydney was not only overwhelming but extremely stressful and poor Sophie was always homesick and restless. She hated the big smoke and the concrete jungle but she also missed her mates. To Sophie, we were family and there was no going back from there.

Our group may have been slightly dysfunctional with our secrets and hidden pasts but we all banded together to help each other and were firm friends. None of us had any airs and graces or pretended to be anyone else other than who we were. We stuck together and never talked behind anyone's back. If we had something to say, we would say it to the person and nobody else.

Sophie used to say that you can move away and live anywhere in the world but at the end of the day you never forget your roots, as that's where you learn your values in life. She was outspoken and said exactly what she thought, and was as adventurous as the rest of us, with plenty of charisma and charm. You always knew when she was around by either her loud high-pitched laugh or the roar of her car as she made her way down to the beach. As soon as she arrived, she had an audience. When she pulled up by the car park, and jumped out of the car shaking her wild red hair, everyone would rush over and gather around her.

All the local guys, who usually kept to themselves, would run over whistling and laughing, welcoming her as they checked out her awesome car. It was easy for everyone to like her as she was such an extrovert with oodles of confidence and wit. She could hold a conversation with almost anyone she came across and I am sure she would have been able to talk underwater without a problem.

Once the car was safely parked and she had said all her hellos to the local boys, she would race down the steep grassy escarpment of the hill to where we were sitting, squealing and giggling, and shouting a greeting to anyone who came across her path. She was always so excited to come back to her old stomping grounds and couldn't wait to catch up with all the local gossip. From the way she went on, it seemed as if she had been away for years instead of a couple of weeks. We were always delighted to see her enthusiastic face and couldn't wait to give her a big hug and welcome her back into our small community of friends. In those days friendships were special, and we stayed together no matter what. There wasn't one person on the beach who didn't love Sophie. We thought she was a goddess and all looked forward to her brief overnight visits, mostly on weekends.

We also looked forward to driving around in her car and would squash in, clutching each other for dear life as she tirelessly ferried us around at top speed to wherever we wanted to go. Even though we would squash in as many as possible, we had to take turns and, because there was so many of us, it would take up most of her day. It was all very innocent and tremendous fun for us checking out all the beaches and different guys, but the burn marks from the screeching tyres were another story. No one bothered to change, we just jumped in wearing only a pair of skimpy bikinis, our trade mark.

One thing that always puzzled me though was the fact that I never once saw Sophie go in the water for a swim, even on the hottest of days. She never surfed either, which was rather odd as most of us were mad surfers and crazy mermaids who never spent much time out of the sea.

The other girls and I would surf from dawn to dusk and hardly ever missed out on a wave. Once we had entered the mystical sanctuary of Mother Sea, we would literally forget everything in "our" life as nothing else seemed important and time always seemed to stand still. The sea's divine magic can only be described as a soothing tonic to the worries of the world and was like a life force to me, as it was always so refreshing and made me feel on top of the world.

Once I entered the water, I was one with the elemental energy of nature and the pulsating rhythmic forces that healed and caressed all scars and wounds from deep within. Like a small child from I would feel happy and carefree way down deep in my soul. The beautiful realm of the sea remains a healing experience for me, as it always washes away any problems or worries I have picked up and carried in my psyche. For hours afterwards I feel centred, calm and re-energised. I still carry happy memories from my days as a mermaid and draw on them whenever I am feeling low.

No matter how enticing or good the surf was on the day, Sophie would never want to go into the water and made it a point to ignore you, or tell you off, if you ever asked her to come in. Even on the hottest of days she would just lay spreadeagled in the sand, basking in the sun like Cleopatra on her multi-coloured beach towel.

She would lay all day and chain smoke, a cigarette hanging out of the side of her mouth and sipping Coke from a can. No matter how hot the day was, she was always carefully covered from head to foot in a long-sleeved shirt and blue faded jeans. Whenever anyone would ask her to join them in the water, she would just laugh hoarsely and berate them for asking her in the first place. Her excuse was always the same. As far as she was concerned she was a fast car chick, and the salt from the water would tarnish that image.

Once she had laid down the law, none of us ever said anything and it was never discussed again.

What Sophie said gave me a funny feeling as I knew it wasn't true. I always kept my feelings to myself as not to embarrass her, or destroy the tough, cool image she had given herself and how others saw her in their eyes. Life is often an illusion and often people pretend to be someone else just to fit in. Even if I wanted to believe her I couldn't, as once I am close to someone I am always able to sense things about the person even if I don't want to.

My intuition told me that what she was saying was just a cover-up for something "dark" she had hidden because, even though she was always laughing and telling jokes, I could feel a deep sadness within her. I wasn't sure what it was, but I knew in time that I would find out as people you love can't hide the truth forever. She was such a funny character, ordering us around affectionately and telling us what to do like a sergeant major and pretending to be really tough.

Some of the names she would call us were "mad stinking surfie chicks" and "warrior whores from the sea", although quite vulgar were really funny too and made me laugh. I often wondered where she got those names from. Looking back, I see that she used to mask her emotions with all her jokes and candid comments.

One day when we were finally alone, my curiosity got the better of me and I took a deep breath and dug deep for some courage and asked her straight out why she never went in the water. Without missing a beat, I decided to be really honest and opened up and told her all about my stuff, and my gift of knowing things before they happened and my conversations with spirit people.

After a few minutes she turned and looked me square in the face. With a serious look on her face and a cigarette hanging out from the side of her mouth, she just looked me up and down as if she was thinking about what she wanted to say next. I was a bit taken aback at first, as I had never seen her so serious before.

After a rather long awkward pause, she began to speak to me in a really soft voice, like a child, as if her thoughts were now miles away and in another place. As she spoke, something in her seemed to lift and her whole expression changed as she began to open up. It was one of those moments in life that you never forget. In great detail, she began to share and tell me of the terrible tragedy that had happened to her in her early life. Tears filled my eyes and I found it really hard not to break down and cry but I knew that she needed me to listen. As she spoke, she seemed to be relieved that she could share her secret with someone.

I was her silent witness and I felt on some level it was an enormous honour for her to pour out her heart. Sophie told me she had been in a serious car accident and nearly been killed when she was small. Apparently she had been knocked unconscious in the accident so it was just about impossible to remember anything at all. She was so young at the time that the only thing she could remember was waking intermittently in the arms of a stranger who was dressed in a uniform.

She also remembered being wrapped in blanket, her body aching all over with incredible pain. Even though she had this excruciating burning pain she kept feeling an overwhelming sense that everything would be all right. She could also hear a voice, which was herself screaming and yelling, but it was as if the voice was coming from somebody else. It was almost as if she felt herself floating above her body and was watching the whole scene like it was a movie.

Everything around her was incredibly bright and the brightness soon began to envelop her whole body. The only thing which was really annoying was the incredible sound of a loud whirling noise that seemed to be going around and around inside her head.

She was later told that she was rescued just in time and pulled from the burning wreckage before it blew up in flames.

It was a miracle that she had survived. The debris had flown all over the road and lay scattered around. Bits and pieces of her father were also scattered everywhere. It was one of the worst accidents ever on the south coast. If she hadn't have been safely pulled from the back of the car, she would have ended up the same as her father. God was on her side that day.

Her father did not escape the carnage, and was killed instantly when the car he was driving hit a tree. His body was seen slumped on top of the bonnet before the car exploded. The police told Sophie's family that he was killed instantly and would not have felt a thing.

At least she knew her father never suffered which was one redeeming thing. But the grief she carried for years never really went away and was especially bad when she tried to go to sleep. It haunted her for years and it wasn't until she got into her teens that she could sleep without a light on.

Lifting up her shirt, she showed me her terrible disfigurement and the ugly, deep scars that were etched and intertwined all over her badly burnt body. The scars were everywhere, running down the back of her neck, all over her back and chest to even all over her arms. She had more down her legs as well, but I begged her jokingly not to show me as I had seen enough. I nearly fell over backwards with shock and felt sick and wanted to cry when I saw the extent of the disfigurement. I managed to pull myself together and pretend that it didn't bother me in the slightest.

I must have been really convincing, or she must have been way off in another place as she didn't seem to notice how affected I really was. All I could think of was how lucky she was that the flames hadn't burnt her beautiful face that was wise beyond her years.

How she survived from the fatal accident was a miracle because most people with her extent of burns would never have survived. I nearly gasped in horror when she then pulled off her wig, to show me her burnt head and scars on the back of her neck.

Never in a million years would I have guessed her beautiful hair was actually a wig. All she had on her head were tiny soft patches of thin hair in clumps. The rest of her head was shiny and covered in scars.

Choking back tears, I stumbled to the ground as if I had a stake in my heart and sat speechless and in silence, a million thoughts rushing through my head. I felt numb with shock and hot tears ran down my face. Wiping my tears I took a deep breath and continued listening to her, not knowing what to say. Even though she told me she felt lucky to be alive, the worst was yet to come because afterwards she had to endure years and years of painful operations and countless trips into hospitals for operations and procedures to mend her burnt and broken body. It was no wonder she had wanted to be a nurse because hospitals had become her second home.

I began to understand Sophie much better after our talk. She was always chatting about her father and the sports cars he had when she was younger, but I hadn't realised that he was dead and she had been subjected to so much pain and stress at such an early age. It made me realise that we all have our secrets in life and often there is always so much more than what people project or actually tell you. Often when you dig deeper there is so much more.

After our discussion, I learnt so much more about my good friend. For a start, I realised why she constantly talked about fast cars as it was obvious to me that Sophie's father was still an integral part of her life. I also understood how important it must have been for her to own a sports car as well. It was probably her way of keeping her father's legacy alive in her own mind after the fatal accident that not only destroyed most of Sophie's body, but must have ripped the whole family apart. It was no wonder that she spoke about him all the time when we drove around in her car. She was always making reference to his old Ferrari and other cars he had in his garage.

Later, whenever we were alone she would also make comments in our conversations about the vivid dreams she often had about her father. She was convinced he was always around her, guiding her in her daily life. If she had an angel to watch over her, it was definitely her father. Whenever I had a go at her about showing off and her speeding in her sports car, she would simply answer that her father was looking after her and she had nothing to worry about.

She later made me promise and make an oath that I would never tell a single person about her secret past. That made me realise we all have hidden things that we did not want others to know about. To look at her and be in her company no one would ever know the hidden tragedy that lay beneath her jovial mask that she shared with the world. Not only was she able to hide the terrible burns under her clothes, she was also an expert at covering up her real feelings with her big personality and crazy, stupid jokes.

It was remarkable how she did it as she always had us in stitches with her funny comments and remarks on people's problems and life. She was a born comic, the life of the party, and there was not one person who could succeed her because she never missed a beat.

Life was always a party when she was around. I always felt her good humour was Sophie's saving grace and that it really kept her going. She must have realised at a very early age that she had been given another chance, was extremely lucky to be alive and was going to make the most of it no matter what. As far as she was concerned she was blessed and happy to have the chance to live. She may have had a few disabilities but she certainly learnt to cover them up well.

All she could talk about was to travel the world and experience everything and anything that came her way and was part of her journey. We used to sit and chat for ages about all our dreams we had collected over the years. We were so young and naive, and wanted to do so much with our lives. We even made a pact to meet up one day, somewhere different and in a foreign land. We decided we wouldn't make any plans but just wait and see what happened.

As we were both planning to be nurses, we knew this would be possible as we both wanted to go and live overseas to experience as much as we could and become other people. Anything was better than the south coast as it was like living in the country and everyone thought they knew everything about you and your business. We felt so isolated and trapped from the rest of the world and were dying for new experiences. We both had the same philosophies in life and ideas and there was just too much to do with places to go and people to meet.

Sophie was not only one of the first real friends I had ever met, she was also one of the bravest people I had ever known, a real survivor. Not once did I ever hear her complain or feel sorry for herself, something I really admired. Other people these days can whinge about all their so-called problems that are trivial compared to what she put up with from such an early age. She was the type of person who just got on with it and was too proud and independent to ever want energy or sympathy from anyone.

Nothing in my life and what I had gone through with my own confusion with being able to see dead people in the middle of the night could ever compare to the horror she had experienced in her short life. We both knew that sometimes it is best to say nothing to anyone about your personal business as people can sometimes take great delight in ridiculing others to make themselves feel better. As I said, that's human nature.

As fate would have it, about ten years later, I bumped into my good friend Sophie again on a cold winter's day at Central London railway station, a madhouse of disorder and frenzy at the best of times.

I had just arrived from a horrendously long trip from Norway and felt jet lagged. As my boyfriend and I got off the train we could not believe our bad luck to see a frustrated crowd of bustling people in front of us, all lining up and trying to get out off the platform and into the station. Trains seemed to be pulling up from everywhere at once, with people jumping off and everywhere was chaos and disorder.

By the time we got off our train, we were trapped with hundreds of people in a long line that seemed to be going nowhere. Everyone around us was pushing and shoving, just wanting to get out, an angry sea of fed-up, dishevelled people lined up like cattle. I was so tired and I could only think about having something nice to eat, washing my hair and soaking in a welcoming long hot bath.

Not wanting to be there, I mustn't have been paying much attention to where I was going, because suddenly I slipped head first over some woman's big foot that seemed to appear out of nowhere. As I hit the hard cold concrete that nearly rendered me unconscious I looked around, bewildered, to see what had happened.

I must have been in a state of shock as I had no idea what was going on as I lost all concept of time and place and was beginning to feel tremendous pain in the back of my head and lower back. Both my hands were bleeding and I had scratches all over my palms, which I must have used to break the fall. Everything had happened so fast it was hard to understand what was going on.

As I lay on the ground not knowing what to do next, a strange woman from the crowd rushed over to my side and stared down at me. It was like time stopped and we were frozen in that moment. Her face seemed vaguely familiar and I kept feeling that I must have known her from somewhere, but it was all so confusing. My head kept aching and I began to feel numb all over. All I could think of was to get out of there and into a nice warm bed.

Everybody else around us just stopped what they were doing and just stared down at me. I must have looked a sight as I lay sprawled helpless on the ground. My bass guitar was lying on top of me and my small suitcase had opened and all my things were scattered everywhere. Strangers were picking up my clothes and underwear and bringing them back to where I lay asking me if I was OK.

Pulling me slowly up, my boyfriend gently helped me to my feet. Thanking him, I began to dust myself down and tried taking a few steps to get my balance. The woman standing next to me now began to apologise profusely, saying over and over again that she was sorry. At first I didn't recognise her until she started talking excitedly at the top of her voice in a loud, high-pitched Australian accent.

Dumbfounded, I stopped what I was doing and looked up at the woman. Strangely, she looked very familiar so I took closer look and stared into her face. Then suddenly, to my utter astonishment it dawned on me that this woman was none other than Sophie, my old mate from the beach. I could not believe my eyes. I had not seen her in years and that lifetime where we once knew each other seemed so long ago and so far away.

"Oh my God, is that you Sophie ... From the old beach days?" I yelled at the top of my lungs. Confused and overwhelmed, I could not believe my eyes and thought I was in a dream. Even the pain that had filled my body seemed to suddenly disappear. Of all the places in the whole world, I could not get over where I caught up with her again. It was almost too good to be true! Without missing a beat, I gave her hearty hello.

"Thanks very much old friend," I said. "Why don't you try and kill me next time?" I laughed until I almost choked. "Nice to see you as well but I find all this really hard to believe," I joked, hugging her.

The chance of seeing her here was one in a million and quite a coincidence. Everything felt so surreal; I was starting to feel like I was in a dream. I always knew we would bump into each other again, but this way seemed so obscure yet really funny. Just the way it had happened was ridiculous and I thought I could not have planned it any better if I had tried.

"Err, yes, Kerrie?" she answered meekly, not knowing what to say at first but obviously processing what was going on. "Oh my God! I do not believe my eyes. I thought I had killed somebody and it ended up being you. Wow what can I say?" she laughed in her booming voice, becoming really excited.

The whole situation was plain ridiculous and to see her standing there with her hands on her hips really cracked me up. She was still the old control freak and the look on her face was priceless. Her eyes were bulging out of her head and her expression was hysterical. Without another word we both screamed out loud and roared with laughter and nearly wet our pants.

"Wow is that really you?" I continued, laughing. "Imagine meeting you here of all places."

"And look how YOU have changed," she gasped, looking me up and down. "Oh man, I don't believe it! If I hadn't tripped you up, I would never have recognised you."

It really dawned on me what she meant because I was thinking exactly the same thing. I couldn't believe it was her either, as she didn't quite match the person I had pictured in my mind and had loved so dearly so long ago. I knew she had gone to Hamburg, but I could not believe how much she'd changed. She now looked extremely right wing and quite conservative from the girl I had once remembered. I could not help but think that she must have eaten too many German sausages or something, by the looks. Her appearance had changed almost beyond the point of recognition. I could not believe my eyes and wondered to myself how it was possible she could change so much. Sophie was now a woman and dressed in the most expensive outfit I had ever seen in my life. In her place was somebody that I did not know at all.

She was wearing a neat pair of pressed pants and matching jacket and coordinated with matching shoes and handbag. Her long flowing red hair was now replaced by a short blonde bob that she wore with a thin headband and around her neck was a string of pearls and a silk scarf. I would never have recognised her in a million years.

Gone were the old blue faded jeans, colourful headbands and long baggy flowing shirts. Way back in the good old days, she dressed like a complete slob but now she looked so prim and proper. I just stared in awe.

Then it was my turn to cop it, because she must have been feeling the same, as she couldn't stop giggling hysterically and laughing and pointing at me. "Check you out, who are you now, babe?" she said. "You look like that German rock singer Nina Hagen," she laughed even louder, not able to hold in her emotions any longer. She must have been having the best laugh she had ever had in years. I didn't mind though, because I was just so over the moon and delighted to see her.

I was in a different head space too from the days I had first met Sophie and was also dressed quite differently. From head to toe I wore smooth shiny leather with a tight silver belt tied around my waist, bangles on my wrist, but no tattoo on my arm. On my feet I wore high boots and my now auburn hair was teased high on my head and worn long down my back to my waist. My face, which in the old days was always red from the sun and covered with thousands of freckles, was now heavily made-up with thick white, greasy powder. I had smudged black eyeliner drawn thickly around my eyes but now running down my face from the tears in my eyes from laughing. My lips were bright red but that was now smudged all over my face making me look like some type of clown.

Poor Sophie must have thought that I looked like the devil, and got the shock of her life. Luckily for us we both saw the funny side of it. I was no longer the shy, blond surfie girl I had been and she had changed from a fast car chick with chains into my mother. Underneath we were still the same and Sophie's great sense of humour was still there. She said she was glad I had found my artistic expression. We must have looked ridiculous to anyone watching as we screeched at each other at the top of our voices in excitement.

"Is that really little miss pink zinc Kerrie from the beach?" she screamed, slapping her sides and jumping up and down. "When I knew you, I couldn't even see your face because it was so red and covered in pale pink cream. Now look at you." She laughed with her hands on her hips.

Finally she took a long deep breath, pulled herself together, and we hugged tightly. "But you really look like bloody Nina Hagen, the punk rocker from Berlin. Oh no, I think I have wet my pants," she chuckled.

"Oh sure Sophie and you look like Doris Day," I replied. Our plan or dream, which at the time might have seemed impossible, had come to fruition. It made me think to be careful what you ask for because in the end it will happen whether you are ready for it or not. Seeing her, I felt like I was 15 again.

We decided to stay together in London to catch up for a few short days, and discovered what each other had been up to. Sophie had gone to Hamburg and I to Norway. Both of us had also married foreign men and worked in local hospitals, just as we said we would.

It was incredible how we had both stuck to our childhood plan that we made so long ago, even though we had lost contact with each other and had no idea what we were even talking about at the time. It was if our plans and dreams had taken on a life of their own and it was our destiny that we should meet again if only once and briefly.

That was the last time I saw Sophie. I still think of her occasionally and wonder what she is up to these days. As far as I know she still lives in Hamburg. We never did make plans to catch up again because that's not the way we operate. We just know that if it is meant to be, the universe will organise it.

The home front

Life at home was not good as my mother was not impressed with my new lifestyle, or friends for that matter. She saw all my good friends from the beach as nobody but uneducated beach bums, only after money and whatever they could get out of you or get their hands on. She also made it a point to complain about the way I looked and the terrible manners I seemed to have developed overnight. She tried everything in her power to remove me from this environment, and it was not long before I was marched off to deportment school to become a lady.

The first thing the school did was to change my appearance as it was said not to be appropriate for a lady to look so unruly. After much deliberation they soon cut off my beautiful long blonde hair and turned it into something ridiculous like a little tea cosy on the top of my head. By the time I had finished the fancy stupid school and got back to the beach, all my friends laughed at me as I must have looked ridiculous.

They all thought my new look was the funniest thing they had ever seen and I was the joke of the beach for months. All I wanted to do was to crawl under a rock and die as I have never been so embarrassed in all my life. Unfortunately, I had no choice but to just put up with it all as it was either face the music and be laughed at or sit at home by myself which I was not going to do. Nothing in the world was going to ruin my new-found happiness and freedom.

As soon as the sun was up and I wasn't going to school I would head down to the beach and surf to my heart's delight in the fresh and calming waters of the ever nurturing sea. Life soon became a pattern of long and lazy summer days spent lounging in the sun listening to music on the radio and eating hot potato chips with plenty of salt and tomato sauce. I could never understand people who preferred to live in cities. What did they do in their spare time, especially on hot days? Hanging out in nature under a perfect blue sky and swimming in the cool blue sea was the only place to be. How and why other people preferred to live in hot and overcrowded cities was almost incredible to believe because everyone knows that the best things in life are free. The daytime was great and like a great big party, but the night-time became a nightmare for me.

A visitor in the night

The visitations from the spirit man began as far back as I can remember. For a child, it was a terrifying experience and there was nothing that I could do to make it stop. Not only was I scared to death but I felt helpless and unprotected.

My sister Debra was in the bed next to me but no matter how hard I tried to wake her up, she seemed to sleep through it all as if she was under some type of general anaesthetic. Every time I poked her with my foot to wake her up she would snore even louder. So much for getting a bit of help in the middle of a crisis I always used to think to myself, terrified that I had to go through this experience completely alone, night after night. Sometimes I even used to think that I must have been dreaming, so I would pinch myself to see if I was awake just to make sure, but this only hurt.

Every night was like a ritual. As soon as Dad's old ship's clock in the kitchen struck one, the persistent spirit would appear making his way slowly to my bedroom until he reached the side of my bed. I would always be awakened by the sound of his loud steps gradually making their way to my room. They seemed to start from the laundry in the middle of the house, out to the veranda and into the room I shared with my sister. As soon as the sound stopped, I would look up and see that he had arrived.

What I saw was the formation of a spirit man dressed in a dark suit with a tie.

Once he arrived, time seemed to stop because he would stand for what seemed like hours staring down at my head to see if I was awake and, after a while, I would hear the footsteps again which soon disappeared until the next night. Too scared to do anything, I would just hide under the hot, heavy blankets pretending to be asleep.

I would wrap the blanket around my head so tightly that it seemed almost impossible to breathe and I would pray with all my might for God to make him go away. My heart would race madly and pound loudly in my chest and my ears ached from ringing in both ears. Terrified, my whole body would shake out of control. I tried to scream out for help, but nothing would come out because I was paralysed from fear.

The strange thing was that each night he came he was always dressed the same in the dark suit and tie. My father was a simple waterside worker, and we never knew anyone who wore a suit, let alone a tie.

Once I had the courage to stretch out my hand to see if he was real, but my hand went right through his body, which consisted of thousands of little black and white dots. When you touched them they felt frozen and icy cold and seemed to disappear. This experience was horrifying, and I never tried it again. It was better to pretend to be asleep and just wait for him to go away.

One day I told my good friend Samuel who lived across the street. He was one of the kids I grew up with and part of the gang of kids I hung around with when I was small. He only became angry when I told him my secret about what was going on every night in my world and ended up calling me a liar and a freak.

He eventually refused to have anything to do with me and must have told his mother because every time I went to his home afterwards, his mother would come out, put holy water on my head that she carried with her in a tiny thin bottle. Then she'd tell me that I had the devil in me, and not to show my face in her house ever again. Her behaviour must have rubbed off on the whole family because after that I was banned from ever playing with her kids. Every time I saw Samuel after that he would throw stones at me or pretend he didn't know me.

Soon I didn't have any friends, but it didn't matter as I always had my imaginary ones who I'd play with in my cubby house up the back of the yard. I realise now that they must have been my guides who always kept me entertained. I remember talking in many different accents and pretending to be certain people so it was no wonder I became an actress many years later. I also must have been accessing past lives as I had a ridiculous exaggerated English accent and an imaginary husband called John.

My mother would always come up the back to see what I was up to, poke her head in the tiny doorway of the cubby house when I was little and ask me who I was talking to. I would never tell her anything as she always said I had an incredible imagination and she never believed a word I said anyway. She still says this to this day, but I have learnt not to listen too hard to her constant criticism, as her heart is in the right place.

To my relief, my visits from the spirit man calmed down to a degree, because my family finally agreed to let me keep the hall light on all night. They were sick of the disruption and had had enough of my stories, which they never believed anyway. The nightly visits still continued, but with the light on they seemed to ease. At least I could see who was there and no invisible fingers would be prodding me in the middle of the night or creepy spirits lurking in the shadows. I never once thought to ask any questions of the spirit, because I was too scared especially when my hand went through his body. Once fear sets in there is no way you can rationalise it as it will always take on a life of its own.

As a trained and experienced medium, today I am fearless as I have a very good understanding of what spirit is about. When you work with the power of love, which is the source, you have nothing to worry about. I know now exactly what I am dealing with, how to work with the light and, importantly, how to protect myself.

I know for a fact that I am never alone as spirit is always with me talking in my ear and guiding me along the path. These days, I would simply tell the lost soul that he was dead, not to be afraid and to open his eyes and go into the light. Once there, he would receive healing and meet his loved ones waiting for him on the other side to come home. Sadly I never knew anyone in those early years who knew anything about what I was experiencing. If it wasn't for my cat, Cleve, who slept with me every night, and the hall light, I don't know how I would have survived. It was a subject nobody ever talked about or was interested in and I knew not to share my experiences in case of further ridicule.

On a visit to my parent's house many years later, I finally found out where the man in the suit lived. In the past, whenever I told my mother about what I was seeing in the spirit world, it would only scare the hell out of her and she would shrug her shoulders saying it was just my incredible imagination, which I had developed after I fell on the floor when I was born.

When all the kids had left home, my mother hated to be alone in the family home and was always upset when my father went away on one of his fishing trips. She complained that she felt she was not alone and that something or someone was watching her. Was this retribution for her not listening to me when I was a kid? She never actually saw or heard anything, it was just a feeling that she had. Whenever I tried to talk to her about it and to get to the root of the problem, she would get angry or upset and change the subject as anything to do with the paranormal would make her hair stand on end. I always believe that things always work out in the end and sometimes when you stand back, any problem that you have in life will always sort itself out in the end.

My parent's home had a small indoor toilet in the laundry and there was a small manhole in the corner of the ceiling, which had a tiny hole in it the size of an eye. Once, when I had stayed overnight and was washing some clothes in the sink, out of the blue, I suddenly felt a strong spirit presence in the room. It felt like somebody or something was staring at me from above in the roof. Turning slowly around, I stopped what I was doing and looked up to the roof to see what or who was watching me. Peering up I saw the tiny hole and felt something like an eye staring back at me.

Within seconds, the temperature began to drop in the room and I began to shiver. All the hairs were standing up on my body and I could feel my third eye opening up, which always happens when I am working with spirit energy. Without warning, the spirit stood beside me.

Surrounding myself with white light for protection I demanded to know who he was and asked him what he was doing in my parent's house. At first he said nothing and just stood in front of me, confused and frightened as if he didn't understand what was going on. He appeared the same size as me but was very fuzzy. Shocked beyond belief, I realised that it was the same spirit that used to visit me nearly every night when I was a kid.

For years I had convinced myself that it hadn't really happened and must have been a terrible dream as nobody ever believed me. Again I asked him loudly who he was and what was he doing in my mother's house. He told me telepathically that he didn't know where he was or what was going on for that matter. As far as he knew, he had lived in the roof for as long as he could remember. He had no idea that he was dead and he didn't know who the other people were living in the house. This is often the case with earth-bound spirits. He wasn't an angry spirit, and seemed more afraid of me than I of him.

He knew I could see and hear him and I sensed he had known me from my childhood. He was so confused; he couldn't even give me his name. All he could say was that he had lived in the house for as long as he could remember. He had tried to get my attention for years as he knew that I could "see" him but as I grew older my inner vision diminished and I became more what we call clairaudient, or clear hearing, instead.

Why he had not crossed over when he died and where he came from I will never know, as I was not given that information. It doesn't really matter and sometimes there are just no explanations in life and it is something I never wanted to dwell on. Sometimes spirit just works this way and I do not have all the answers. It will always remain a mystery. I can only speculate that he must have lived in my parent's house before he had died and, instead of crossing over, came back to the house instead for whatever reason.

Slowly turning to him, I gently told him that it was time for him to cross over and reassured him that everything would soon be OK. Calling on my spirit helpers and God, I asked Great Spirit to open up a portal of love and light so I could send him home, which is back to spirit. Next, I lovingly told him to open his eyes and go into the light. I told him he was dead and it was time to go home where his loved ones would be waiting for him on the other side. Once he stepped into the light he would understand as he would receive healing. His loved ones would be waiting for him and he would have the love and support of his guide.

Within seconds the energy shifted in the room, and he was gone. The temperature was warmer again and there was nothing left but little dots all over the room, which also soon disappeared. I did not bother to tell my mother that her noisy ghost was gone, because she would have just told me that it was my incredible imagination again.

I realise now that earth-bound spirits are attracted like moths to a light to spirit mediums, even when they are children because of the inner light or vibration they radiate. People who are natural-born mediums often attract this type of phenomena as they have a very high vibrational energy. If the person is not trained as a medium or healer, you can imagine this would be a real disability as they would be attracting spirits all the time and would be overloaded and drained of their natural energy.

It was unfortunate for the man in the suit that I was not able to help him sooner but in spirit time there is no time. Looking back I had no idea of my gifts or my abilities or how to use them for that matter. All they seemed to do then was to create chaos and fear, making my life a burden. At that age I was not able even to help myself, let alone an earth-bound spirit who had lost his way. I only wished I knew then what I know now, and perhaps I could have helped him sooner.

The ghosts in Balmain

Balmain is one of the oldest and most historical parts of Sydney so it isn't surprising that most places like this are often full of spirits who had lived there when they were alive. My grandmother's place there was an example. Not only was it an old house, that smelt peculiar but it had its own history of human tragedy as well. The old terrace home that nanna lived in by herself in those days was not only miserable but haunting as it was full of so many sad memories. It had two levels joined together by an old staircase that led up to an old attic at the top which was kept locked as the old house was falling down. Most of the rooms I remember were locked and nobody was ever allowed to go in there. It was a sad and lonely place, full of so many unhappy memories from my father's past from when he was a child.

I could understand why Dad wanted to get as far away as he could and move down the south coast. Whenever I sat in Nanna's sitting room, I could hear voices coming from the adjoining wall of the house next door. We always knew whenever anyone was home and it almost felt as if they were in the same room as you. Whenever the family next door was having a fight we could hear everything.

My grandmother, Edwina, was from Lancaster in England. She was a wonderful woman and I loved her very dearly as she was always so very kind and generous to me. She was a small woman with fair hair and glasses and had a large wart on her chin. On first meeting her you might think she had just arrived that day off the boat from England as it was hard to understand her as her accent was so thick, even though she had lived in Australia for many years. She was also a widow who lost her husband from cancer when he was in his early forties, leaving her to bring up three children herself. She was also a chronic alcoholic who often stuttered when she spoke.

Now I realise she must have been quite psychic herself because of the number of spirit people I saw that lived in her house. I have never in my whole life seen such a large collection of spirits in one place as often when you are psychic or have mediumship qualities, your "energy" or what I call "light" will always attract a lot of spirit people and paranormal activity around your house, whether you like it or not.

Nanna would not have been able to talk to anyone about her gift or abilities because it would have been frowned upon as being evil or bad back then. People would have looked on her as a social pariah and she would have been more isolated than she already was because of ignorance and lack of education.

As a society today we often treat people who are different really badly because of our own ignorance and prejudice. People who are different will often find it takes time for others to really accept and acknowledge where they are coming from as, very sadly, a lot of us still live in fear of things we do not understand. It is only starting to improve today because of the many gifted mediums and psychics who are speaking out. It is hard-working and selfless people like Doris Stokes and John Edwards and many others who have made the whole spiritual movement really progress into the public arena.

I often think that, perhaps, if Nanna had been born in a different era, or somebody had only taken the time to tell her that she was not alone and that they loved her, things may have been different. She would perhaps not have had a terrible drinking problem and drowned herself and all her sorrows in her addictions. Instead she may have found happiness and not ended up dying in a nursing home from chronic alcoholism. I know this as a fact as I have spoken to her many times since she has passed over and she always tells me how sorry she was and how she could never cope with what life brought her when she was alive.

Whenever our family visited from the south coast on the weekends, I would often see spirit people sitting on the front veranda. One of the spirit people was a very old grandmotherly spirit woman, who always sat on an old rocking chair. She had long white hair that she wore tied back and always stared straight ahead of her as if she was looking at something. It always seemed really weird as I never knew what she was watching. We always pretended not to see each other, but both knew each other was there. Whenever I would take a long sneaky sideways look at her, she would instantly disappear into thin air. The old lady lived in one of Nanna's locked rooms upstairs and I had seen her on several occasions as well when I peeked through one of the keyholes.

Sometimes, when nobody was paying attention I would creep upstairs and just listen to the sounds coming from the old rooms. I knew that they were spirit people talking, as there was supposed to be nobody inside and I always felt they were as nervous as I was.

I sensed other spirit people that came from other houses in the street and a couple of young spirit children. I believe they were waiting for me because they knew that I could see them. I suspect they also brought their spirit friends along as well, as there would be so many of them lined up at the front of the house, as if waiting for me to arrive. Nobody else in the family could see them, of course, except for me. Whenever I said anything I was told it was just my incredible imagination again.

As you could imagine, I was only a young girl and not impressed at the time as it used to scare the living daylights out of me. The mere thought of having to spend time there or even stay overnight in the house was a living nightmare. I was always grateful that my mother never wanted to stay as the energy in the house was empty and depressing and my mother never liked my grandmother and always insisted on going home almost as soon as we had arrived. On the rare occasion we did stay overnight, I never got any sleep as there was always some type of drama happening in the spirit world.

Once I saw a small spirit boy crying at the end of my bed. At first I thought it was Peter, the son of my dead cousin who had killed himself. The spirit looked like Peter, only years younger. Sitting up sleepily and rubbing the sleep from my eyes, I tried to ask him what the matter was. As soon as I did this he just disappeared only to reappear again once I lay back down in the bed. This was very frustrating as the noise kept me awake.

In the end I did my old trick of just burying myself under the blankets pretending I was asleep. Peter was only ten, the same age as me at the time of his father's death. After the incident, I never saw him again because the tragedy had eventually split the family. Dad said that my cousin's death was an accident, as he was depressed and terribly unhappy at the time and did not mean to actually kill himself. Anyone who has ever experienced a suicide with a loved one will understand the pain and deep sadness that goes with it as it is incredibly hard to comprehend. As a small child, it was almost impossible.

Years later, I was given more clarity into the circumstances around the situation of my cousin's death. Apparently he was having difficulties in his marriage at the time and was extremely depressed and in a poor state of mind, often the case in most suicides. On that eventful day I could only imagine what he must have gone through. He must have been in incredible pain and confusion to have taken so many sedatives. It was later found that he had tried to vomit them all up but, sadly, was unable to do so. Instead, his young, athletic body was found dead, lying tragically over the bath. By the time they got to him, it was far too late.

I often wondered when I was older, if this is why my grandmother drank so much because every time I saw her she was always so merry with a jug of beer in the kitchen ready to pour. She had already lost a husband in her lifetime, but to lose a grandchild as well would have been a terrible tragedy and a heavy cross to bear.

Whenever we arrived to visit my grandmother, it usually took quite a while for my poor parents to pull me out of the back of the tiny Volkswagen as I never knew from visit to visit what was going to happen next. Even though I was often exhausted from the long drive and carsick from the fumes of my mother's perfume anything was better than going inside my grandmother's creepy, haunted house.

As soon as I stepped inside the door, I could feel the spirit energy like raw electricity in the air. I would start shaking and cold shivers would run up and down my spine, making my hairs stand on end. Once I had stepped over the threshold of her house I would immediately begin to feel anxious, in case my parents decided to stay. As far as I was concerned the place was crawling with dead people or spirits, all making useless efforts to grab my attention and I wanted no part of it.

"Why doesn't she get out of the car?" my mother would ask my father as soon as we pulled up in front of the old terrace. "What's going on? Come on, not again. What is your problem?" she would screech at the top of her lungs. "Stop being difficult and get out of the car at once!"

Finally she would scream through gritted teeth with her arms firmly crossed in front of her. "Now, listen to me young lady! Get out of the car," she would repeat, tired of the same routine every time we arrived at grandmother's house but she'd also be dying to get inside for a cup of tea.

"Can you hear what I am saying? Listen to me when I talk to you. You are just being your usual highly strung self, aren't you?" she would moan.

Nothing she could ever say or do made any difference in the world. Under no circumstances was I going to move until I was good and ready. As soon as we had arrived my parents were always arguing anyway, so I had no reason to want to stay.

"Just let her sit there and come inside," my father would say, not wanting to get involved with all the stress taking place. "She will come inside when she is good and ready."

The last thing he wanted was an argument as he already seemed to have so much on his mind. It was his duty as the eldest son to keep an eye on his aging and very sick mother and nothing on earth was ever going to change from that responsibility. When I felt I had the courage, I would let myself out of the car silently and finally go inside the house. It was something that I dreaded doing each time I went there but I knew I had no choice in the matter. I knew a lot of things about the house already as I had visited it so regularly over the years.

There had been two deaths in the family already and you could really feel the sadness and emptiness as soon as you stepped inside nanna's home. Dad had not only witnessed his own father's ill health and untimely death from cancer when he was in the prime of his life, but he had also been a witness to his cousin's death from suicide.

The only thing that made me laugh was the old toilet which was way up the back yard, and it felt like everybody was watching you whenever you walked up the small path to pay a visit. All the houses were in a row and so close together. They had small windows up the top which you could look out of. Nanna used to have what she used to call "a dunny man" that used to come and collect the toilet pot. He was always really friendly, and whenever he talked he would have a cigarette hanging out of the side of his mouth. He only ever wore a tiny singlet, on the coldest of days which was tucked into a pair of little shorts. He also wore a pair of thick woollen socks and a pair of sandshoes as he was always running.

Whenever he arrived in his huge truck, I would hold my nose and try not to breathe as it stank so much. He was a friendly man, who used to laugh and tell jokes to anyone who would listen, while he got on with his business. The smell was intense and horrible, but we all used to smile, and pretend none the wiser, to be polite. It must have been a terrible job, but he didn't seem to mind. I often wondered how he did it.

Another thing that always bothered me was no matter how much you warmed the house, it was always cold. My grandmother was always complaining about all the coke she used to use, which she had stored out the back. She also had a gas meter which you had to put coins into. It is not often that you will find an earth-bound spirit in a lonely house unless of course they once live there or have an attachment to the home. I am sure a lot of the spirit people in Nanna's house had lived there once before.

Years later when I was a nurse, later on in life in my twenties and thirties, I would often feel and hear spirits walking around hospital wards whenever I did the rounds on the lonely dreaded night shift. Working those types of shifts can be really draining as you usually do not have time to have a proper sleep and it takes a lot out of you as you become so sensitive.

At first I thought it was my imagination, but it happened so many times, over and over that you could not just put it down to nothing or a loud cockroach. There were definitely spirits running around the buildings I worked at, as I am sure many people must have died there. So long as they did not come near me, I was happy. I had one touch me once and it scared the living daylights out of me as it was so ice cold. The other nurses that I worked with all felt the same and had similar situations happen to them. When we got together we would all joke and scare each other to death just to keep each other awake, with horrible scary ghost stories. Usually we worked in pairs and walked around in the dark corridors of the old hospitals clutching torches and shining them into the dark whenever we heard any noises … Almost every single nurse I have ever spoken to have all had paranormal experiences in one way or another.

The spiritualist church

By the time I was 18, I was drinking gallons of herbal tea, reading as many spiritual books as I could get my hands on by authors such as Lobsang Rampa, and I was astral travelling out of my body. I was so dedicated to leading a spiritual life that I would try just about anything to become enlightened. Every morning I would read the *Desiderata* which I had plastered with thick sticky tape on the back of my bedroom door. As soon as I opened my eyes, I would stare up at the poem and ponder about my life and where I was going. Like most people of my age at that time, I had so many dreams about what I wanted to do with my life that I started to worry how I was going to fit everything in.

My early days of astral travelling, which was an awesome experience and I recommend everyone to try, soon came to an abrupt end when I had a slight accident one day. My mother, always wondering what I was up to in when I locked myself in the room I shared with my sister, starting screaming out my name to come and eat breakfast while I was astral travelling. Startled on hearing my name called, I suddenly lost concentration and found myself, for a split second, stuck in the bedroom door. The next thing I remembered was lying back on my bed with the taste of wood fibres in my mouth. This awful experience really frightened me but when I tried to tell my mother about it she would have none of it.

With no one to encourage me to push myself with my spiritual studies, I never attempted astral travelling again until later in life. I now travel all the time and in my sleep state as well. Now that I am well practised I no longer have any problems as I know I am safe and always protected by spirit.

At the same time, I was also reading tarot cards. Somebody had given me a pack for a present and as soon as I picked them up and tuned into their energy I had a feeling of déjà vu that I had worked with them before. It is a great responsibility reading the cards for others, however. I soon learnt to be careful with what I said, as my friends took every word I said as gospel, and were always amazed at what I came up with.

As soon as my predictions came true, they would let me know right away and became extremely excited. They thought it was amazing how I could channel information and not really know what I was talking about. I always put it down to the fact that all people, events and actions leave an energy trail that is easily detectable for past and even future events. My new-found gift made me very popular and before long I was in great demand. By developing your psychic abilities, you are placing your soul's energy or aura in contact with another's and establishing a connection.

Whenever I did readings, so-called feelings about the person just came to me naturally and most of the time I would tell them things I couldn't possibly know about. Even to this day I still find it all quite extraordinary. I don't recall how I knew how to channel or what to do, I just did it. As soon as I looked at the pictures on the cards, I had an inner knowing of what they meant as well. I now put all this down to past lives and I believe I must have been a witch and burnt at the stake, as that's what happened to many intuitives or healers as their skills were considered evil.

People who do not understand things often choose to go into fear. Luckily for me, I was able to carry the information quite easily in my soul's memory and carry on the work or life path that was intended for me.

As soon as I relax or centre myself, I open my third eye and tune into the other person's energy. Then the information just flows and I am able to pick up or channel information from the person's guide, or what we call communicator. This can be a spiritual guide or a relative or friend in spirit.

I have always been attracted to the paranormal and everything it has to offer as well as learning as much I can. Back then, I was also a member of the spiritualist church so I was not alone in my beliefs and abilities and enjoyed being surrounded by lovely and helpful like-minded people.

The spiritualist church was a safe haven for me but, more importantly, it's also a sacred place of learning and development for those wanting to develop their spiritual beliefs while working with white light, which is love and Christ consciousness or what we call the "source".

The church and its people, who work tirelessly for the sake of this way of life, will always offer a sanctuary where like-minded people can open their spiritual awareness. The church has seven principles of spiritualism which it teaches to all its members.

1. The fatherhood of God.
2. The brotherhood of man.
3. The communion of spirits and the ministry of angels.
4. The continuous existence of the human soul.
5. Personal responsibility.
6. Compensation and retribution hereafter for all good and evil deeds done on earth.
7. Eternal progress opens to every human soul.

Finally, I had found a place where people could help me with my abilities and, more importantly, where being psychic was accepted and quite common. I was relieved to find others who spoke my own language and who were willing to teach me everything there was to know about being a natural medium. To me, it was a lot better than the Christian church because the people were kinder, listened with patience at everything I had to say, and genuinely interested in spiritual matters. Each time I attended, I heard similar stories to my own that others were going through or had experienced themselves.

The spiritualist church down the south coast was just a couple of suburbs away and took me a good 45 minutes to get there by car. When you live in the country you are used to driving long distances and one of the first things you do when you leave school is get a licence.

This church was run by a medium and clairvoyant, who was also the minister. She was a kindly woman, well into her seventies, with the face of an angel and a mischievous twinkle in her eye. There wasn't a mean bone in her body, and she encouraged all her students to believe in their gifts as being natural and given by God. She was a great inspiration to me in the early days and appeared at the right time in my life because no-one else I knew had any idea what I was on about.

She taught me to believe in myself and my abilities and had a profound influence on me. I believe that everybody on the planet has some type of spiritual gift, whether it is healing, channelling or psychic abilities. If you want to develop these, it is just a matter of believing in yourself and spending time to do so by learning to meditate to still your mind and finding a good teacher.

As you learn to work with your powers, you will gain confidence. Your ability to tap into things will give you much insight to your inner world and the world around us. The more time you take to work on yourself will help you release negative patterns and karma, by connecting and working with your higher self.

You will also learn to stay focused which, in turn, will help you take less time to do things. Meditation also helps you become more aware of the people around you and teaches you everything there is to know about Great Spirit. Spirit always works in so many wonderful ways and always uses us for the good of mankind in a way that we may not even know is possible.

I am still amazed when I go to other spiritual churches or groups and find out later that some of the people who congregate there are often not who they say they are. I always tell people and clients to trust their own intuition and to only work with people that they feel they can trust and who are working in the light. There are too many people out there who are only into ego and power and make it their life mission to disempower everyone else they come across by stealing their energy. Often, these "energy grabbers" are so caught up in control issues and their own needs they are not aware of what they are doing and forget why they are there in the first place.

I always protect myself by wrapping white light around my energy field, a most effective practice. Yet again, there are also wonderful true earth angels out there who work tirelessly for the spirit world and who would do anything for you. These people are few and far between but I never give up hope, knowing that they are out there.

I will always be grateful to this kindly minister for teaching me to trust in myself and my own inner voice and power regardless. Our prayers to God and spirit are always answered, no matter what we think or how difficult our circumstances. What goes around comes around for every single living person on the planet, no matter what they believe in. It is a universal law that every action is followed by a reaction as we are all energy.

When you ask for assistance you will always receive it as spirit is always with us every single second of our lives, and we are connected to spirit through our love. I also believe that when you are ready to learn about yourself as an immortal soul, the teacher will appear.

When I first walked into a spiritualist church, I had never seen anything like it in my entire life. I was used to seeing spirits or dead people hanging around, but never so many and all in one place. As I looked around me in awe, I saw great gobs of energy whirling and swishing around in the room in the air above people's heads as they sang. This really frightened me as I had no idea what I was seeing. Now I know this was energy or spirits congregating in the hall.

As the congregation sang, they built up the energy to create a bridge or link, making possible for the medium sitting at the front of the church to connect to loved ones on the other side. I could also smell something like old dirty socks. Some lower types of entities or spirits often have a funny smell about them. These spirits have a lower vibration and dwell on what we call the lower astral level. Not all spirits are highly evolved and when you go into a spiritualist church there are all types hanging around.

Just because Freddy the old alcoholic and drug addict has crossed over to the other side and is in spirit does not mean that he is suddenly an ascended master or someone special because I or another medium can contact him. Once he is dead and has passed safely over he, like everybody else before him, will have the same personality he had when he was alive.

Once he is in spirit, he will receive healing like all incoming souls. He will also get to stand in front of the council with his guide and review how his life went on earth. He will have time to heal and be able to reflect whether he accomplished his spiritual lessons as an immortal soul. We all have free choice, so it was entirely up to him.

The next time he decides to come back and reincarnate on earth, he will have the right to make other choices on what he wants to learn on a soul level to heal and grow, and raise his own vibration.

When I read for someone, I often smell smoke if the spirit was a smoker or alcohol if they liked to drink, although some spirits smell like perfume. When I am doing spiritual healings on people, I will often smell a sweet perfumed flower which signifies a mass of angels are in the room, which is a blessing as the energy is always beautiful, loving and serene.

The spiritualist church and teachers I was attracted to, not only taught me how to meditate, but also about all types of healing, including trance and platform mediumship. For this I am eternally grateful. The rest I already knew and remembered as I must have worked with these abilities in other lifetimes and it was easy to utilize as it was already downloaded in my memory cells. Over the years I have worked tirelessly for spiritualist churches all over Sydney and parts of Queensland on the platform as a medium giving messages, healing and survival evidence.

Spiritual healing

I have also over the years worked as a practising healer for Australian Spiritual Healers Association or ASHA. It was first founded in 1964 in Melbourne by the late Arthur Kendrick with the help of the late spiritual healer, Harry Edwards. The ASHA, now defunct in NSW, was founded with a vision of uniting Australia spiritual healers and aspired to promote spiritual healing here and overseas.

ASHA members practiced spiritual healing by the laying-on of hands, and by attunement through meditation and prayer, seeking to induce a beneficial effect upon a client's life force at all levels of their existence. Spiritual healing may be given for any disease, illness, stress or injury as a therapy that has no side effects and complements other therapies. The medical diagnosis of an illness doesn't influence the outcome of spiritual healing as you learn to work with detachment. The healer acts only as a conduit of pure light energy from the "source" or "God" energy.

For many years I was part of a group of like-minded people who would hold free healing every month for the elderly and sick down in Manly, on Sydney's northern beaches. I met so many wonderful healers and like minded people in those years who gave up their Sundays to help the sick. It was a very humbling experience which taught me a lot and we enjoyed getting feedback from the willing participants. This was also a great learning curve for me and taught me a lot about a healing and the way it works.

Life and travel

As I grew older I was always guided by an inner spiritual force within. I always used to know things before they ever happened, though I kept this information to myself so as to not spook my friends. But there were always other people around who were keen to discover what was going on in their lives.

Rosie was one of those friends. She was about eight years older than me and she had an uncanny knack of getting involved with the wrong people and would pester me to find out who or what was coming into her life, whether they would end up together and how handsome he would be. I could understand the way she behaved as her mother and father were old fashioned and tried to stop her from being outspoken and a rebel. Everything they tried to do, however, just made her go in the opposite direction as she was so strong-willed.

Unfortunately for her, none of her so-called relationships ever lasted. She was "a real romantic" and forever falling in love for the sake of it as all her men were utterly creepy in my eyes. My mother had little time for Rosie because she was so much older and always dropping in and borrowing my clothes and never bringing them back. Mum didn't like this but she was also concerned that Rosie's other friends were too old for me.

One day she arrived at my place unannounced, and begged me to come and meet her latest conquest. I was having a cup of tea with Mum and our next-door neighbour when she arrived. We couldn't stop giggling, and my mother started to roll her eyes as Rosie began to describe her new boyfriend in exaggerated detail. We had heard the same story many times before and were tired of them. Even my cat, which was sitting under the table, couldn't stand Rosie and ran and hid in the bedroom until she was gone. Bored to death we listened in silence as she describes her latest conquest.

"He is short, but really sexy. Mmmm," she said, thinking deeply and looking as if she would like to eat him. "He is into lots of things and I have never ever met anyone like him before," she purred, looking delighted.

Here we go again, I thought to myself, wishing she would just give it a break. She was always on the same roller-coaster, forever looking for love in the wrong places and always falling for creeps.

"And how long have you known him, dear," asked my mother, passing her another cookie from the jar and soaking up the entertainment for the day. I could see by the look on her face she was enjoying herself as she always loved gossip.

"Oh, only two weeks but I know he's the one," said Rosie.

"That's a pretty short time, Rosie. Are you sure about that?" Mum asked hiding her sarcasm. "I wish Kerrie would meet someone and settle down. If she only kept her mouth closed she would have lots of boys after her, just like her younger sister. She frightens them off because she has too much to say."

"Oh please give it a break, Mum," I answered, starting to feel sick in the stomach.

I was used to mum berating me about getting a boyfriend and I usually just ignored her, but I was starting to feel sick as I was not getting a good feeling about Rosie's new man. Just listening to her made me feel sick to my stomach, my heart was pounding, and it was hard for me to catch my breath. It felt like I was going to have an anxiety attack. I was starting to get the feeling that something was about to go horribly wrong.

In the past when something bad was going to happen I could sense it in my body. It was a type of anxiety when something did not feel right. It was always the same: my throat would get dry, my foot started to get restless and I would feel irritated and nervous, and start to wind my hair around my finger.

Against my better judgement, I finally gave into her demands. No matter what I said she wouldn't listen so I decided to go and meet him so she would stop pestering me. All she wanted me to do was just check him out and I knew she was desperate for my approval. I was also starting to get a little curious as to why I felt so negative.

"I can only stay for a short time as I have exams coming up," I told her matter-of-factly.

"Cool, no worries, we won't take long," she squealed with delight, with a wild look of excitement.

Jumping in her tiny Mini, we turned on the stereo full pelt and made our way to his house. He must have lived about an hour away, and I remember sitting in silence and listening to her rave on about how special he was and how I would think how lucky she was to have met someone like him finally.

He lived quite a distance away, so we had a good old laugh for a while until a feeling of anxiety began to wash over me again. I laughed along with her, but all I could think about was how I wished I was somewhere else. A voice in my head kept telling me to be careful. I even started to make up excuses in my mind about turning around, but I did not want to disappoint her. By the time we pulled up outside his house I started to feel really terrible as the feeling of impending doom became stronger, almost overwhelming. When things weren't right or when something bad was about to happen they sort of took on a life of their own.

As we walked up to the front door of the house, I had goosebumps all over my body and it became harder to breathe. I was also starting to feel weak at the knees. Fear and trepidation flooded through me. Something in the house was definitely wrong, but I had no idea what it could be. I tried to tell Rosie how I felt, giving her subtle hints that something was not right, but she wouldn't listen. She was far too gone into her own little world.

Ivan, her new boyfriend had given her a key to his house so she could come and go when she liked. Turning the key in the door, she let herself in and started to give me a tour, proudly displaying his house as if it were her very own.

Hesitantly I shuffled slowly behind her, looking cautiously all around me. Everything seemed OK, so I couldn't understand why I felt this way. The house had a funny feel about it, but I couldn't figure out at this point exactly what it was that was bugging me.

"And finally we come to the meditation room," she proudly announced, smiling happily from ear to ear and opening up a door to a locked room.

Peering in, I glanced quickly around. It felt creepy and ice cold and all the hairs on my arm stuck up. Something wasn't right. The room was completely black, and it was hard to see anything at first. My eyes adjusted to the darkness and, feeling agitated, I quickly scanned the room.

The room smelt stale and musty so I breathed through my mouth, holding my nose. I wanted to run away, as it smelt as if something like a rat had died in there. Determined to know what was going on, I found the light switch and screamed in horror at what I saw. I could not understand why Rosie would not put on the light and now I understood why.

"Are you insane?" I screamed pointing to a large grotesque statue in the corner of the room, hardly able to believe my eyes.

"What the hell is that used for?" I gasped and pointed into the room that looked like the set of a horror movie.

Standing in front of us was a life-sized dummy dressed up as Medusa, with painted blood running down her mouth, long black hair, and a sharp bloody dagger in her hand. She was dressed in ancient robes and no matter where I stood I felt like she was staring right back at me. At her feet was an altar with bottles, candles, matches and weird-looking objects placed on it. It looked as if some type of animal was also cut up as well as there were bits of fur and dried blood splattered all over the place.

Stepping back I glared at Rosie, dumbstruck and in shock as if I was really seeing her for the first time. Not saying a word, she stood meekly beside me and said nothing. She started to softly cry and was slowly turning pale. Not knowing what to do next she began to shake and stared at the ground, avoiding eye contact.

"You never told me your boyfriend was into black magic and spells," I screamed into her face, unable to control my emotions and finding it really hard to believe what was I was seeing. What had she got herself into this time, I asked myself.

"Oh yeah, it's cool isn't it," she whispered, unsure of my reaction. "Ivan does lots of spells and he has even asked me to go with him next time to the cemetery to collect more old bones and things for his altar." Her voice faded and I could hardly hear what she was saying.

"He loves nothing better than to dress up in ancient robes and chant and sing strange words in a funny language. That is cool isn't it?" she asked, not sounding as confident as she would like. "There are a few of his friends who are really nice and who do it with him. I feel I really understand him." she purred, caught up in her own world, unwilling to see the look of revulsion and fear on my face.

"Sure, Rosie, if you are into demons and ghouls!" I screamed back, not wanting to hear another word. "You are absolutely and truly bloody insane. You have gone too far this time you stupid bitch," I shouted into her horrified, face unable to hide my emotions. I knew she could be a bubblehead but this was way over the top. "What in hell have you got yourself involved in, you stupid bitch?"

I could not believe what I was seeing or even what I was doing there. This was insane. No way was I going to get involved with this as it was way out of my league and was crazy. Frightened and in shock, I turned and started running out of the house, feeling like I wanted to vomit. My legs were turning to jelly and my heart was thumping. Straining for breath, I screamed at Rosie. "Get me out of here now, you bloody idiot. I knew you were crazy but, shit: you have gone way over the top this time! Let's go now! I want to go home, I feel like I am going to be sick."

Without saying another word I hurried to the car and jumped into the safety of the passenger seat and started to shake uncontrollably. All I could think of was to get home to safety and to get away from this horrible place as fast as possible. I had never seen evil before but this had to be it. I had read about these types of things in books but had never experienced it first-hand. Just to be in the house had made my skin crawl and I felt dirty. My ears were buzzing and my stomach ached.

The experience made me feel like I had witnessed something dark and sinister. The awful cold energy was crippling and overwhelming. Nauseated, I started to vomit out the car window. Yellow pale fluid, which missed the gutter, began to run down my chin and the window. The dreadful pain in my stomach felt incredible and seemed to come in spasms. It was if somebody had stuck a knife in my stomach and turned it slowly around. Negative, frightening thoughts filled my mind and I kept thinking if I didn't get home I would surely die.

The worst part about all of this was Rosie had no idea what she was getting herself into. I found it amazing that she could get it so wrong. Surely, I asked myself, she must have some commonsense to realise the truth of the situation. She was obviously dating an evil nutcase who was taking her for a ride. Even worse, she may have been brainwashed or under some type of spell.

I couldn't understand how anybody in their right mind could be so insensitive and not understand the difference between right and wrong? I could not get it out of my head how she never got it as it was pretty obvious to me and anyone else who walked into that awful room. What was her problem, I wondered, hardly able to think straight.

Covering my mouth, I started to breathe deeply to calm myself down. After a while, Rosie joined me in the car. We sat in silence for what seemed hours before we spoke. Calming myself down and regaining my strength and composure, I gently patted her on the back of the neck and shoulder, trying to be reassuring. That was really hard for me because I can sometimes say the wrong thing. "You have no idea what you have got yourself into, Rosie!" I said.

Quietly sobbing, Rosie kept her head bowed and stared at the ground, tears filling her eyes as she listened in silence, not knowing what to do. I was obviously upset and she had no idea why.

"You have been my good friend now for years, Rosie, so we have known each other for a long time." Awkwardly, I continued, carefully searching for the right words so as not to upset her even more. I needed all the tact and diplomacy I could muster.

"I feel I need to tell you that what you are doing is very wrong," I explained. "I don't know how long you have known him, but it is obvious to me your so-called boyfriend, or whatever he calls himself, is not only weird but dark and evil. It looks like he is into some type of dark and creepy black magic!"

"So what?" she huffed, stiffening her body defensively and not wanting to listen to my warning. "He is nice to me, you know, and that is all that matters," she whispered, crossing her arms angrily but not daring to look at me in the face.

Scratching my head irritably, I continued trying to find the right words to make her understand the reality of the situation but realising at the same time that it was useless. She had her heart set on him and that, as far as she was concerned, was the end of the matter. She had always been looking for love ever since I had met her.

"Come on, don't you get it Rosie? Hasn't it occurred to you that what Ivan is doing is rather odd?" Rosie just stared back at me blankly, tears pouring down her face.

"What does your intuition tell you?" I went on. "Can you honestly tell me that you don't find any of this really strange or weird?" I pleaded, trying to make her come to her senses. "Have you even for a minute had a good think about what he is doing? Hasn't it occurred to you that what he is doing is kind of bad and certainly not normal? And that house, surely you must be able to feel the creepiness inside it. It is so cold and the energy is so thick and sickening," I said pausing. "If you don't, then I think you have been smoking too many drugs because this is really bad!"

"But I think I love him," she wailed, sniffing and drying her eyes with a used tissue she had stuck in her shirt and looking at me trying to make me understand her feelings.

"You hardly even know the guy," I hissed back, fed up with the whole situation. "How long has it been? A couple of weeks I suppose?" I moaned, wishing I was somewhere else. Swallowing hard, I continued. "Well, if that is the case, I don't know what else to say, except please take me home. I am sorry for upsetting you. And, please, under no circumstances tell your boyfriend that I have been here today as I think it is best that we do not meet."

"But I have told him all about you and your gifts and I wanted us all to be friends. It's just not fair," she wailed, not liking what I was saying and starting to behave like a child.

I was starting to lose my patience and it was difficult not to show my disgust and distaste for what she had got herself into. All I could think about was to get away as far as I could and not have anything to do with her. My inner voice kept telling me to be calm and not to show my real emotions. "Well, between you and me we are obviously into different things."

I was becoming impatient and did not want to discuss the matter any longer. What she did with her life was her business. It was not my responsibility to tell people what to do. If she was attracted to that type of sinister and evil dark energy, then perhaps that was her lesson and journey. It was totally beyond me why she had gone this way.

"I am not interested in any type of witchcraft, spells or black magic. Do you understand? I said patiently, trying to hide the fear in my voice. "I do not want to meet him, OK, and that is final," I said.

Refusing to even talk to her any longer, I sat in silence for the rest of the trip home. We had both realised that we were not going to change our minds on the subject. I wanted nothing further to do with her. Sure, I had known her for years, but people change and our lives were taking us in different directions now.

Taking a deep breath and feeling still shaken by the experience, my mind continued to race a million thoughts as we drove slowly along. I still felt sick to the stomach and could think of nothing better than to get to the safety of home and tell Mum everything that had happened because I knew she would be as shocked as I was. She had never liked Rosie from the start and had warned me not to get too involved with her. She made a point of telling me I was never good at picking friends and this time she was probably right.

Feeling sorry for myself, I tried desperately not to cry. I felt so overwhelmed and anxious and worried she would tell her boyfriend what I had said. I slowly became paranoid, thinking that he would come after me or, even worse, put some type of spell on me. My brain and whole body felt like it had gone numb as my mind raced overtime thinking of terrible things. The worst thing of all was that this was over a man Rosie hardly knew.

All I could think of was to get as far away as possible and not have anything to do with her and her crazy evil boyfriend or whatever he called himself. Luckily for me, I was leaving town and heading overseas to work in the next couple of months so I would never have to see her again. I would also be far too busy with my studies to socialise so that was a good excuse. My nursing finals were coming up and once I had finished my studies I would be registered as a nurse and working overseas.

The journey home in silence seemed to take ages. After what seemed to be a terrible trip, we finally pulled up outside mum's house. Turning to face her, I gave her a hug and said goodbye. As I opened the door of the car and stepped out on the pavement, I turned and faced her one last time. "You need to step back and have a look at the bigger picture here, Rosie," I said. "In my opinion I think you can do a lot better for yourself."

Trying to keep the conversation light, I started to try and make a joke of it all as humour can sometimes get you out of the worst scenarios. "I don't think he is really your type anyway. From what you have described, he is too small and you know how you have always had a preference for really tall men. Please don't ever tell him I was at his house, OK?" I laughed, trying to hide my fear.

To me this was some type of black magic and you don't need to be psychic to work that one out! Anyone who would want to do anything like that would have to be insane and not of sound mind. To want go into a cemetery in the middle of night and steal some innocent person's bones from a crypt or grave is utterly wrong. What the hell was she thinking?

Besides being incredibly gruesome and disgusting, she wouldn't like it if someone came and desecrated her family's grave. Then to cut up some poor animal into tiny pieces and let it rot on an altar and have dried blood everywhere was another matter. That was the last time I saw Rosie. I have no idea whether she stayed with her boyfriend Ivan and I did not particularly care. Everybody has to find out their own lessons in life, and if she was unwilling to listen to anything I had to say, so be it. If she had chosen to live on the dark side of life, that was her journey and not mine. All I could do was send her love and compassion, and hope and pray she would come to her senses one day. I sensed from the first time I met her that she would probably find out things the hard way.

With so much going on in my life, I made a point of remembering all my dreams as they were so vivid in those days and luckily for me remain so even till this very day. When you are told continuously you have an incredible imagination, why not use it. One of my recurring dreams was of a strange place, covered in ice and snow. The place I dreamed about reminded me of Sweden or the northern countries in Europe that I had seen in magazines and on television.

Even though I loved the sea, I was always talking and fantasising about these dreams and certain places that I had never been to in my life. Without knowing why, I felt I wanted to travel and live there one day even though they were on the other side of the world. This obsession I had used to really irritate my mother, as she couldn't comprehend what I was on about. She often complained she could never understand my fascination with these countries as I had never once seen snow or travelled further than the south coast and Sydney.

On the south coast, where we lived, the only time it got cold was in winter when we would get wind and rain but never snow. I realise now that these vivid dreams were from other lifetimes in past lives and other incarnations I must have carried through in my memory cells. Throughout my work with past life regression, I have met many people from my days as a Viking in the longboats. We have now all become good friends. When I heard the Swedish band ABBA, I loved all their songs. Unfortunately all my heavy rocker friends begged to differ and thought I was a bit crazy.

After I finally finished my nursing exams, I packed my bag and bought a one-way ticket and headed overseas with nothing but enthusiasm and joy in my heart that I was escaping and off on an adventure. I had just finished three years of hard study and was desperate to let my hair down and have a good time. I was now ready to go the countries I had dreamed and yearned about for so many years even though I had no idea what I was getting myself into.

Finally on the road

Once I landed in France, I visited an old friend for three months, then said my goodbyes to everyone and bought a Eurail ticket and started travelling by myself all over Europe. I ended up meeting so many lovely people on my travels from all over the world. My experiences, although not entirely wonderful, taught me a lot about myself and other people as I had such a sheltered life back home in Australia. After all, I had come from a small town and was quite naive in many ways but I always felt protected by my angels and a guiding force.

My inner voice continued to warn me if I ever was about to get into any trouble. All I had to do was listen to it. Whenever I chose not to I would always end up in some type of sticky situation, but nothing I could not talk my way out of. Learning nursing from such an early age taught me so much about people and what they were like. You can learn so much by just standing back and observing and listening to what people have to say. It is amazing how a little bit of kindness can go such a long way.

On my travels, I hit it off with two fabulous sisters I met from Scandinavia, Berit and Helena, from an island called Harstad which is way up at the top of Norway, in the land of the midnight sun. They were quite different from one another. Helena was the youngest and sweetest of the sister's as well as being extremely intelligent. She had an interest in music and politics, so we hit if off straight away.

Berit was older and much more intense. She was quite moody and it was hard to read her at times as she was always thinking about something. She had a great sense of humour, though, and was really funny. As soon we met, we had an instant connection. It was hard to explain, but I felt as if I had known them my whole life and it didn't take us long before we became inseparable as we all had so much in common and couldn't stop talking and laughing about every subject imaginable.

It did not take long for the sisters to talk me into going camping with them down the Adriatic coast of Yugoslavia to a beautiful place called Dubrovnik. They had been there many times before for their summer holidays and it was a favourite destination for many Norwegians to holiday in the cold winter months.

As I had no plans other than to eventually find work when my money ran out, I just went along and agreed to whatever they wanted to do. Berit ended up in a romantic rendezvous with a very talkative German called Herman. He was happy to be our chauffeur and slave, and her boyfriend for the summer. He ended up driving us merrily up and down the coast in his little Citroen. I don't think I have ever laughed so much in my whole life.

Everything was great except for the times Helena and I spent fending off the amorous overtures of local Croatians who wanted us to be their girlfriends for the summer. One thing was certain, they certainly had no understanding of the word no, or get lost, in whatever language we tried to express it. No matter how many times we told them off, they would still persist and seemed to be extremely oversexed. We found this extremely frustrating and they very quickly became the enemy. I remember carrying a big stick around with me for protection which I would wave in their faces if they came too close. This of course did not work and they just laughed at me. Luckily we had Herman who we affectionately called "Wolfe" with us for protection and for our getaway route.

Other than that, we had so much fun together, travelling around the place. Before long I ran out of money, so they very kindly invited me back to Norway, where they insisted I would have no trouble getting work at their local hospital. I was thinking of going to England at the time, because that is where most nurses end up. It didn't really appeal to me though, so I was quite happy to take them up on their offer, without thinking of the consequences. I was always so fascinated with the Scandinavian countries anyway so this would be my chance to explore. I had a good feeling about it all so I just followed it.

Once I arrived in Harstad, within six weeks I was able to speak the language fluently, from just studying Mickey Mouse comics. Within a few weeks I was working in the medical ward at the local hospital and finally earning good money. All the medicine was in Latin so it was easy for me to understand. Most of the staff at the tiny hospital had never met anyone from so far away and were fascinated to meet a girl all the way from Australia. They very kindly went out of their way to help in whatever way they could. The patients, curious to meet such a celebrity, loved me as well and practised their broken English with me, plying me with questions about what my country was like and what was I doing there so far away from my own home and people.

Looking back it was really very funny as everything just fitted into place and was all so easy and simple. It was if I had lived there before and had come home as everything seemed so familiar. I was treated with the utmost respect, as nobody had ever met an Australian girl before, and everybody went out of their way to please me. The only thing they had ever heard about was *Skippy the Bush Kangaroo* and *Jaws* the movie. It really made me laugh when I heard that Norwegians were convinced that we had gigantic killer sharks everywhere living and breeding on our coastline. I didn't have the heart to tell them that the movie *Jaws* was, in my opinion, a propaganda film made by the Americans to make millions from people's fears.

I loved all the people I met and could not get enough of the clean air, country and the incredible natural world that surrounded me. Everything I saw, from the midnight sun to the northern lights that seemed to move in the night sky when you waved your hands in front of you, was truly an amazing experience and something that has stayed with me forever. I felt honoured and still do to this day to have had that experience as the northern lights is truly one of God's fabulous creations.

Years later, I found out through a past life therapist that I had actually lived in that area in many of my past lives.

The move from the north

After I finished my contract at the hospital in Harstad, I sadly said goodbye to the sisters and the land of the midnight sun and travelled south to a city called Trondheim. This is situated in the middle of Norway and was a much easier place to live as the weather there is relatively good compared to the extreme climate of the north where there are three months of darkness in winter and in summer there is light all the time. The long winter months had done my head in and I had become quite depressed as I was not used to living without sunlight. It'd be hard for anyone to live in such conditions.

I had a friend in Trondheim called Livy, who I had met in the north when she was visiting some relatives. We had got on really well and she ended up asking me to come and stay with her and her friends when I had finished my stay.

She wanted to spend more time with me as we had so much in common and I was a rarity being from the other side of the world. Livy was an amazing person who talked a lot about feminism. She wrote for an underground magazine, which she loved with a passion as she was very political and like me cared about righting injustices in the world. We were both interested in music and she was at university studying writing. She is now an author and writes historical romances that are published in Norway.

I had decided to take up her offer as I had had enough of the north and it was time to move on. One always knows these things as you will often get a nudge from spirit to let you know and Livy was that signpost.

It didn't take me long before I got a job in the local hospital which paid really well. It was easy for me to work now because I was able to speak the language more easily and was now registered as a nurse in Norway. I had loved my experience in the north, but my time was up as there were people to meet and places to go.

A few weeks after I had moved into my new home with Livy and her friends there was a knock at the door. Everyone was out at the time and there was nobody home except me. I had been working afternoon shift and didn't get home until late. I was tired and half asleep and must have overslept. At first I just ignored the knocking but then realised it could be some friends wanting to come for a visit.

Everyone had been really kind and friendly and welcomed me when I had arrived. Once they had met me I was invited to stay as long as I liked. I got on with everyone and I had so many wonderful new friends who were all part of my new life. My whole social life had changed and, although I was overwhelmed and everything was so intense, I was starting to feel really at home and was making very many wonderful new and exciting friends. I felt as if I must have been doing something right.

Jumping out of bed half asleep and rubbing the sleep out of my eyes, I rushed clumsily to the door and half opened the latch. I was still dressed in my pyjamas, and must have looked a real sight. To my surprise, when I stuck my head around the doorway I saw a rather creepy, strange-looking young man staring back at me. He seemed confused with glazed eyes, and was dressed from head to foot like an old hippy. He looked to me as if he had just stepped out of the musical *Hair*, or stuck in a 60s time warp. He wore a long white robe with a belt around it, jeans, and a dirty pair of worn sandals. He had colourful tiny glass beads around his neck and smelt of incense. His greasy dirty hair looked like he hadn't washed it for a week and reached his collar that was also covered thickly with a shaggy beard that blended with his hair.

My impression of him was not good as he seemed to me as if he thought he was some kind of crazy prophet, or holier than holy. The last thing I wanted so early in the day was a conversation with somebody who was going to give me a speech.

"Hello, are you the young girl all the way from Australia?" he asked with a wide stilted smile on his wooden face, looking me up and down with his downcast eyes.

I could not believe my ears. How could this strange person, possibly know who I was, I wondered. I hadn't been in town long, and already I was attracting the freaks I thought miserably to myself.

Without missing a beat, he carried on talking, seemingly unbothered by my lack of enthusiasm for his company or visit. "Sorry if I have woken you," he said. "Can I come in?"

Unable to believe my ears, I continued just staring at him, unable to think of anything to say, wishing I was somewhere else. Neither of us spoke for a while, standing in silence staring at each other. It was one of those awkward moments where you are not prepared for what to do next.

I did not have a good feeling about this man. I did not know him, for a start, and he looked really strange. There was something about his manner that did not sit right and it annoyed me that he had the audacity to just arrive at my home when I did not know him from a bar of soap. My long shifts at the hospital were starting to get to me as I hardly had anytime to sleep with all the partying, let alone meditate. I was burning the candle at both ends and the last thing I wanted was some weirdo standing on my doorstep, wanting to come in.

Hesitating and speaking very slowly in broken Norwegian, I finally spoke. "Yes I am, and what can I do for you?" I replied, irritated, looking at him from behind the large wooden door and wishing him just to disappear.

The last thing I wanted was a crazy guy chasing me because I was someone different from another country. My mind started to race, and I wondered how this weird guy had found out where I lived. At first I thought he may have been an undercover policeman, but that did not make sense as I was registered at the local police station, and allowed to work in the country. Then I wondered if he was someone checking up on my friends as they were very political and he may have thought I was an overseas activist they had imported to help them with their political campaigns. My cautious and suspicious mind went into overdrive.

There was a long pause as he continued to stare rather rudely with a confused look on his face. I could feel him sucking my energy like a vampire as he looked me up and down. My stomach hurt and my head began to throb. Finally gaining confidence, he grabbed something from his pocket. "Do you know what this is?" he asked as he pulled out a tarot card and shoved it in my face.

"Yes, that's the hanged man..." I yawned becoming very tired of the whole procedure. "Oh yeah! And so what?" I asked, starting to become really annoyed and irritated.

Then he started to tell me in broken English, while clapping his hands like a madman, that he was looking for the foreign girl who was very spiritual and I was "The One" that he was looking for.

He then went on to tell me he had many dreams about me and what I could do and that he was sent by his group to meet me. He wanted me to sit in his meditation group as a guest, with the rest of his friends so they could lift their vibration as they were stuck and in need of my help.

The whole idea sounded pretty weird and I wasn't going to wait for him to tell me to take off all my clothes next, so I quickly shut the door in his face and yelled through the keyhole not to bother me again or he would be sorry.

Refusing to give up, and not taking a "no" for an answer he relentlessly pursued me for a good couple of weeks until Tor, one of my flatmates, decided to take action and threatened to beat him up and call the police.

The situation was rather awkward at the time, and I was paranoid about going out and meeting people, but I still managed to meet like-minded spiritual people like myself along the way, who weren't so intense. Why I attracted him into my life I will never know but perhaps spirit was teaching me about boundaries.

At that time I made a conscious decision to put my spiritual life on hold and get more involved with music, theatre and serious dating. I was young and fancy-free and I had no time to commit myself to my spiritual work as I wanted to live my life, fall in love and have some fun like everybody else. I was sick of attracting spirit phenomena into my life and knowing things before they happened. I just wanted to be like everybody else around me and have fun. I made a conscious decision to block everything out and take no notice of the strong voices or messages I constantly received. Spirit would just have to give me a break so I could find my own way.

Little did I know then that the gift I had was the best thing I had going for me and was my only true salvation in life and always kept me out of trouble. It is only when you lose something you realise how important it is. Within a week I was listening to my higher guidance again.

Tina

Another girl I had met in the land of ice and snow was Tina, an exchange student from New Zealand. She was in love with one of my flatmates, Tor, the playboy, who was always falling in love with every girl he met. He was a great guy but was always getting himself into trouble with his disastrous love affairs. A real romantic in every sense, no matter how hard he tried, he always got involved with the wrong type of woman and the affair would end in tears.

There were five of us living in the house. Livy lived with her boyfriend, Egil, who toured a lot with a local rock band and had a penchant for other women. We also had a friend who was a poet and writer called Arne, who visited frequently, drank till all hours of the night and recited poetry to anybody who would care to listen. We were all heavily into politics and music in those days and all of us, when we weren't working, played in bands in our spare time so we were always meeting people and travelling all over the place.

One day Tor told me in confidence that he was worried about Tina, his new girlfriend that he had recently picked up, as she seemed to be suffering some type of depression and spent hours sitting alone, chanting and reading occult books. She was also into spells, as he had seen magic books lying around the place, and bits and pieces of strange things she had cut up or put on her little altar she had by her window. He felt very uneasy about her behaviour. He had thought of breaking it off a couple of times but every time he did he could not stop thinking and lusting after her.

After he confronted her about what she was doing, he discovered a strange piece of dried fruit wrapped in coloured string in his shoe and when he asked her about this she only became even more secretive. He was a very spiritual person like me as we always talked about such things together and he said his inner voice kept saying that something was not right. In the end he talked me into meeting her to find out what vibe I got from her.

Besides being an intuitive, he also knew I was a nurse so he wanted me to suss out what was going on in her mind. I began to worry about him, as he was becoming more and more smitten with her every day. He also told me that he was becoming obsessive and jealous, which was not like him and he was finding it difficult to stop thinking about her all the time. This was very unusual for him because he had a sex life like a rabbit and was always on the go with a few women at the same time. I would wonder where he found the energy and how he did it as he had women running after him all the time from all over the place. The rest of us used to laugh and call him "the Bull" behind his back because of his bad habits. In the end he had me convinced that I had to help him get to the bottom of it all as he was not himself and was feeling quite frightened.

Time passed, and I soon forgot about our conversation at the breakfast table until I accidentally bumped into Tina at the local bookstore in town, a great place to meet and greet friends. She introduced herself and told me she had heard all about me and was desperate to chat as we both spoke English. This was a relief as speaking Norwegian all day used to make my mouth ache.

At first, we seemed to get on really well as we had the same sense of humour. I could also see what Tor saw in her as she was one of the most beautiful women I have ever met, reminding me of a life-sized Barbie doll, but with brown long hair instead of blonde. She was tall and thin, with a beautiful face with large pink lips to match and, from a distance, the most beautiful eyes. But when you got up close and looked directly into her eyes, they were completely empty. I used to shudder whenever I looked into them as it seemed to me that sometimes nobody was home but then she would smile again and it all seemed to change.

I found her very confusing and, at times, forgot who I was talking to as she seemed to have two distinct types of mood personalities; one was bubbly and happy while the other was sad and withdrawn. I now realise that she must have been suffering from some type of depression but she never wanted to talk about it so I just let it go. Often when I thought of her when I was alone, my feelings would tell me that things were not right. In the end I decided to give her a little nickname, "Loving Tina who just wants to kill you." Which made me have a good laugh to myself, as it seemed so appropriate at the time? Poor Tor, I could really understand what he was going through.

I believe people's eyes tell the story of what they are really like as they truly are the windows of the soul. At first, I was overwhelmed by her beauty and fantastic personality, and wanted to hang out with her all the time as she was so much fun. I could understand what Tor saw in her as she was fantastic to be around if she was in the right mood. She had poor Tor wrapped around her little finger and it was funny to watch in a way, because I had never seen him so fixated with anyone before. In hindsight her only motive to have me as a friend was so she could get closer to my infatuated flatmate who thought he was hopelessly in love.

I also couldn't help but sense there was something a little strange about her energy but I could not put my finger on the nagging feeling that things were not what they seemed. Whenever we met for coffee, which was often on a Sunday after she stayed the night with Tor, I always felt extremely drained afterwards, and this worried me.

Tor on the other hand was over the moon and so excited that we had become friends. He wanted me to accept her because he said he loved her so much and that he wanted us to be close. My real feelings, however, were becoming very different. I was too afraid to break his bubble and tell him what I thought, as she was really strange. No matter how hard I tried to just go with the flow, and put it at the back of my mind, that horrible feeling haunted me.

Tina lived out of town so, whenever I was free from the hospital, which was not often, I'd catch a tram out there, which usually took about 45 minutes. Her one room apartment was small but cosy and nestled neatly above a family's home in the middle of a forest. She had lived alone, except for her cat, for a couple of years as her parents had gone back to the US and she needed to finish her university studies.

The room was big and bright and she had hundreds of books crammed into an old bookcase. On closer inspection, I could see she was heavily into the occult but more the dark arts than spiritual. When I tried to speak to her about this, and my concerns, she became angry and annoyed and refused to talk about the subject.

She also had several books on spells and even told me once that she used them for everything in her life. This really worried me after a while because while it seemed innocent at first, she wasn't who she said she was.

To my horror, I began to realise she was not a very nice person and I wondered why I was so involved with her. She was so clever at hiding things about herself but after a while all the cracks started to show giving me a bigger picture of who she really was. Whenever we would have a conversation about her life and what she thought about people or situations, little things would just slip out making me shudder as she never had anything nice to say about anything or anyone. Whenever I spoke about myself or what I thought she never seemed interested.

Her cold mannerisms when she was playing "happy" began to make me feel uneasy and a little afraid. I was starting to dread even being around her, as her energy felt really toxic after a while and I could feel waves of anger under her emotions. I even saw that she was not really my friend but probably using me to get to Tor. That was ridiculous as I had no hold over him and was not interested in him in any way except friendship as I knew him too well.

Even though I am not into magic myself, I do not condemn it as I know some who use it wisely and would never in a million years hurt anyone or anything. However, it was a different scenario for Tina.

She used magic spells she read about to manipulate everyone and everything in her life, even her boyfriends. She did not care about the ramifications or the effects it might have on people. She wouldn't allow things to happen naturally as she always wanted to be in control, so she used magic and spells to do this which is really against the universal laws. Everybody on the planet should have free will.

The more I got to know her the more I could see that her beauty was just a mask of the real Tina. She always had continual dramas in her life that I would hear about on a regular basis and on many occasions was cruel to her cat, which was a real sore point with me as I found that despicable as all our pets are like our children, very innocent and vulnerable.

I should have ended the friendship then and listened to my intuition, as it is never wrong, but she always would say she was sorry, so I would feel sorry for her. She was stuck in the "poor me" syndrome and gradually wore me down and I began to dread having to see her. I decided to end the friendship, using my work as an excuse. She was upset of course, but said she said she understood as I was studying at the time like her and had so many exams. Tina never had friends who stayed in her life for long because she always said they bored her, and she was used to people leaving her all alone.

After a while Tina broke up with Tor. He cried like a baby and was devastated for ages until he met a German student who swept him off his feet. Anna was a beautiful girl and everyone in the house loved her.

Not long after all of us heard that Tina had left town and went to live with her parents. I felt relieved, as I knew she would get the help she needed, as she was so lonely and had many problems. Both Tor and I could look forward to having fun in our lives and not having to find any bits of dried fruit or strange things stuffed in our boots. When I think of Tina, I really believe my guides and angels were looking after me. She was definitely a troubled soul, though perhaps misguided might be a better word.

The Sydney move

Shortly after I arrived back from overseas, I divorced my first husband, who I had married hastily in Norway, got involved in a few bands playing my bass guitar and finished my university studies. Within a few years, I met and later married my true soul mate, Andrew. Some time after meeting him we moved into a small apartment in Marrickville. He is a really funny guy and I met him when playing a gig in a backyard for a party. I did not fancy him at first but when I heard him laugh, he stole my heart and we have been together ever since.

After living together a few years, we ended up buying an old house which was a deceased state in the inner western suburbs of Sydney. An elderly couple had lived in the house and as far as we were concerned were very happy and had lived there for years. Eventually, like the rest of us they became too old and sick and later died in a short time space of each other. As they had no children we inherited what was left of their estate, a collection of bits and bobs that included everything from an old commode to pictures of kittens on the wall and a really old walking stick. It did not take us long to get a good impression about how they had lived their lives and what had happened to them. If anything the old home was very homely and welcoming.

We also inherited a friendly widow called Tess who lived next door. She was extremely bright and intelligent, like a detective who knew everything there was to know in the street. You would never in a million years be able to pull the wool over her eyes.

She often told us stories about the history of the house and the lives of the couple she was neighbours with for many years. She was lonely herself as her son had moved interstate and was overjoyed to have a young couple with a child move in next door to amuse her and to give her some company.

This worried us all at first, but the ice was broken when we both realised that we all loved cats, so we all soon became good friends and neighbours. It also did not take long before she became part of our family.

Whenever I pulled up from the hospital where I was working in between acting jobs, she would be waiting for me in her front parlour to have a cup of tea and tell me about her day. She would then enquire about my day and ask me what I had been up to. It made me realise how extremely lonely it must be for old people, especially when their health fails and all they can do is sit at home because they no longer have the strength to want to go out. I also never had to worry about anyone ever breaking in as nothing ever got past Tess's watchful eye. Some people may have found her irritating but I could see she had no family so it did not bother me and I welcomed her with loving arms.

As well, there were other rather strange and unexplainable things that were going on inside our home. This experience taught me how spirit people can also influence us in our daily lives. Every day, around the same time, just when I was about to cook dinner for the family, something very strange would happen. As soon as the clock hit 5pm, a stinking smell of urine would manifest from nowhere and appear in a wet puddle on the lounge room floor. The smell was so strong and so rancid, almost as if somebody had urinated right there. The awful smell would gradually waft its way from room to room and no matter where you were in the house you could always smell it.

At first I thought it was the cat and kicked him outside a dozen times until I realised it wasn't his fault, because whenever I looked for him I could see him sitting on the back fence fast asleep. Kaja, my eldest daughter, was only a teenager at the time and she would yell and scream with annoyance that the awful smell was back, asking me to do something about it. In the end we put it down to visitations from old Mrs Robertson who once lived in the house. She seemed to make it a habit of visiting every afternoon and letting us know by going to the toilet, on the floor.

This was later confirmed by our neighbour, Tess, who told us in few words that the old girl was quite incontinent before she passed. This made sense because one of the things that we had "inherited" was an old commode which the old lady must have used until she died later in the hospital.

I also remember hearing a dragging noise occasionally, which must have been the spirit lady dragging around her old walking frame. It hadn't struck me that she could still be in the house as the house had a welcoming feel, as if it wanted us to be there. Except for the strong smell of urine on the carpet she never bothered us and we all used to just joke about the incident.

Kaja is also a psychic and a healer, and felt it was the old lady's way of having a little joke and letting us know that she was around. As far as we knew she was harmless but probably just a little curious about what was going on in her well-loved home, as we had made so many changes when we moved into the place and there was always so much activity in the once quiet home.

My mother, who is the matriarch of our families and is always not so far from our lives, grew more open to spirit phenomena as she got older. Perhaps this was because of my influence as I would often discuss these matters with her. When she found out about the incident she became really annoyed because she had often had the same problem occur in her home.

Over the years she was often visited by her deceased uncles and aunties, who would leave smelly things behind. She also complained of hearing things in the night that kept her awake. Whenever this happened, she would just tell them to "buzz off". Funnily enough, this always seemed to work because she never had problems again. I will also never forget that a couple of years ago on Christmas day, I saw her own mother in spirit, who I recognized from old photos standing by the kitchen table. She had come in to give my mother a message about her health and her habit of overeating. As soon as Mum heard this she went on a diet and lost 15 kilograms because her own mother had died of a heart attack when Mum was only five. Since then Mum has always kept a good figure and has never been overweight again.

When Kaja was telling her about the incidents one day on the telephone, Mum started yelling angrily at the top of her voice and threatened to visit to shoo the old woman away. Poor Mrs Robertson must have heard her yelling and was frightened to death, because not long after my mother's call the smell suddenly vanished and never came back again.

I have come to learn that smells are often a sign that spirit people are visiting, not that they're earth-bound spirits which are entirely different and I will discuss this later.

Another strange thing was that we found out that her husband once had a beautiful garden in the front of the house but it was now choked with weeds. All his old garden tools, still in perfect condition, were locked up neatly in a row in his shed. There was even an old gardening hat that he used to wear, sitting high on a dusty iron hook.

After he had died, his garden bed soon became wild and eventually disappeared amongst hundreds of prickly weeds and vines. The once beautiful and exquisite prize roses were now old and rotting and being strangled by weeds. Soon we too became avid gardeners, even though my husband and I had absolutely no idea about gardening and had no interest in the subject previously. Once we got the urge it did not take us long to bring the once-magnificent garden back to life.

Weekends began to be taken up with activities such as travelling to the city's botanical gardens to check out all the different types of roses on display. We wanted to know which roses were best to plant and what they looked and smelt like. Our little hobby soon turned into a major project and, in no time, we were rewarded by the beautiful scents of our blooms wafting through our bedroom window when we awakened from a good night's rest.

Suddenly, we had the best-looking rose garden in the street. When we finally sold the house and moved on a few years later, I found that I was never able to grow roses like the ones we had back then. Perhaps we had heavenly help.

Michelle

Around the same time, a beautiful kindred soul came into my life called Michelle. She also had experienced a similar childhood to mine, but had suffered much cruelty from her mother who had no understanding of her daughter's paranormal gifts that she had been born with. Instead of listening to what her daughter told her and trying to understand her frightened daughter's experiences, she treated her only child like a leper, telling her she had the devil in her and sending her off to psychologists and psychiatrists. Exhausted and feeling as if there was something seriously wrong with her, Michelle closed down. Her childhood was a nightmare because of the human tragedy of non-acceptance thrown her way. In the end, the psychologists could not find anything wrong with her so she was sent home and learnt to live in silence and not tell anyone about her inner feelings and experiences.

This made Michelle very untrusting of people who came into her life and, for many years, she found it difficult to have friendships or allow anyone to be too close to her. Her relationships with men seemed to suffer too and, as a young adult, she was subjected to abusive relationships. To me she was one of the most talented and remarkable energy workers I have ever met. Her talents from spirit to this day are exceptional and she has worked as a tireless energy healer and medium for many years with great success.

We met one day at a healing centre in Balmain. I had just finished some shopping, when I decided to go inside and ask for a job as a reader. She was standing at the counter and smiled, and from the moment we looked into each other's eyes, I felt an overwhelming connection as if I had known her my whole life. As our eyes met, I smiled back and felt genuine warmth that I had not felt in a long time. Feeling extremely relaxed and assured, I told her I was a reader and trained in mediumship and healing. Straight away, she told me that they were looking for people with my experience, and asked when I could start. After accepting the offer, I agreed to start on the following Sunday.

Whenever this kind of synchronicity has happened before it is always a signpost or message from spirit that I am on the right path because it all happens so easily. Over the years I have worked in many healing centres around Sydney and they have been a great training ground and learning curve for me as a light worker.

I have met and worked with so many wonderful talented like-minded people, and there is always enough work for everyone. Most have integrity and I have only run into a few rotten apples or charlatans. Once you are on the spiritual path, your journey never ends and you keep on learning. That is what I love about this work and I find I am constantly challenged by my clients to work on myself more and never stop reading and studying.

Work with people from all parts of life teaches you about compassion and non-judgement. Some of the best friendships I have ever had have been from these types of places. In fact everyone I have met to this day has taught me something that I needed to learn, which has helped me become a much better person. I feel humbled by this and there is not a day that goes by that I do not thank spirit for all the blessings I have in my life.

Michelle and I gradually became good friends and started spending time together in between our busy lives and working in the shop. We had so much in common we spent our precious free time talking for hours. To me, she was like a soul sister.

I later discovered she was also a gifted trance channel, healer and clairvoyant. Like me, she was trained by her guides and helped on a daily basis through meditation. Even though you may study the fundamentals at different colleges and schools, sometimes the most important things are only learnt from your loving guides who are with you 100 per cent of the way. Books simply will not have the same information that your guides can give you because the best spiritual information does not come from the earth's plane but a higher consciousness.

Once you train the voice, or voices within you, and learn to trust yourself with your innate abilities, you get to have control of your gift and it grows. With discipline and focus, your vibration or energy will steadily grow as your guides are with you every step of the way. It may take years of dedication but it is worth it in the end. I often hear people complaining about how they feel stuck and cannot become any better than what they already are. They do not understand that it takes years of working on yourself to understand how energy really works and you have to trust the process. A healing course on a weekend is not going to get you there because you need to incorporate what you learn into your life and work with the energy.

Patience is a key factor you have to learn and spirit will only move you and teach you more things when you are ready and have learnt the lessons. If ever you do anything wrong that can harm anyone and that includes idle gossip, the universe will give you a big bump on the head with a stick and things will not go as smoothly as you want.

You will continue to remain stuck and disappointed and others will fly past you. As well, you will only attract the same type of people into your life as we all mirror each other. I have even known people to lose their gift as they have misused it in an egotistical way. Everything comes at a price in life so it is important to stay on the straight and narrow and not step on anyone's toes. If you want to be treated well and respected that is exactly how you need to treat everyone who comes into your life because what you give out will come back. I know it is easy to be angry and disappointed with people, as I have experienced this many times in my life, but the only way to heal this situation is to send love and forgiveness. This is the basis of all healing.

Michelle lived far away from me in the Snowy Mountains with her two sons, so whenever we wanted to catch up I would have to drive for miles just to see her. When we got together we'd spend a lot of time going for bushwalks as the nature in the Snowy Mountains is beautiful and so healing. I always felt like it was heaven walking in the bush, smelling all the fresh aromas and listening to the birds and the wind in the trees.

We used to go for glorious bushwalks together and "talk" to all the flowers and trees in the natural surroundings and she would tell me many stories about her life and the many encounters with extra-terrestrials in some caves in the mountains as well. This amazed me because I have only ever seen "ships" in the northern night sky. Whenever I told my husband about my world and the people that I used to meet, he would just shake his head his head and say, "Look I don't care what you do, but just don't bring any of these people home or tell them where we live, OK?" I thought this was hysterical, as I often thought of the TV show *Bewitched* where the white witch Samantha is married to the mortal Darren.

Michelle and I were like sisters and I had the most knowing feeling that I really knew her as we had much in common and understood each other so well. Before she ever said anything I would know what she was going to say. In hindsight, it did take her a while to trust me because of her horrible past. Sometimes I think this could have perhaps have been karmic debts she was paying back from other lives with the same people but possibly she chose that contract with them so she could learn as a soul to believe in herself and her strengths.

We were friends for quite a while until she packed up everything and moved to France, where she later married. She had an English passport so she was able to live in Europe without any difficulties. Sometimes I think of her and our great connection and wish that she was still in my life but I have come to realise that not everyone stays in your life forever.

Michelle came into my life to teach me about using my skills and working with them. I never wanted to be what my mother calls "a fortune teller or a nutcase who can talk to dead people", as your life can be like a circus and you are up for ridicule as people can be so insensitive and treat you like you are a black witch.

For years I tried to suppress my gifts by reading girly magazines and getting involved with bands and creative projects but the restlessness would never go away unless I was helping people. The last I heard of Michelle was when she wrote and told me that she had a thriving practice in Paris, and had married a local man who had visited her in Australia when she lived here. She also was madly trying to get pregnant and asked me if she would and I told her I saw her having a baby girl. I was going to visit her one year when I was overseas with my husband, but for some reason it never happened. I realised, sadly, that our paths had gone in other directions and our contract was over but our love and respect for each other will stay forever. I am left with just very fond memories of Michelle.

Part Two

Spiritual Path

Doing the work

Once you are on the spiritual path, you will never want to come off it. There is no other way to live life, as it is a continual journey of discovery. Spirit really opens you up and you learn to open your heart and listen to that wise inner knowing. Spirit also teaches you to trust the subtle feelings you have inside you and how unconditional love is so important in your life. Learning to love yourself for who you are and others is one of life's main principles.

Another one is the principle of forgiveness. I have tried to be "normal" and ignore the silent messages that I constantly receive but whenever that happens, without fail I always get into trouble. Everybody has this sixth sense; you just need to learn how to use it and a good way to start is by listening to your inner voice.

I always wonder how people survive without using their intuition and inner wisdom that spirit has given them. When things have gone wrong in my life I have shaken my fist and blamed God for not being fair, but I know now this is just a waste of time. I could never live my life any other way. You not only get to meet the most amazing people along the way and your life is an exciting journey.

The more you work on yourself, the more you grow and lift your vibration. As you clear your emotional body through meditation and spiritual growth, your outer world will change for the better. Nothing will stay the same. You may find that you are no longer attracted to the same people or situations anymore. This process may even affect your marriage or partner. You will also become extremely sensitive to most things, if you aren't already, and smell is a big one for me.

You will become attracted to more like-minded people and this always makes life interesting. You may end up being lonely for a while, but that will soon change as others will come in who are on the same wavelength as you, as in the law of attraction. As a child I spent a lot of time by myself, because nobody, even members of the family could relate to me and what I was feeling and experiencing but I still survived. I learnt to become self sufficient. Isn't that what happens when you are the black sheep of the family? I am sure there are many others with a similar story to tell.

Another change in your life will be your diet. I no longer eat red meat as I do not like the way the animals are killed. After seeing the live export trade in the Kimberley's first hand I had a major life change. I now eat only fish or free-range chicken but, most of the time, my diet is mainly vegetarian. Because of my work and my vibration, I am no longer able to drink large amounts of alcohol as it takes me days to get over it. Cigarettes are also out the window, as my body prefers no toxins but, if ever I am really upset, I will sneak one occasionally. Old habits never die!

People on your wave length will not only understand you but give you support with your work and goals or contracts you made in heaven before you came down to earth. There is always enough work for everyone and plenty of opportunities to go around. Sharing the fruits of life is a blessing. Friends who walk the same path as you will be more loving and more fun to be with. Spirit is your teacher, and you just have to trust, have a good life and do the best you can.

Before she died, Joan, one of my old teachers, always used to say, "Once you surrender to Spirit, Spirit will always look after you. You will always have food on the table, wonderful supportive friendships and someone in your life who loves you unconditionally for who you truly are."

I do this work because it brings so much healing and love to so many people. It not only connects to your loved ones that have passed over, but it also helps people move on, to know that their loved ones are safe and well, and no longer in pain or physical discomfort. I am able to connect with them, as if I was on a telephone. This is **clairaudience,** or clear hearing, which involves hearing guidance coming from outside or from inside your mind, the still small voice within. To me, it sounds like my own voice but others may be different.

I am also **clairvoyant** or clear seeing where I am able to see still pictures or miniature movies in my mind's eye either inside or outside my head and I am also **clairsentient**, which helps with my mediumship as it involves receiving divine guidance as an emotion or a physical sensation, such as a smell, tightened muscles, or a touch.

All these skills help with proof of survival, when I contact somebody who has passed over and they want to give evidence that they are around. All I have to do is just relax and trust the gifts. If I become nervous or stressed it can be very draining because what most people do not realise is that this type of work can be very taxing as it requires much focus from the medium.

We also suffer a high degree of sensitivity with the work we do so we have to be careful who we mix with. Toxic people and toxic substances do not mix. Some of my friends and acquaintances I have collected over the years have had to go because they have no understanding of what I do and are not on the same level. I just put it down to being on a different path. It only makes things complicated as you become so sensitive to energy and it is really a disfavour to yourself to have to put up with harsh criticism, unfair judgement and total ignorance from people who don't work on themselves and do not understand who you are as a soul. I have come to realise that some of these so-called spiritual people are really teachers and, even though the lessons were tough, I have blessed them all and forgiven them. I have found that I have to continually work on myself and my emotions as the work is an incredible responsibility.

I have also studied all types of spiritual healing from Reiki to hypnotherapy and was even a registered nurse in both Australia and Norway. Studying for me is a passion and I am forever learning new things on a daily basis and how I see the world around me. When you work on your abilities you learn so much as spirit is always using what you learn to teach you more things. If for example, you are into astrology, you might get a picture or symbol in your mind's eye of the spirit of a Ram, which may in turn mean something for the person that you are reading for. And because I have been able to read tarot from an early age, spirit will sometimes show me one of the tarot cards in my mind's eye which, in turn, may be a symbol for something meaningful in that person's life. For instance, one of the Tarot's major Arcana cards is the Tower, which means big changes. As I write this short book of my life to date, I have a few interesting case studies of people further on in the book that I have worked on and other topics that I am passionate about. I hope to give you insight into the role of a light-worker, as life as a medium and healer is never boring.

Meditation

Come into the silence of solitude, and the vibration there will talk to you with the voice of God, and you will know that the invisible has become visible and the unreal has become real. Just beneath the shadows of this life is God's wondrous Light ... When you meditate, you will find doors opening to Him everywhere.

Paramahansa Yogananda

Meditation is the golden key to spiritual growth as it connects you to your inner light and eternal soul. Once you master this art, you will discover the secrets to your inner wisdom. You become more aware of yourself and everything around you. Meditation teaches you to stop stressing, ground, focus and stop the constant mind chatter that goes on in your head on a daily basis.

Everything you need in your life you will be drawn to you easily and manifest as we are all energy but vibrating on different frequencies. You just have to learn to surrender and go with the process. By just meditating 20 minutes a day you can bring so much peace into your life and it helps to keep you younger as you are able to let go of the stresses and anxieties that life brings.

I tried so many times when I was younger to meditate but never had the discipline to even sit still as I was hyperactive and my mind was always in overdrive. My parents used to call me "the fly" as I could never sit down and finish a cup of tea without wanting to race off and do other things. There were always people to meet and places to go, so much so that I used to just about wear myself out by trying to keep up.

My way of meditating in the early days was by swimming in the sea and staring at the clouds in the sky, or taking long walks in nature and being aware of everything around me as this always gave me so much pleasure and energy. Just to be one with nature is rewarding and calming.

Often my friends and I would head off down the coast on surfing holidays at Easter or summer holidays to check out other surfing beaches and hidden bush enclaves. We would drive as far as we could in one day, heading down the NSW South Coast to Green Point, Ulladulla or Pambula. Once we got there we would set up a little camp and spend quality time in nature away from prying eyes, sitting around a campfire and telling stories of what was happening in our lives. If we were lucky there would be nobody except us and other kindred spirits who always kept to themselves. It was always a blessing and simply refreshing to camp under a canopy of bright twinkling stars and listen to the sounds of the waves pounding on the beach while you slept.

When I was heavily into music it was great playing with other people in bands as we were all on the same wavelength and heavily committed to our art. It was always a "high" to play my bass guitar with other musicians and get lost in the energy of loud rock music waves. For many years, all I ever thought about was music and songs and different riffs and bars that would play through my head.

Music opened up another world for me where nothing mattered except the band and the passion we had to get our music across. The only trouble was we were all highly creative people with massive egos and sometimes we did not want all the same things. Whenever that happened, it always ended really badly and some would go their own way and start something else. Somebody once told me that being in a rock band can be like a marriage gone wrong as it is such an intense experience.

One issue for me was that often when I walked into pubs I could feel a lot of spirits around me, not always the loving kind. Because of the toxic people who use heavy drugs and excessive alcohol who go to hotels and clubs, there can be a lot of dark energy around. Often I have felt some lost souls in these places that can play havoc with my energy. At the end of the day, too much bad energy can cause fights and with alcohol it can be a very toxic situation where people can get really hurt. Whenever this has happened to me, I would leave and go home and shower to wash off the unsavoury energy I picked up.

I once met a medium, a really lovely lady, who worked as a barmaid in a really rundown rough hotel. When I asked her what she was doing there and how could she work in such a place, she told me that she felt it was her job to help lost souls that came into the pub to pass over into the light. She was a strong, tough woman who was easily able to stand up for herself and what she believed was right for her, and keep everyone in check. On some level, she felt it was her destiny in life to do such work in an environment most of us would only want to avoid.

A couple of years later, when I was an actor working for a travelling theatre company and on the road, I would chant to calm myself down and centre myself. The other actors in the company were not really my friends and, as you could imagine, I found it difficult to be with people that I had nothing really in common with for weeks on end. When you do so much touring to so many different places, you can become extremely wired and fragmented so it is essential to find some way to be able to tune out from what is going on around you all the time. This way you can avoid disagreements or unsavoury altercations that can be stressful and uncalled for.

Now I cannot live without meditation and wonder how I ever survived without it as it is an integral part of my life and helps me on a daily basis with everything. If I don't do it on a regular basis, I can be a bit of a bitch and have what I call a really bad hair day where everyone suffers, even the cats. Everybody has to duck for cover as I can go a little bit hyper if anyone gets in my way.

When I first started meditation I used a mantra for a while to get rid of what's called monkey talk. I think it was something boring like SO HUM, which was nevertheless effective and helped heaps. I was also told by one of my many teachers that 20 minutes of meditation is equivalent to four hours sleep on the theta level.

A journey of constant changes

When I was in my 30s I was really stressed out and was working part-time in a hospital as a trained nurse so my husband and I could get a loan for a house we wanted to buy. I hated my job with a vengeance as I had finished with nursing. I just wanted to be an actor because I had just finished touring with a travelling theatre company called Sidetrack Theatre for nearly a year and the last thing I wanted to do was end up back in another hospital as a nurse.

In the show I played bass guitar and wrote my own scripts, playing all the different characters that were needed in the show. Once I finished my contract, however, it was almost impossible to get any type of acting job in town as it was over-saturated with models and housewives wanting part-time work.

I remember sitting for auditions with famous actors on one side and housewives on the other, as the people hiring us never had any idea of exactly what they were looking for so they used to just herd us in like cattle. Most of the jobs were only commercials for dog food or small parts on television shows or what they call 50 liners which is basically "hello" or one-word syllables. Occasionally, we were allowed to improvise but this was only if we were lucky. I found this situation extremely frustrating as all I could think about was getting back on the road and doing my thing. My husband wasn't impressed, of course, and was tired of the drama queen within me so reluctantly I went back to what I call the slave mines to get enough money to pay for the mortgage. Anybody who has been a nurse in an under-staffed crumbling old hospital will understand my sentiments as the government has no idea of the worth of nurses even now.

After I had my second child, Anna, I decided it was time to develop myself more and immerse myself into the spiritual side of life so I enrolled in as many courses as possible and started to meditate on a daily basis. This was one of the most rewarding things I could have done and I have never looked back as I was opened up to a whole other world. Everything I was looking for was inside me, even all the questions and answers I wanted to know. My whole inner world opened up, and I started to meet my guides, receive information and have better control of my gifts I was born with. Instead of trying to suppress them I started to understand more of who I was as a person and started to love and embrace the real me.

I didn't care what people thought of me anymore and did not try to hide my gifts and natural talents. For years I hid in the closet, trying desperately just to fit in. Now, I didn't care if people thought I was a witch or somebody evil or weird. If people could not accept who was and what I could do, well, that was their problem. Five months after I had my second baby, I was headhunted for a community television program by a friend I used to work with.

My friend had kept coming around to my place and telling me about a community television show I would be perfect for. They were looking for a presenter with acting skills and the producer wanted to see me. Every time she asked me to go down and talk to the people, I would just fob her off as I had a small baby and was breast feeding at the time. I was also disillusioned with the acting world and not interested in doing television or stupid ads. The whole experience had been humiliating and I was sick of dressing up as different characters and not getting any work. One lady up the street even asked me if I was on medication as she had seen me walking up and down the street to the train station in different outfits all the time.

When I finally gave in and went to the studio and introduced myself to the producer, something really strange happened. She looked into my eyes and smiled. Without any hesitation she grabbed my hand, gave me a hug and asked me when I could start. I was startled and wondered what I had got myself into, but whenever these strange occurrences happen to me in my life, I just go with it and see it as a gift from heaven.

In two weeks, I was working on the show she produced without even having to do an audition. I could not believe it and thought myself to be the luckiest person in the world.

My segment was called "Let's have a chat with Kerrie". On the show I must have interviewed hundreds of healers, psychics, and alternative therapists from all over Australia and overseas. It taught me so much about what was going on out there and I was very humbled to be in their presence. I also had to learn really fast how to do all the research and write the scripts for each episode of my show. It was a totally hands-on production where we did everything. Also being live-to-air did not help matters as you could never make any mistakes and had to improvise if anything went wrong or your subject became tongue-tied. I loved meeting others like myself, but it also taught me about believing in myself and doing my thing. It was always easy for me to run my own business and be creative as I did not need other people like I always thought I did.

I feel this was all set up by spirit, as there are never any coincidences in life. I had so much work and study I wanted to do I did not know where to start. All the doors began to open and everything became really easy. Everything I was meant to do was just given to me as if I was led there by an invisible force. I kept hearing the words in my mind from very deep inside, "Remember who you are."

The higher self

The more you work at raising your vibration and your awareness, the more you are in alignment with your higher self, which is your soul energy and is with you in every lifetime. When I first came into contact with my higher self, I was told that she was a like an angelic being or light being called Cassandra or Saku. This makes sense to me as I have always since I can remember been driven to help as many people as possible and I have always known what my path is. I find her energy patient, compassionate and extremely nurturing, considering I have had such a varied and colourful past. The more you work on your own lessons and issues, the more you are connected to your higher self which can be an all-empowering experience.

In metaphysics we learn how to recognise the various levels of consciousness. In mediumship we learn who our main guide is, or gatekeeper, who looks after and guards the soul. We gradually form a friendship as we learn how loving and kind our gatekeeper is and how we have a strong and protective trusting bond with all our guides. We come to understand our guides, and even though some will come and go, they are our spiritual teachers and friends. They guide us with love, compassion and gentle coaching. I have learnt not to be afraid about surrendering the need for attachment to the ego.

It may sound paradoxical but letting go is not about losing self-empowerment but is about gaining it and this process involves trust. When you remove the needs of the ego and allow your true destiny, through the will of the soul, to guide you through life, then life itself becomes a rewarding journey.

Trance classes

A trance medium or channel is a person who enters a state of trance in order to produce mediumistic phenomena. This person, or channel, will be able to set aside their conscious self in order to allow another being, a non-physical or spirit being, to speak through their body.

When you speak to an entity or enlightened being who is being trance channelled, you are speaking directly to that entity without the channel's personality acting as an intermediary or translator. The experience is like having an interactive conversation with a wise and loving friend. Remember that each entity has its own distinctive personality, and no one is the same. Trance channelling also allows less distortion of any information that you may receive.

Trance, or light trance (as channelling is also known) is something I have done for many years both by myself and with groups of like-minded people. It is also what I call a type of meditation. It is something that has to be worked at on a regular basis. Like anything in life, if you want to be good at it and get results, then the only way is to have a good and clear contact with your guides, who are our true spiritual teachers.

We may have many teachers here on earth who teach us many things but our real lessons come from our loving guides that are within us from the time we are born. We may have different guides throughout our development, who come and go, but our main guides or guide remains with us forever.

The first time I learnt to be a channel was an incredible experience. I was sitting in a class or what we call a "circle", in a darkened room with three other mediums. We were with a highly qualified teacher who was leading the group and were sitting close to each other, and surrounded by a beautiful energy of light that our leader had set up.

Not long after, relaxing with my eyes closed and paying special attention to my breath, I was suddenly what we call over-shadowed by a big loving male energy or entity. Never in my life had I felt such a strong connection to anyone as there was so much love being directed to me all at once and I felt overwhelmed. My guide's energy was so enormous and strong it felt as if somebody really big was sitting on top of me.

After I asked my guide to move aside, I felt a lot better as any fears I had just disappeared. Tears of happiness and joy filled my eyes with the love I was feeling and the deep connection taking place with this being and I.

When I asked intuitively my guide's name he told me that he was an Indian chief known as White Feather. He also called himself "father" and showed me pictures in my mind's eye of the life we had lived together as father and son. This did not surprise me as I have always had infinity with the indigenous people, especially native American Indians. (This may also explain my love of horses. I know now that many of my cats have been my horses in other lifetimes.) I soon had the urge to play an imaginary drum that sat in my lap and went with the gentle flow that was happening. I felt as if I was being teleported to another time and place where everything was just simple, easy and free.

At the same time my mind was in overdrive about my breakthrough and I just wanted to learn everything there was to know that he was talking about. The energy quickly changed, though, as I began to hear a funny noise coming from the other side of the room. Even though I opened my eyes as my curiosity got the better of me, I was able to stay in the energy because some entities you channel come through with open eyes and others closed.

I almost burst out laughing at the sight of my friend Lorry, who was crawling around on her stomach like a big caterpillar or worm making strange noises. This sudden change in energy and my laughter brought me straight back into my body. The teacher, realising that the energy had shifted, decided to bring us all back into the room and close the circle. Our first lesson was over.

I have since discovered that some people may take longer to make a connection to their guide. They may even just fall asleep and think they are channelling, but by their snoring this is not the case. Some even vomit and make loud horrible noises when they first begin to work with the energy while tappng their legs or hands, or walk around or dance. With one of my Indian guides, I feel like I am riding a horse bareback over the plains. My whole body rocks and it must look a sight to others to see. Some people may even feel a very heavy energy in their throats and feel as if they are choking. Everyone is different and no-one ever has the same experience as this is all part the journey in their teaching with spirit.

These days I much prefer to work solo and run my own group, but when I go through change I will get together with other like-minded people as the group energy is usually a lot stronger. It is also important to have a good teacher or leader and someone highly experienced who knows what they are doing. This energy work will take you to higher levels with your spiritual work as it is very uplifting.

I decided long ago not to work in the deep trance state as it does not appeal to me. (In the deep trance state you are completely overshadowed and you do not remember anything as your guide takes over your body.) And not everyone can do deep trance work as it takes a lot of time and energy, nor should anyone feel they have to do it or be forced. I once witnessed a woman force a young man to go into a deep trance, but he was terrified each time he did it and would scream and shout before going into the state. When he awoke and came back into the room he could not recall anything that happened. I spoke to her of my concerns in private, out of respect, but she assured me that he had wanted to be the channel.

As one who was sitting in the circle, this did not feel right to me as I felt he was not ready to do this type of work in his development. It was not long after my guide, White Feather, who is main guide, or gate-keeper, advised me that perhaps it was time for me to move on from this group. While I was there, I kept getting the flu and was unwell for many months, so something wasn't right. I had continued there to get a better connection with my writing guide, Leon, who usually stayed in the background as I always had so many healing guides around me all the time because of all the previous work I had been doing.

Once I learnt to ask the others to step back, my writing guide Leon stepped forward more and my mediumship guide, Romanov, came forward. As a result of this my writing became stronger and my mediumship went to new heights which was quite an interesting experience. If you are meant to do something, spirit will make it happen for you anyway, no matter what. When I finally left that particular group, my health improved so I felt I had done the right thing.

Now whenever I want to speak to my guides, all I have to do is just gently close my eyes and my loving and wise friends are always there. For others, all you have to do is find a good teacher and sit with a like-minded group. It may take a while to get there but it is worth it in the end to learn who all your guides are and for them to come in and talk to you, or through you.

If anyone ever asks you who are you talking to, you will be able to tell them precisely who the being is that is giving you your information. From my experience, I can say that trance meditation or mediumship is an integral part of your development as a serious psychic, medium or healer.

Can animals or insects be channelled?

This is a very good subject for debate. Many people may not relate to it but plants, animals, birds, insects and just about everything on the planet is made up of consciousness. I have channelled dogs and cats and even have a whale I sometimes make contact with. I also have experienced many people that have had past lives as animals in my hypnotherapy practice. (By the way my whale, which does not have a name as I receive the messages telepathically, has told me that one day there will be an end to the slaughter of these most magnificent mammals.)

Not long after I channelled my first cat, I had a stray cat land on my doorstep whom I adopted as he had nowhere to go and had no intention of leaving anyway. My other cats were not impressed with his arrival and still have their noses out of joint but they had no say in the matter. I ended up calling him Harry Stavros (all my cats are Greek) as he was and is still really big. It never ceases to shock me the number of animals that are dumped on a day to-day basis. Some people do not understand the meaning of responsibility.

A friend of mine often channels trees or plants and I once sat with a girl who only channelled angels. I have also channelled small sprites and devas or nature spirits. One of the guides I channel is a tiny water fairy, or being, called Erin.

Animals also have living souls as they too have a circle or cycle of life, and they incarnate as humans do but we have a higher vibration than animals. Trees as living beings also have a soul as does everything that lives. Animals do incur karma just the same way humans do, because for every action there is a reaction. It may also surprise many of you to know that certain animals incarnate specifically to be companions to certain souls.

How many times have you seen an animal or pet that is highly intelligent, just like a human? This idea has been frowned on by some people who have a small-minded belief system and think that you can only channel ascended masters or guides. Every living species on Earth and other planets is connected to the divine source of love and has its own intelligence. As we evolve as humans and learn to raise our vibration we become more open to other concepts and start to be more open in other ways.

As souls we are continually learning lessons of tolerance. Once you reach the end of your life cycle, your own loving guide who is always with you, and usually family members who have passed over to the other side, will come to be with you at the time of crossing over.

Meet the gatekeeper

In mediumship, our gatekeeper is usually a spirit guide we have had a past life with, perhaps a relative, friend or someone extremely loving and caring. Commonly, with clients we will discover they have a relative with them in spirit who has taken on this role. The rapport we build up and the contracts we make with our gatekeeper help protect our aura and chakras from unnecessary and inappropriate energies when we are consciously doing the light work.

Our gatekeeper stays with us always and protects our soul until we pass over to spirit when we are joined again with our protector and our own soul group. In some circumstances, my guides will occasionally go and work with other healers and mediums. We are multi-dimensional beings and well-known guides can be present in many dimensions and places at once.

Another psychic who I have worked with on and off for years will often ring me and say, "I worked with your guide Margaret last night in trance. She came through and started bossing us all around."

Another time, the same women told me that she was sitting in another healing group when she felt my guide White Feather come in and show her a few things. "Is he a big Indian fellow with a funny laugh?" she asked.

These comments are common and I have heard them many times. Can I help it if my guides want to work with other people? No, but seriously, it is common to trance or channel other guides from other healers and mediums. I have often sat in groups where a few of us will channel Jesus, other ascended masters and, occasionally, the archangels.

Automatic writing

Writing has always been an important part of my life and is a way for me to be more creative and to express myself. I call it "food for the brain and soul" as when writing your life, it can be reflective for you to look back on things but also very cathartic as it helps you sort out your emotions, which all helps in the healing process.

Much of my creative writing is generally information channelled from spirit, known as automatic writing. When I wrote my first book, *Magical Tales from the Forest*, I had no idea what I was talking about as it was mostly information that was just coming through when I meditated. Somehow I had become an expert on nature spirits while I researched other details, creating a story to go with this information. As my first serious book, it was a fascinating process even though it took years to complete.

One day, I was in a coffee shop having a laborious discussion with my husband about the difference between goblins and gnomes. I was explaining how a goblin couldn't be trusted as it is generally a greedy, lazy and selfish creature that is only interested in itself and gold, whereas the gentle gnome is a more compassionate, gentle creature who thinks only of their family. After I finished, he asked me with a puzzled look on his face how I knew this, and where I got the information from. Suddenly I stopped in mid-sentence, thought about it for a while and confessed I had no idea at all. As far as I was concerned, I just knew things. I didn't know how, I just did.

Our spirit guides talk to us all the time, even though we may not all be aware of it. Most people unintentionally do not listen to the messages they receive any more than they would listen to what their loved ones around them said. Most of the time, when a thought or message just pops up in our consciousness, unbeknownst to us, we let it go or don't take any notice.

Our beloved angels or spirit messages are here to guide us throughout our life so we are never alone. If we just took the time to listen we would be far better off and able to avoid some of life's entrapments without falling over or getting hurt. When you learn to channel your guides not only will your world improve, but you will join a whole network of other light workers on the planet that are connecting to a higher energy of consciousness and helping Mother Earth become a better place.

Practising automatic writing

Automatic writing is one of the oldest forms of divination. By connecting to your heavenly guide or guides, loving messages will easily come from out of nowhere if you take the time to practise with an open mind and heart. It is important to do this work at the same time every day as you are setting up an appointment with your loving guides to do this work.

Create a sacred space or just a quiet place where you will preferably not be disturbed and clear the room with white light or burn sage so the energy is clear and clean. (I find if I don't do this, as I am so sensitive to energy, I will pick up somebody else's problems, and it will be harder for me to tune into my guides.)

Make yourself comfortable, light a candle and get yourself a pen and paper. Before I open up to spirit I always say a little prayer and ask for protection. The last thing I want is to invoke troublesome spirits, or what we call dark energy spirits who will try and play games with your or attach themselves to your energy field. One of the prayers I repeat three times out loud is "I ask only to work in the light of the Christ consciousness within. I am a clear and perfect channel of love and light."

Breathe deeply three times and open yourself up. Gently close your eyes and place your pen and paper in position and open your mind to let whatever wants to come through happen. Some people write with their eyes closed, but this is not necessary. Just write everything down that comes into your mind and don't be surprised if you even start to draw, as I did once when I was shown a picture of my main guide, White Feather, in my early spiritual development.

Success will only come with clear intention and dedication to what you want to do. There is no guarantee that automatic writing will work for you straight away, but like anything, if you persist you will get results. Only ever listen to loving positive messages as this is an indication that you are channelling light beings. Anything else, like a spirit telling you what to do or any negativity directed your way, is nothing other than mischievous spirits taking you for ride. Learn discernment and feel the difference.

Teachers and guides

The best teachers that you will have in your development on the spiritual path are your own loving guides and angels who stay with us from birth until we die. I repeat, even though it might seem that you are all alone at times, that is never the case even for a minute as the love of spirit is always with you.

As we develop with our spirituality, we are given different guides along the way. Often they will work with us and when we have worked our way up spiritually to another level, or vibration, they may depart or simply stand back. As I have worked in different areas on my path, I have worked with different guides. There was a time when I did a lot of healing work and psychic surgery in a trance state. This phase soon passed as I went in a different direction. My own spiritual guides that I have worked with so far include the following:

Dr Lee

Dr Lee is a healing Reiki guide who first appeared when I studied and became a Reiki master some years ago. He works with energy and meridians within the body. He is quite serious, dedicated and very bossy. He is a small Oriental gentleman with tiny little hands who wears his hair in a long plait. He has a restless nature, similar to my own, and is a curious intelligent being who likes to get on with the job at hand.

When I began working with his energy, I was attracting numerous clients who may have had cancer, or other serious

problems with their body. I found I also started doing psychic surgery with my healings. I had no idea what I was doing, but just surrendered to the energy and acted as a pure channel for the work that needed to be done.

Spiritual psychic surgery is a non-invasive event to the physical body and operates by drawing negative energy out of the energy body or field, removing deep-rooted blocks of stagnant and negative energy out the body and energy centres or chakras. It also removes thought forms and memory implants or what we call soul retrieval. If not removed, these energies can create disease leading to strangulation of the organs and body parts on an emotional and physical level as it blocks the life force and can lead to long-term health problems.

This type of hands-on healing is completely different to the psychic surgery that is practised in the Philippines and other areas in the world where tumours and other diseased tissue is actually removed from inside the body.

Reiki energy and other methods of spiritual healing works successfully with all types of conventional healing and can accelerate the healing process. I would never suggest to a client to go off their medication unless their doctor told them to do so.

I also learnt to do many good crystal layouts using crystals as grids and laying the stones on the body's energy centres. The more I did this work, the more the clients came. It was if I was in training with my spirit guide, and I ended up spending years perfecting this ability.

As soon as I developed myself further and became attuned as a Reiki Master and Seichim Master, Dr Lee came straight into my energy field and I began to do a lot of psychic operations on clients. Dr Lee was very forthright and wanted to get me doing psychic surgery more and more as the phone never stopped ringing with clients wanting to book. I was shown and taught so many things about the human body through this wonderful guide. I found I could sense things about people and their diseases and was encouraged to learn more at different courses and schools. I found that as soon as I sat down and closed my eyes, healing energy would be channelled from this guide.

Having studied spiritual healing, and being a qualified Reiki master as well, I basically already knew the fundamentals. I have cut back with my healing work now because I lost a lot of inspiration when a good friend of mine became ill and died. I know it was her contract but an event like that seemed to a sign for me to move on and find another way to help people. I thanked Dr Lee for his fantastic teaching and asked him to stand back. I still channel this wise guide's wisdom and use his energy in other ways.

Margaret

Margaret is an older wise woman guide who once worked as a clairvoyant and healer in England. When I connect to her energy through light trance she speaks with a distinct English accent. She works with flower essences and mediumship. She has also taught me how to remove entities from the aura, how to do spirit rescue, which is removing lost souls from houses, and how to get rid of spells and curses.

Margaret lived in the 18th century, and did not like the church as it condemned her type of work, even though all she ever did was help people to heal or reach their loved ones on the other side. I have had the most amazing insights by working with this very kind and humble guide as she is constantly teaching me things I could not possibly know or even have read in a book.

I have worked with Margaret on many spirit rescues, which is when a person does not pass over to the other side and becomes what we call "earth-bound", often not knowing they are dead but in some cases they are too scared or may not know where they are. This can happen if, for example, they have been in an accident, were suddenly killed, or even if they have behaved badly and think they are going to end up in hell, which is a make-believe place anyway.

When somebody dies, they are usually greeted by a loved one and their guide, who guides them over to the other side, which looks very similar to Earth, where they receive healing. Those who have died from cancer usually go straight to spirit hospital where they are healed by lying on giant crystal slabs.

When I had my first near-death experience, in my early 20s, I could feel myself speeding like a bullet through the cosmos, way beyond Earth. Suddenly I was taken back and jolted heavily back into my body, as it was not my time.

Everything happened so fast, it was unbelievable. I remember waking up and I was lying on the ground, with people standing all around me. My girlfriend had just given me CPR, which made me jolt back into my body. I did not even get the chance to see anyone as everything happened so fast.

With my guide Margaret and her assistants I am also able to remove what we call entities, which are lower vibrational parasites from the aura, the energy around the human body. We sometimes pick up these energies when the outer layer of our aura becomes thin and breaks or rips. This can happen through drug use, shock, long-term sickness, trauma, alcoholism, accidents, and stress and so on.

Once I have scanned an aura with my hands and third eye, I am able to send these pests into the light for healing. I am also able to remove curses that may have been around for centuries and can be very harmful for people. Most people know when they have a curse on them, as nothing works in their lives, no matter how hard they try, and they go around and around, never getting anywhere. Often their love life is a shambles as well. These people usually know something is wrong, but do not know what to do about it. Luckily for them, once they are onto it, they will find someone who can help them who works in this department, as their loving spirit guides will guide them to a reputable healer who does this work.

I always feel safe when Margaret is around as she is very competent and knows exactly what she is doing. My interest in vibrational flower essences comes from this loving guide and I used these essences since the early 70s. Often I will know how and when to use them as I can communicate with flowers. This is a gift I have always had, and I put it down to a strong connection to energy and nature. Shells and the corals from the Great Barrier Reef also possess an amazing pure energy and are very therapeutic when used in healing.

Three of One

Three of One is a delightful and highly intelligent star person or starlight being. He is an unusual tall character of sheer pure light that comes from another dimension or galaxy. Unfortunately, his own planet was destroyed long ago so he lives on spaceships with other light beings who all communicate telepathically to one another through sound waves.

Like the other beings from other planets here on Earth, he is helping mankind with the changes we are experiencing on the planet. There are many beings like him on the planet today, helping and working with the ascension and growth of our sacred planet, mother earth.

When I studied with the Michael Newton hypnotherapy school, with the Life Between Lives program, I found I have had many past lives on other planets and am what he calls a hybrid soul. It did not surprise me to know that I have a beautiful guide from the stars.

Three of One's interests include teleportation, healing with symbols, and teaching people to become empowered and to be more aware of their own abilities. He has given me a few symbols for different uses, which I use with all my healing work. These symbols are not cures but simply ways to attract the right energy for healing the client may need in conjunction with other conventional therapies the client may be using.

Cancer

Arthritis

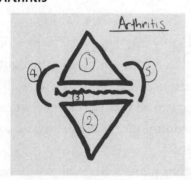

Longevity	Clearing or detox
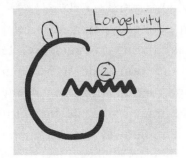	

All these symbols are drawn in the same way as you would draw Reiki symbols and have been very effective and beneficial for a lot of my clients. If the energy is not needed by the client, it is simply dispersed from where it came, as in any healing modality or vibrational healing.

I feel humbled that I am able to pass on these symbols to you. To use them, simply place them energetically with love into your client's crown chakra. If they work for you then it is meant to be as all healing works through your good intention.

If they don't work, this is part of your karma or contract, and is God's will.

On a personal level I have always had a great interest in teleportation and have used the technique many times throughout my life. Teleportation is the process of physically relocating the body from one place to another site without touching it in anyway, or using any mechanical device.

American hypnotherapist Dr Bruce Goldberg describes it: "What we find in true teleportation is that the psychical body dematerialises (disappears) from one location and subsequently rematerialises (reappears) in a different spot in an instant, often accompanied by a "pop" sound." (*Time Travellers from Our Future*)

It can also be used for time travel and should not be confused with out of body experiences (OBEs) or astral travel.

My journey with teleportation is ongoing though I feel I have not mastered this craft as yet. With my main guide, White Feather, I have often travelled to the "other side" in a dream state or deep trance meditation and met up with many of my deceased relatives. I have imagined myself going to the spirit hospital which is really just a dimension away with its quartz crystal slabs or beds of light for healing and I always feel better when I come back.

Cassandra

Cassandra is a beautiful, kind and gentle angel whose main concern is to help mankind and as many people as possible. She talks of love and kindness and has a yearning to help children, animals and all mankind. The first time I channelled this being I felt very honoured. As I told my small trance group, I can't believe such a beautiful being would want to work with me as she is so gentle and loving whereas I can be blunt and direct, like a typical Aries.

This delightful light being has not only graced me with her presence but has taught me on so many levels how important it is to honour and love yourself as an eternal soul and to never feel for one minute lesser than others around you. When you learn this simple lesson, people around you will respect you more as this is the energy that you will ultimately give out. What you believe you become.

She also talks about taking time out to nurture ourselves, something many of us find hard to achieve as we are so busy trying to make a living and trying to please everyone else around us. We forget to make the time to just chill out or meditate. Now, I am slowly starting to learn to reserve time in the day just for me, and make sure I do something enjoyable each day.

Cassandra has taught me about the value of chanting, which raises the body's vibrations and clears out the chakras.

Here are two simple chants. Say them slowly just like they are spelt.

AUH   (Sounds like R-OO-HAR)   which means God is here.

AUM   (Sounds like R-OO-MMM)   which means God is love.

I first started chanting aged 16, when I joined the Hare Krishna's for a while. I was initially attracted to their philosophy and vegetarian diet and, when I was overseas, I often ate at their wonderfully clean and economical restaurants which are everywhere in the world. The more we work with healing sounds such as chanting and toning, the better we will feel on all levels of consciousness. Not only are they a great tool to enlighten you, they will also help:

Clear heavy internal energy (it can help with depression, though is not a cure);

Clear out your energy points or chakras to help you feel wonderful and lifts your vibration, helping you attract like-minded people and beneficial situations. You can find many great books written on chanting and sound therapy at your local bookshop.

Leon

This guide is quite a character and one of my favourite enlightened beings in my spiritual team of guides I work with. He has a similar personality to mine as he is a practical joker and likes to see the funny side of things. Too much gloom and doom is not a good thing, as it only drags you down to places that you really do not want to go. Your life will become dark and bleak and you will not have the energy to get out of bed in the mornings. The same goes for hanging around with judgemental righteous people, watching negative or violent movies, or reading dark, depressing books. The energy can drag you down and fill you with anxiety or unknown fear, which is such a waste of time.

Laughter and good cheer is the best type of medicine to fill and nurture our souls. The first time I channelled Leon, I could not wipe the smile off my face as he was so pretentious and snobby. I realised that this amusing and creative guide has been part of my life for as far back as I can remember, as I was driven to express myself in an artistic way and always wanted to be an actor.

Creative writing was my favourite subject at school because it gave me time to daydream.

I also played in bands when I was younger as music has been another way to express myself. Seeing the Sex Pistols in Trondheim, Norway in the late 70s was a turning point and got me on the road for many years as a bass player as they were revolutionary for the times. Sid Vicious and Johnny Rotten were my favourite rebels as they tried so hard to be bad. It was just part of their so called image and was very theatrical and way over the top.

Eventually this led me to the theatre and I was a professional actor for more than 22 years, never quite making the big times unfortunately. But a few dog food commercials along the way paid the bills and had a trip around Australia in a travelling theatre company. I really enjoyed dressing up as different characters and getting paid for it. As long as I didn't take myself too seriously!

My friend Kathryn, a talented psychic artist, picked up on Leon's energy one day and being a medium herself was able to draw a picture of this quirky character. Staring at the drawing I laughed to myself when I saw he actually looked like a little "gay" beatnik from the 50s. He wore tight pants, a polar-neck jumper and a black beanie and had a cigarette hanging out of his mouth which was set in a large mischievous grin, like a naughty little boy. He is also a chain smoker, with a cantankerous wit.

Leon is "an artist", in every sense of the word. When he talks he is loud and bombastic to the point of hysterics, waves his hands around and talks with a plum in his mouth, something I would never do. He writes (he must be helping me with this) and was an actor himself in the 50s and loves music, especially jazz. I prefer drumming or new wave music myself. He helps me with all my creative pursuits and theatrical ventures and gives me the inspiration to direct my own "shows" and subtly suggests how to make it look visually entertaining.

On a more spiritual note, he tells me when I channel him how important it is to take time out to smell the roses and to stop pushing myself to study or do things all the time. By simply freeing my mind of clutter and worrying thoughts helps me to relax and daydream. I just have to trust in the process and wonderful, creative ideas fill my mind.

To regularly sit and meditate helps creative expression and will open doorways to other realities that you cannot even imagine. By simply using your incredible imagination, so to speak, your dreams and thoughts will lead you to your own loving reality and all your dreams can come true.

Romanov

A big man with a turban and a beard, Romanov lived in the time of Ancient Egypt when he worked as a mystic. Later this spirit entity also appeared in the 15th, 16th, 17th and 18th centuries. I am still getting to know him, through my meditation, and am proud to have him as part of my team. He is a wise spiritual teacher who shows me how to be strong and to use more discernment with people, instead of just rushing in before I really know who I am dealing with. Too many times I have befriended people who have really no interest in me at all except what I can do for them.

He assists in my personal readings at the spiritual churches and the Rainbow Show, a vehicle for learning and raising money for sick children. He works only with what we call overheads and survival evidence. I listen to what I am getting for the person, and then give the message directly to their loved one. This is called connecting to spirit through voice, which is clairaudience.

When I came to read the flowers for psychic messages in the churches, which I was able to do for years, he said he could not help me and I was only to work with overheads or voice. I saw this as a progression with my mediumship and am very grateful I have been taught to go to a new level. Luckily for me, I still have Margaret to help with my psychic messages. It really is quite amazing how much help I get from these wonderful spirit helpers, which I call team spirit, when I ask for it. Spirit is always there to help us and teach us things in our daily lives.

Erin

Tiny Erin is a mischievous nature fairy or undine who likes to travel around on the back of birds. I have enjoyed channelling her over the years as whenever she comes through, the room fills with mirth and gaiety. This wise being helps me appreciate nature, as I always feel her around when I am walking in the bush or in our garden.

When I channel this sprite, I am full of giggles and feel like a child again. Her personality is utterly charming, innocent and sweet. I also feel that she helps me with my inner child by teaching me to play and not take life so seriously.

Her energy is light and grounding but it can change dramatically as she becomes enraged at the injustice of mortals polluting the rivers and forests of our world. I feel the same and it saddens me when I see the abuse of our natural resources and the little respect for nature's gift and how precious it is in the way it heals us.

Whenever I am clearing my own yard or making changes in the garden, I always say a little prayer or ask permission of the nature spirits before I go ahead with major work such as renovations or tree or shrub removal. I have noticed that people who have not done this have later had major problems with water and electricity. Whenever this happens I always put it down to a disgruntled sprite. I also have a lovely fairy garden in the front of my yard that is hidden amongst the trees and bushes where I place my sick plants for the nature spirits to heal. They always end up becoming healthier and happier than ever before.

About eight years ago, when I wrote my children's book on nature spirits, *Magical Tales from the Forest*, I channelled lots of information about the elemental kingdom and nature spirits from this tiny enlightened being. Erin also knows a lot about flowers and their energies, and helps me with their use in my vibrational healing practice.

Red Hawk

Red Hawk is a gentle energy and guide who works with my mediumship by helping spirit people cross over from the the spirit world to give messages to their loved ones. To me, he looks like a young American Indian with long dark hair and wears simple clothes. He stays very much in the background, saying little, but is happy to give assistance when needed. He is very humble, and I feel I have been a brother to him in a past life as an American Indian.

He was first seen by a very good and well respected medium called Marcia Quinton who gave me a reading from him in a spiritual church in Sydney.

Every time I channel him in trance, I feel like I am also riding a horse bareback on a great open prairie. He always comes with great messages of reassurance that in death we are never alone in our journey to the other side.

White Feather

The first time I met White Feather, my main guide or gate-keeper, I was meditating in my healing room when from out of nowhere I heard a gentle voice talking to me in my head. In a male voice he told me that he was my main guide and had been with me since birth and that I was to call him White Feather or Father. Gradually I began to channel him more clearly and picking up a pen and a piece of paper, I began to draw him, a beautiful old man with deep kind eyes with a full set of feathers on his head. He explained that we had been in a past life together, and that I had been his son. That made sense to me as

I love nature and dreamed of owning a horse. He said he was looking after me with my mediumship, and not to be afraid as he would guide and protect me. He told me that the work I would be doing was important for many people. At the time White Feather made himself known, my good friend and spiritual teacher at the time, Joan, had just lost her husband and was beside herself with grief.

As I sat and meditated I suddenly heard a male voice say, "Ring Joan and tell her that I am doing fine, and not to worry will you, love?" I was frightened at first so

I asked who I was talking to. The male voice replied it was Joan's husband and that he was trying to get in contact with her as she was so distressed.

"Ok," I said. "Give me some evidence."

"Just tell her, 'Hello chicken legs!' will you? She will know what that means," he laughed back at me.

Feeling rather coy, I quickly jumped up from my meditation and called Joan. "I have some information for you, Joan. I hope you don't mind but your husband is here and wants to say hello." Joan was stunned at first but after a long pause she asked me to go on. Feeling rather sheepish, I gave her the message. "He said to say, hello chicken legs."

Straight away I heard her softly crying. "Thank you darling, you have no idea how much that has meant to me," she replied. "I told him to give me proof that he had gotten over OK, and that has helped me immensely."

Signs or signposts from spirit

The divine source is always with us. We are always with spirit in everything we do, even our sleep state. Because we are so busy with our lives, we may forget this. Not only do we have our own loving guides with us, we also have angels, spirit friends and helpers, and loved ones that have passed over to the other side. Our deceased loved ones and all our spirit helpers, usually visit us in our dreams, through music, touch, our senses, or just situations.

We may feel them around us at certain times. They hear our prayers and know exactly what we are up to, but usually we cannot hear them. It always amazes me when I read for someone and they often ask something like, "How could my uncle, or whoever, possibly know that? They died before that happened to me." Believe me, our loved ones know exactly what we get up to, whether we like it or not. This is all a constant reminder that love is eternal and that they are still concerned for us, like they were on earth.

Spirit can manifest in many ways: a certain smell, memory, feeling, even a favourite song, are signposts our loved ones are around. I'm so grateful for my guides loving support as it is a constant reminder that I am not alone, and a way of "knowing" that I am on my spiritual path. I always make it a point to thank spirit for the help they have given me, and the wonderful blessings that I am given in my life. Signposts can come in many varied forms and different ways.

Feathers: When I started to open up and trust in spirit, I was inundated with feathers. I used to think it was because my Indian guide was called White Feather and he was trying to tell me that he was around. Often when out walking, I would pray or ask spirit for help and, sure enough, I would find a feather right in front of me, a sign that all was okay and I had nothing to worry about. Sometimes I would even find one in my home, as if an invisible force had placed it there.

Once, when a friend was very sick I prayed for a miracle and, sure enough, a feather appeared on my lawn, sticking up in the middle of the grass, as if someone had just stuck it there. This was conformation that my friend would be all right and I had nothing to worry about. Even when I would test my new found ability of manifesting feathers, they would appear out of nowhere, sometimes several at a time.

Numbers: I was driving home from a meditation class one day and I was worried about a fight I had with my sister. We'd had a really big argument and I was feeling really sorry for myself. I prayed for a miracle, and just as I finished saying it in my mind, a large black car drove past with the number plate ANGELS. I couldn't stop laughing and nearly crashed the car as it came out of nowhere. When I got home my sister rang me and said she was thinking of me and apologised for her behaviour.

House numbers are interesting too. I live at 33, the age Jesus died, and I work as a spiritual medium. People laugh when they see this as they can see the humour in it.

Messages: These may be repeated several times until we hear them from our friends, neighbours, or even total strangers. (I get it now. I will leave my job as I know it is not good for me, and I need to move on to bigger and better experiences.) When I was working as an actor, I was really getting sick of the work I was getting considering my training and experience. I would turn up for auditions for TV commercials with models or housewives with no experience in stage work or acting. It was a large cattle call, and the advertising companies could not have cared less if you were a trained actor or not.

It was a very humiliating and humbling experience and I was becoming more and more dismayed with the rejection each time. My friends kept telling me to give up my dream of becoming an actor and to start reading professionally as I was so good at it. The last thing I wanted to do was to become a fortune teller and talk to dead people but once I tried it the floodgates opened and I was on my path. Little did I know the work that I was meant to do had been right in front of my nose.

Dreams: These are incredible, especially when they are vivid and you can remember every little detail for some reason. Often these are hard to shake off as they feel as if they really happened. If you have a prophetic dream and you can't handle it always ask spirit to take them away, because spirit never gives you a gift you can't handle.

Buy a good dream book, and write everything down before you even put your feet on the floor in the morning. Your guides, if you ask them, will help you remember, just ask them before you go to sleep. I have had a dream book for many years and often discuss my dreams with my husband before we get out of bed in the morning. It always gives us insight into what is going on in our lives. I once dreamt my mother died and awoke really upset. This dream, of course, means nothing of the sort. It turned out that she was going through major changes in her life, which turned out for the better. After the dream, my relationship with her became closer.

Sometimes I have overheard conversations where someone is talking about the wonderful trip to Sedona that you might have been thinking about doing for years. Then you realise that you are not the only enlightened being in the village after all. Many times I have been thinking of doing something and will be sitting in a café and overhear people talking about something that I want to do or am truly interested in. It never ceases to amaze me, as it is as if you are meant to hear it over and over again till you finally get it.

Songs, tunes, music: How strange is it when you are thinking of someone and a certain song comes on the radio or you are out somewhere and you hear a particular song playing? Music can also activate memories of people you once loved, or had a connection to, not only in this life but past lives as well. Every time I listen to certain songs they take me back to a time in the past that I can never forget. Music is such a great prompt. It is amazing how sentimental I can become.

Names: These can be the names of towns or cities, people or animal's names, bird names, or whatever. On many occasions I have had so-called coincidences about certain people in my life. Out of the blue, I will hear news about them or they simply appear from the past.

An example of this occurred when I had a new female client turn up called Gordana. As this is an unusual name, I asked her if she was from Croatia. When she replied that she was, I smiled and told her that I had been to university with a girl called Gordana from the same region. My client thought this was unusual as her name was certainly not common. After work on the same day, when I was out at dinner with my husband and some artist friends of ours, I received a phone call from a man I knew, who told me that my friend , whom I hadn't seen in about 25 years, had died from a brain tumour. I felt spirit was giving me a little warning that I would be hearing news from my old friend but to hear she had died was a shock as she was way too young, in my eyes.

The time: Seeing the same time repeated around you frequently, for example 5.55, is a signal our loving guides and masters are around. When I look at the clock and I will often see the same numbers such as 2.22 or 3.33. I may be asleep and will wake up at the same time every night or when I'm driving I might see the same car number plates or numbers on buildings. Or the address of a job you are going for may have the same numbers as your house or birth date.

These are all signs from spirit saying they are with you.

Synchronicity: Being in a particular place at a particular time and seeing someone you haven't seen or heard from in ages. Ever had the feeling that you had to go a particular place and that it was urgent? That has happened to my on many occasions. Some people call this synchronicity.

One day I was sitting at my computer thinking how I needed to expand my business. Suddenly I felt like going for a walk down to the local shops. I didn't really need to buy anything so I just went along with the feeling. As I walked into a shop which sold beautiful crystals to buy a music CD, the manager, a young girl I had worked with before asked if I would be interested in doing readings in her shop as they needed someone urgently, because their last reader had just left. I didn't take the job, but I told her I knew of a woman who needed work and could start straight away. My friend was grateful for the work as her husband was unemployed so it all ended up being just as it was meant to be.

Thinking of someone: Often someone will just come into my mind's eye then, without warning, in the next 24 hours I will see them or accidentally bump into them. That applies to the telephone as well. I usually know someone I am thinking about is going to ring me and, sure enough, they do so not long after.

One of my closest friends, Rachel, has a habit of ringing me just when I am going through a hard time in my life. I may not hear from her in ages and just when I need someone to talk to she calls. This has happened to me often and I am always grateful as we all need a shoulder to cry on occasionally. I often think of her, even though she lives miles away, and I can feel her energy as I know she is always there for me.

My client Sophia was good friends with Adam, a male she had met in a meditation class. As they got to know each other they looked forward to their meetings together which had gone out of the class situation. She was very attracted to his energy, and he to hers, and they both felt that they had past lives together and had even been husband and wife. They were both very happy to find one another but, unfortunately, Sophia was already married to a man she loved and had been together with a long time.

Adam was single and seven years younger than Sophia. He was still finding his way in life and seemed lost and confused. Being an intuitive in her own right, Sophia knew that in this life she was not meant to be with Adam as she had dedicated herself to her work and felt that that should take priority. The fact that she was married but was attracted to him as well did not help matters, and she found herself more and more wanting to be with Adam and even started to fantasize about them being together. This distressed her as she started to feel really guilty, even though she was doing nothing wrong.

She soon developed problems concentrating with her work and found it almost impossible to sleep at night. All she could think about was Adam and what he was doing when he was away from her. It also started to affect her marriage, as her partner could sense something was wrong, but she didn't want to hurt him so she kept it a secret from him. It soon became obvious that she had to make a decision and decide which man she wanted to be with: the father of her children or handsome young Adam, who was single and fancy free.

Her commonsense soon told her she needed to cut the ties with Adam so she came to me for help. I could instantly see the attraction between them but that it would not last for long. Adam was a traveller and an adventurer who was still finding his way in life. If Sophia had gone off with him, the relationship would have been over soon, as he had an eye for the ladies, and she would have been left high and dry. Not long after she left for the United States to live with her family and children. It was very sad for her but she soon began to love her husband again and realised that it is possible to be in love with two soul mates at once.

A certain knowing: This is when that feeling you keep getting over and over is correct and turns out to be exactly what you thought. Remember, the first moment of thought is the moment of truth. Whenever I meet someone for the first time, I will always get a pretty good impression of what they are really like and it usually ends up being correct. This "knowing" is your intuition at work. It never fails you and is like a tracking device which transmits information for you. All you have to do is listen to it, if you choose.

Shooting stars: Seeing a shooting star is often a sign that everything is going to be OK. Watching a beautiful sunrise and feeling energised by it is another reason that Nature and everything in it has always been my favourite escape. It is a place where I would also like to spend more time if I had it. It is the only place I know where you can get a healing just by being there, as the saying goes; the best things in life are free. I have made many wishes on falling stars and they have all come true. I have also had a telescope and spent much time researching the stars and looking at the night sky. I have seen spaceships in the night sky as well so I am convinced that there are other star beings who visit the planet. This will be revealed by our governments in years to come.

The media: An answer to something you have been waiting to hear about might appear in the newspaper or on the television, as confirmation that you are right on track. It is amazing how your guide can send you a message answering a question or problem you have been thinking about. I have often asked my guide for confirmation and received messages this way. For example, "move on, the time is now."

Watching clouds: Cloud-watching has always been a favourite pastime of mine, especially when I was a child. You can get all kinds of information and messages from the sky, which reminds me of a gigantic stage, and the cloud formations. Sometimes I have even seen the shape of an angel in the sky watching over me or other faces.

Messages in your head: You keep getting a certain idea that pops up in your head that won't go away until you do it. My intuition kept telling me once, over and over, not to put the towels on the heater to dry as it was dangerous. One night, I nearly burnt the house down doing this and we were saved by our cat meowing and waking me up. Luckily, all that was burnt was the carpet.

When I first met my ex-husband we travelled to a small island called Fevag, off the coast of Trondheim in Norway to stay in his grandfather's old home. As soon as we arrived, I began to feel sick all over and a tiny voice kept going off in my head telling me to be careful. It was the first weekend away together for Paul and me. We were madly in love and we were excited to have a holiday where we could be alone and get to know one another.

Unfortunately, the old farmhouse had a ghost, which I discovered later was Paul's grandfather. When I walked into the house, Paul showed me a picture of his family in which I saw his grandfather staring back at me. His face looked angry and his cold eyes seemed to penetrate right through me. Straight away, I could feel and sense from the photo that the old man did not like me and I started to notice a cold, frosty energy silently begin to creep in the room. All my hairs on my arms and legs began to stand up straight and I became scared and wanted to leave but it had taken us three hours to get there and there was no chance of leaving till morning as there were no more ferries.

The old man's face looked hard and stern and as I continued to stare at the photo, and I could feel his disapproval as he stared angrily back at me. Looking around, I sensed he was still living in the house. I should have protected myself with white light as soon as I felt the warnings but I didn't as I kept thinking it was all my imagination. Anyway, why wouldn't he like me, I thought, I never even met him.

I should have trusted my intuition and the warnings I was receiving in my head as I had no sleep that night. I could see the old man standing over the bed, staring down at us disapprovingly, and at one stage I could feel something pressing down on my head. Maybe he knew our relationship wouldn't last because within two years it was over.

Watching insect activity: I always know when it is going to rain, as I can smell it, but I can also see the way ants aren't around when we are ready for a downpour.

Birds: Our winged friends have always provided a great signpost for me. Once, when I met with a friend, we were lying in a beautiful park surrounded by enormous trees talking about life and our deepest darkest secrets when we suddenly realised we couldn't hear what each other was saying. Above our heads, we saw we were surrounded by a circle of 14 large black crows, all looking down at us from their perches in the trees. The noise was so loud and so disturbing, it was impossible to talk further unless we shouted. We had over-talked our stay and got the message that it was time for us to depart.

The wind: When the wind whispers through the trees, it's almost as if we are being played a song. When the wind comes, it always brings change as it sweeps all the pollution and bad energy away.

A rainbow: Especially when it comes with much-needed rain, how often a rainbow fills our hearts with hope. To me, rainbows have always been gifts of truth and love from spirit. I have used the name "Rainbow" for a show that I do about connecting to spirit. To me, a rainbow brings a bridge of love connecting to the other side, proving that love is eternal and that our loved ones are always not too far away.

Laughter: How many times have you felt really down and then suddenly hear a loud laugh that sounds so ridiculous that you smile and shake your head and wonder why you take yourself so damned seriously? Laughter will also link you to a memory of someone you once loved. My Auntie Gladys was an attractive redhead and a terrible flirt in life. She worked as a pharmacist, and was an independent woman who loved to travel. Every time I visited her, she always told me incredible stories about all her boyfriends she had collected over the years.

Both her husbands had died, so she was alone, but not really, if you know what I mean. Every Valentine's Day, she received bundles of cards from all over the place from would-be suitors. As far as she was concerned, nobody could resist her charms. She would always display these offerings out on the living-room table, proudly comparing them to one another and smiling happily to herself as if she had won the lottery. As she spoke, she laughed continuously, like a little girl, and every year without fail, would asked me curiously, "Have you received any, dear?"

I could only shake my head in silence. "What a shame," she would say, delighted with her own collection and not noticing my own discomfort. I will never forget her infectious naughty laugh as it echoed around the room as a lovely reminder of the happy times we spent together.

The list of possible signposts is endless and I am sure everyone will have their stories about these messages. It is all about developing awareness and remembering that we can create miracles in the way we think as what you believe about yourself you become. If you truly believe in something it will soon become your reality as the law of attraction dictates. If you want someone to love you, you have to love yourself first.

Once you are aware of signposts in your life they will keep appearing all the time over and over again. That's because they were always there; you just didn't know it.

Once you learn how to recognise and use signposts you will have a new tool to play with. You will be well on your way to a new way of being where amazing possibilities open up, making your life easier and brighter.

Past life regression

I first became interested in past life regression when I went to Norway in the late 70s. Once there, I found it quite extraordinary that I had an understanding of the ways and idiosyncrasies of most Norwegian people I came across and felt quite "at home."

In the large group of international nurses who worked with me in the hospital, I was the only one who understood the language without any problems. Whenever we were called into the office to see the Matron who was our supervisor, to report on how we were going with our work on the wards, I was the one who was pushed to the front of the queue to do all the talking.

We were all working our way towards being Norwegian nurses in those days and were put through rigorous and sometimes difficult tests. The other girls squeezed behind me as I blabbed my way through the interviews. The secret, I found, was to just ask questions so they would do most of the talking. Everyone was most impressed though they were also puzzled as to how a foreigner could speak their language so well.

For years I thought I must have been a "super brain" and wondered why I had not discovered this unique ability before. I have always had a photographic memory, but I knew deep down I was certainly no super brain.

When I returned to Australia a few years later, I went to a lecture on past life regression therapy and learnt how we carry memories deep within from past lives. The lecturer told us that her husband had a session with her and he discovered that he had been on the Titanic. Strangely, he had always been afraid of the sea and feared drowning his whole life.

Past life regression is a technique that uses hypnosis to recover what most practitioners believe is certain memories of past lives or incarnations. I have trained as a clinical past life and Life Between Life Therapist and have assisted clients to resolve issues from past lives in this lifetime.

Often through reincarnation, we have played certain roles or lived in certain places before and are attracted to the same archetype role or country in this lifetime. In past life regression, the subject answers a series of question while hypnotized to help reveal their past life identities and associated events. Often, unresolved issues from other past lives may be the cause of the patient's present day problems. When I regressed one of my clients, we found she had died of consumption and the cold sometime in the 18th century. In this life this showed up as a recurrent problem with asthma and, after just one session, we were able to reduce her attacks.

When I had a past life regression with the lecturer I mentioned, I was taken back to a past life in Norway where I found I was a huge male Viking called Tron. I was horrified to feel thick hair all over my body, something that I really dislike to this day. (Trust me, everything is always waxed off.) In our session I began speaking fluent Norwegian and the therapist asked me to speak in English as she had no idea what I was talking about.

In other past life sessions, throughout the years I have since met many Viking friends from the longboats. One of these souls is a lovely lady called Maggie, who has been sitting and working with me now for many years. She is a special needs teacher and uses her healing abilities and gifts with the children she works with.

In other lifetimes I have been American Indians or living in England and Europe. I use regression regularly in my busy practice and have had the honour to witness many other people's pasts. I have learnt about mankind and the soul using this modality.

Case study 1—Michael

Michael was a friend of mine who worked in insurance. When he decided to finally settle down and marry his long term girlfriend, Lauren, he started having very distinct recurring dreams, which he had during his childhood, about winning a trophy for long distance skiing in a faraway place, somewhere in Scandinavia.

For years he thought about doing just this but had always pushed it to one side, as other things always came up for him. When they finally decided to marry, his dreams about the skiing became more intense, coming every night and keeping him awake. This affected his health and work and he gradually became more and more obsessed about following his dream. Soon he was retrenched from his job and his obsession intensified even further. Every time he tried to discuss this with his girlfriend she would not listen. She had no desire to travel because she was studying to become a vet, something she had wanted to do her whole life. Her dream of establishing a veterinary practice conflicted with his dream of becomming a champion skier. As far as she was concerned she had absolutely no interest in living in Scandinavia and following him all over the place on a whim. She could not understand his obsession as he had never mentioned it until their engagement and she disliked the cold with a vengeance. Also the possibilities of her finding work in a foreign land were minimal as she couldn't speak the language.

Instead of talking to her and telling her how he felt he withdrew more and more into himself and became terrified of losing her. She had no idea of the full extent and confusion of what was going on in his head but was becoming increasingly concerned and frustrated as the man she had known for so many years and had fallen in love with had changed so much and all the fun and excitement had gone from their once loving relationship.

When he arrived I sat in the chair opposite and tuned into his vibration to access his energy. It was obvious that he was a sportsman in the prime of life, as he was very fit and healthy. But his life force energy was telling me another story as it was very low and flat. After he opened up, he told me about his problem and his obsession with his dream. I asked him if he had discussed how he felt with his sweetheart and future wife, as it was an incredible life change that he wanted to make. He said he had but she would get annoyed and would not listen. As far as she was concerned, if he went away overseas to train he would be gone for too long.

I told him about my work with past lives and explained the possibility of memories from past incarnations hindering us in our current life with unnecessary emotional blocks, fears or phobias. I suggested we begin by returning to the point of what is stopping him from moving forward in his life now. I explained that hypnotherapy is really self hypnosis and all he would have to do was to relax and stay connected to my voice. I would act as his guide on his inner spiritual journey to his memories and to the information that he carried through each incarnation as a soul.

I slowly managed to take him down to a calm, relaxed state of consciousness, even though he was feeling uptight and anxious. After a while he let himself go quite deep, as he felt stuck and wanted clear straight answers about how to resolve the situation. He was a straight talking character and was curious to see what his obsession was really about.

I took him back through his present life and down to the womb to his soul state. As I took him to his most recent past life, he looked down at his feet, and in his mind's eye, saw he was wearing a pair of large skis, dressed in warm clothing and typical ski gear. He said he looked to be a tall fair-haired, blue-eyed male and was looking at mountains surrounding him. Everywhere he looked was covered in thick blanket of snow. He was Jan-Eric and was aged 22 and lived with his parents, Tina and Ulf-Gunnar, in a tiny town in the mountains of Sweden. He was a professional skier in training for the Olympics.

The more he spoke about his life as Jan-Eric and the country he had lived in, I was startled to discover I could relate to it in every way as I had also been to the same town myself. Everything he described, including the shop I used to buy my food at, was exactly like he said, including the characteristics of the people he described. I knew that he could not be making any of it up as it was so clear and he told me he had never been in Sweden before.

Asking him to disengage his emotions, I took him to the death scene in that lifetime and asked him to view it like he was watching a movie. Listening to my instruction, he took me to a scene where he had just died in a big ski race. As far as he could remember he was racing down a slope and crashed into a tree. He was now lying dead, covered in snow, and there were people all around him.

As his spirit hovered not far from his body, I brought down energy from the source or Christ consciousness, and made a beautiful light of love. Gently I asked him, as Jan-Eric, to open his eyes and go into the light so he could cross over and be healed. Once he had done this, all sad and painful memories from that lifetime would be healed. He would no longer have to carry the pain, or the obsession, with him any longer and I healed all memories from that life. After we had done this, I asked him, if he wanted to go to other life times but he was happy with what we had already done.

I suggested we do a future life, or time line, where he could access information as to whether it was futile for him to stay with his dreams of training again for the Olympics. He soon saw himself one year in the future training for a race. He was no longer married to Lauren and was alone. He did not seem concerned by this and was happy to be doing what he loved. Taking him further into the future, he saw himself completing his ambition of winning a trophy. Later, he saw himself back in Australia and living with a woman with a small child but wasn't sure whether she was Lauren. He said he felt he was happy and felt whole.

After the session, he seemed more calm and relaxed. He now understood the dream and knew that it was possible to finish something he had started as it was his heart's desire, and not lose his woman in the process.

All his life he wanted to become a professional sportsman and was already in training. It did not make any difference to him afterwards that he had done the same thing in his life before as Jan-Eric, the skier. His only challenge now was to open up a dialogue with Lauren and share his feelings with the woman he loved and wanted to spend the rest of his live with. If they were meant to be together, it would happen, even if it meant they might be apart for a while.

Case study 2—Alana

Alana was a beautiful young woman in her early 40s who booked in with me to have a past life regression, as she felt stuck in her life and had no direction. She was also unhappy in her marriage and told me she had stillborn baby twins. She and her husband had stopped communicating and he told her he was no longer in love with her.

I asked her if she had counselling in the past, but she said this had not helped them. After the death of the baby boys, their marriage had gone downhill and nothing seemed to help.

Sometimes grief can do this to people if not resolved. She felt very sad and angry with her husband and was ready to walk away from the marriage.

As I took her down to the different layers of her life I cleared her chakras and in the healing bubble that I had set up she forgave both her husband and her drug-addicted sister. This was an enormous relief for Alana, as she had issues with her sister going back to their childhood. It seemed as if the death of her baby boys had brought everything up to the surface and she was now ready to forgive and let go so she could move on with her life. Next I regressed her to a sacred space, a beautiful garden full of flowers, birds and trees. In this healing space we can contact guides or loved ones who have passed over.

Straight away she could feel and see her father who had died 10 years earlier. He came in to say he loved her and was always there for her and other personal messages.

Next her guide appeared, an American Indian man with a feathered headdress. This loving guide from the light introduced himself as Red Arrow and reassured her all was well and how important it was that she should come into her own power and to trust her intuition more. She acknowledged this as she had always had strong feelings since she was little about helping others but found this draining as she felt everybody depended on her. Her guide told her about boundaries and suggested this was something she needed to learn.

After she received her healing from her guide, I asked her to call out to her daughter on the other side. She was now older and came forward and told her mother that she loved her as a soul but that she had not wanted to come in. She would return and be born through another member of the family, which is often the case with reincarnation.

After Alana finished her healing with her loved ones I asked her if she was ready to go deeper and to visit the past lives room, where we could enter any doorway or look at any issue she wanted.

The first doorway she entered was the green doorway, which represents the heart chakra. In this past life she was a man and was married to her now-husband who was a woman and lived in England in the 1800s. Most of our past life characters are usually also from this lifetime as they belong to the same soul group. As a couple they had a pretty uneventful life but were good friends. In this lifetime, however, it was also difficult for them to communicate but it was something they were aware of and worked hard at.

This lifetime gave her great insight into her current relationship as she felt throughout the marriage she made all the effort as he was a quiet man who kept to himself. The main thing, though, was that she realised she still loved him and wanted to make more of an effort, but knew that it was all up to her if they were to stay together. After all he was a good provider and father to her other children.

The next doorway she visited was also in England where she was married to a man who was really cruel to her. She did not recognise this person when I asked her to look into their eyes. It was a very unsatisfactory lifetime and taught her how important it was to feel love and not to just marry for name and money. This theme recurred in other lifetimes we visited and she realised it was important for her to know her own worth and to speak her truth. She was a strong soul, who was extremely loving and full of compassion. It was important for her to live her life how she wanted and to explore hobbies and recreation where she could meet souls with similar interests. She especially needed to have fun and not think too much about life's problems.

As the session came to an end, Alana thanked me and I could see her face was clearer and appeared softer and calmer. She was happy to have so much insight into herself and felt that she had cleared a lot of things that had been stuck in her mind. She would take time to be more understanding of her husband and his prolonged grief, look for some satisfactory work that she wanted to do and spend more time with people that she really cared about and more in common with, instead of trying to work out everybody else's problems.

Case study 3—Darcy the dog

Tim was a 56-year-old from Adelaide who booked in for a past life session one day. He was visiting friends with his wife, Sarah, who was also very interested in the subject and also wanted to book in with me for a past life regression. Tim was very interested in finding his spiritual purpose, wanted to see what the connection was with other places he had visited in this life time and felt a connection to and, most importantly, wanted to get in contact with his dog, Darcy, who had died tragically of cancer. They were what he called best friends in this life and were with each other constantly before Darcy died. Tim was finding it really hard to move on with his life, as he missed his beloved pet so much. Not a day went past without Tim crying every time he thought of his beloved dog and mate.

A year had passed and nothing much had changed as he found he was still very emotional every time he thought of Darcy and it seemed he was still going through the grieving process. Their connection had been so strong that he wanted to see if Darcy had been in a past life with him and if he had crossed over safely to the other side.

He carried Darcy's collar with him everywhere and could not stop thinking of the day when he had to make the painful decision to have his good friend put down. He was also consumed with guilt and questioned himself daily whether he had made the right decision.

As soon as Tim came in, I saw an elderly man in spirit enter the room and stand to the left of him. He said he was Tim's grandfather, James. He told me he had been dead for a while and had passed from a stroke.

I asked Tim if this was correct and whether they were close when he was still alive. Tim seemed shocked and surprised at first, and confirmed this was true and that they had spent a lot of time together in the country when he was younger. His grandfather had lived on a farm and he always carried happy and loving memories from the times that he'd stayed with him as it was so much fun.

As he relaxed, the energy started to build up in the room and I saw what appeared to be a spirit dog sitting on the other side of him by his chair. I described the dog in great detail until Tim suddenly started to cry. It was then that I knew that I had contacted his best friend Darcy. He must have made an incredible effort to come over from the other side and knew his master missed him. I started to see him sitting next to his owner without a care in the world.

As soon as Tim stopped crying, he asked me to ask his dog if he had done the right thing by putting him down because he felt so heartbroken and guilty and missed his best mate so much. With Darcy wagging his tail, he told me to tell Tim that he needed to stop feeling so bad and, yes; he had done the right thing. Darcy was in so much pain when he was alive, he was happy to pass over to the other side, even if it meant he had to leave his best friend here.

Tim and Darcy had such a connection that I felt they must have had many past lives together as the love between them was so strong.

Funnily enough I could easily relate to what Tim was feeling as I have always had a very strong and loving connection to all my cats. My husband called me Cat Woman from the day I met him and, when he is in a bad mood, he will complain that I give them all the attention. I have always imagined and felt that they were my horses from my previous past lives as an American Indian.

Thoughts of love washed over me and tears welled in my eyes as Darcy went on to say how he missed his friend terribly as well, but he was happy now in the spirit world and did not want Tim to worry any longer. When Tim was ready to move on, I relaxed him down into a deep regression, the sacred space to meet up with his beloved spirit guides and angels, and also his loved ones in spirit who have crossed over to the other side. Once this sacred space has been created in the mind's eye it is possible to go back there in a meditation, a sleep state or simply by closing the eyes.

In this beautiful garden near a great lake, Tim walked around and described everything to me. We went over to the great lake and met with Tim's guide and his grandfather, who both gave him sound and loving advice. Tim was happy to do this as he had never met his guide before and was thrilled to catch up with his beloved grandfather who he had not seen in years. While in this space, Tim felt relaxed and at ease. He was in a deep mediative sleep and able to receive healing from his own loving guide as well.

Next I took him down to the past lives part of the session, where there is a white room with many different-coloured doorways, which represent the chakras or energy points in the body. After he selected a doorway, he could go in and just look at his feet where he would see he had been transformed into somebody else from a past life. He found this fascinating and had read many books on the subject before he came so he was more than willing to explore his past lives. When we got to this particular place, he told me that he just wanted to go into the lifetimes with Darcy, as he felt this would help him in the grieving process.

In his first lifetime, Tim saw himself as a strong warrior. He rode a great proud black horse that always accompanied him in battle. This horse was Darcy and they had a remarkable connection. Tim felt safe with the horse as he was strong and they were in tune with one another whenever they rode into dangerous battles. When Tim, as the warrior, finally died his horse was with him and they crossed over together.

In the second lifetime, in 18th century England, Tim saw himself as a poor labourer called Samuel who worked in the fields with his best friend Peter, who turned out to be Darcy again. In this lifetime they were together right through to old age. Peter helped Samuel by looking after him when he became sick until his death.

In the third lifetime they were in France and the year was 1788. Tim was a rich landowner and saw Darcy as his only child, a young son that he had fathered with his wife. Tragically the boy died at a very early age from an incurable disease that had infiltrated most of the country at the time. This was really sad as there was nothing Tim could do for his son even though he was a wealthy landowner.

The amazing thing for Tim was that each time he went into a different lifetime, he saw Darcy in some form or another. They had been in many past lives together and probably will continue to do so as they are probably from the same soul group. Tim was, of course, overjoyed at seeing his old friend again and now understood the connection they had. It proved to him that life is a continuous wheel that continues spinning and that love never dies as it is indeed eternal.

When the session ended Tim seemed much more relaxed and happier in himself. His face was full of wonderment and joy and all the pain and stress that he had walked in with was now gone. He said he felt "over the moon" that he had received a message from Darcy that he was okay and that they had been in so many lives together. He was now able to put it all together in his mind. He would miss his old mate, but now he knew that they were destined to meet up again because isn't that what good friends do.

So, until the next life Darcy will always be in his heart forever.

Life Between Lives

Life is always full of fascinating events, so nothing that ever happens in life, as a working medium, ever surprises me anymore.

One day a couple of years back, while working in a busy healing centre, I was patiently waiting for one of my client's to arrive for an appointment, when a book by Dr Michael Newton called *Journey of the Souls* caught my attention. As soon as I picked it up, I could not put it down and knew I had to do this work as it is remarkable research into the afterlife.

Life Between Lives is about what happens when you die and leave your body and travel with your guide to the afterlife. It goes on in great detail about all the stops in the spirit world and so on. I would totally recommend for anyone interested in this topic to read his books as they are so enlightening, educational and informative. If anything it teaches us that death is only a beginning. All I could think of when reading the case studies of how similar it was to my own near death experience (NDE) I had in my early 20s.

Not long after, I was given the opportunity to train at this academy and have never looked back.

Over the years I have worked as a past life therapist as part of my practice and have trained with what I can only call some of the best teachers in the world.

Another really good teacher was Dolores Cannon who is not only an expert in her field, but an inspiring woman as well. She really made me laugh when she told me how important it is to be really passionate about the work you do. I could not agree with her more as the work that connects you to spirit as an eternal soul is never boring and always keeps you on your toes. Nothing is more rewarding than to see what I call "the healing aspect" that comes with the work you do with your clients and to see them be able to move and grow as souls.

Working as a medium already, I found this was exactly what I needed to do next. What happens to you when you die has been a question most of us think about from the moment we are born and is always in the back of our minds. When we are educated about death and know that we will be OK, it takes away a lot of unnecessary fear around the issue. In many ancient civilisations, death has always been a sacred process and seen as a passage for growth, where we live on and grow as a spirit.

I have spoken to many spirit people on the other side but nothing they told me was as comprehensive as the journey of the souls and my session with a Life Between Lives therapist.

Life Between Lives combines all your past lives and takes you back to the soul state, connecting you with the ever-powerful and loving god state or source. For me, on a personal level, it is a humbling and teaching experience to be able to do this amazing work.

A lot of things have happened for me since I finished my Life Between Lives training with the Dr Michael Newton Institute because when you do this type of work, in my experience I have found, it not only gives you information but also increases your rate of vibration and so decreases your karma.

I am a lot clearer about my intention about what I want and need in life, my heart chakra has opened up more and I know what it is like when you go to heaven! (You not only meet up with your faithful and loving guide, but all your wonderful friends in your soul group are there to greet you.)

I already knew that I was here for spiritual service, but the other insights I discovered about my own immortal life as a soul were amazing. As your "energy" or "vibration" increases so does your awareness.

I have discovered through doing work on yourself, that you will no longer be attracted to people that drag you down, such as the poor me's of the world, because you will be on your path and so many doors will open, making your life more creative and exciting. You will no longer have any time to be dragged down by so called "energy stealers" who use your energy instead of their own, leaving you feeling drained. You will feel energised and opportunities you only dreamed about will become a reality.

Other doors may close because you will no longer be attracted to certain energies. People you may have been attracted to before will disappear or you will no longer want to be around them. This is called the Law of Attraction. Those who are no longer on your level may leave your life. Sure it is sad sometimes, but when you work on yourself these things happen. You may feel lonely for a while, but new people on your wavelength will come in to take their place.

As I constantly work on myself to be a better person in the world, I now allow myself to feel free and happy and wake up every day wondering what else could be better than what I already have in my life now because I am so blessed.

The other information I received in this session was my spiritual name, Saku. I was also given insight to my own energy as an immortal soul and tips on how to live my life. I would like to share all 11 points with you.

Personal responsibility.
Loving yourself for who you are.
Treating others as equals.
Understanding and compassion for all.

To honour others as you would honour yourself.

To respect the planet and environment you live in.

To live in harmony with everything around you.

To feel the beauty and energy of your surroundings.

To feel peace and wholeness inside you via the breath.

To see everyone and everything as a mirror for your learning.

We are ALL ONE WITH THE SOURCE.

Meditation

Go to a quiet place by the ocean.

Find a lovely and protected place, by the sea, to just find time for you.

Now, sit yourself down, or lie on the warm sand and gently close your eyes.

Begin to slowly breathe in and out until you feel all your body, completely relaxed.

As you breathe, release all the tension, all the stress, all the heaviness from your body from the day, until you are completely relaxed.

No cares, no worries, just letting go and spending time for you.

Now expand your energy and awareness, all around you and as you do this, imagine you are surrendering and letting go of everything you no longer need in your life that may be holding you back in your life.

Let go of any trauma, negativity, bad feelings or fear, from your mind and cells that no longer serves you.

As you do this, slowly begin to open up all your senses and begin to feel, smell, taste and hear everything that is all around you in nature.

Feel the warm gentle caress of the sun on your body, smell the fresh and invigorating air, taste the salt of the water in your taste buds and hear the many varied cries of the birds, in the sky.

As the sound of the thrashing waves rush up on the beach, feel the tide taking all your worries and problems away.

When you are ready to come back, feel yourself energised and gently open your eyes and see the new day.

A Life Between Lives session

After my first Life Between Lives session with the Newton Institute, I had another session which was quite different from the first. Most people who come to me for a LBL session always want to know about my experience.

After being induced by the Dr Michael Newton script which was done by a therapist trained in this area, I was taken to my last life. I find I am an American Indian called Little Bird, who was traded by her father, the chief of the tribe, for some horses to a kindly white man called James.

Together we have a harmonious life and bring up two children, a boy and a girl. In this lifetime I work with potions and herbs, but it is frowned upon by the local villages as evil and they believe me to be a witch. I can relate to this experience in this life as well as it is just human nature for people to be suspicious and wary of others who are different. Eventually the villagers through their own ignorance fear and prejudices kill me and my entire family.

After coming out of my body at the death scene all I can feel is a deep sadness at being killed for nothing by these people and the love I felt for my husband, children, animals and surrounding nature is overwhelming. Finally, moving away from my body I feel a strong pulling sensation and I am moving very fast. I can see the earth curved below me, and I can see millions of lights spread out in front of me.

Soon blinding light envelops me and I arrive at a big opening with gigantic doors. Inside is a big vast golden city of light and all I can feel is that I am surrounded by love and I have a feeling of "coming home".

My first contact is made with my guide, White Feather. He is dressed as an Indian and tells me my spiritual name is Saku. He feels like an old friend, and is full of compassion, humour and love. We spend some time together, catching up and having a few laughs. Soon I am taken to my cluster group (or soul group). They are a group of 11 lights and I recognize some of them from this lifetime. Most of them are my own family now. It is good to be together again as we all support each other. We are all strong-minded souls and have a high level of energy.

Next I am taken by my guide to the council, which is next to a beautiful lake on the mountainside. There are four wise ones who appear androgynous and are dressed in white robes with silver medallions around their necks, a symbol for eternity. I wear a similar one now.

I am told to believe in myself and learn to shine in my own light. They also tell me it is important for me to step into my own power. My guide laughs as he has told me all this before in meditation.

Among the places I visit are the spirit hospital, the library where I can download some important information for this lifetime and many other places of interest. All around me are amazing clear colours and an endless space of vastness and eternity. I also get to play with my own soul group and have fun. All the time I am surrounded by the source which is a continual stream of unconditional love. I also find that I have lived on other planets where all the beings are just rays of light and who communicate through sound. This was an amazing experience for me, as you can imagine. Each person who decides to have a LBL session will receive a healing and an insight into their own immortal soul energy to help them on their own spiritual path to the truth.

Healing lost souls or earth-bound spirits

As a psychic medium, part of my life's work is releasing earth-bound spirits from entrapment on the earth's plane. There are two types of spirits:

Earth-bound: These are spirits or souls that do not know that they are actually dead or for some reason have not passed over to the other side.

Living: These are spirits who have crossed over successfully into the light or have "gone home" to receive healing. They have already met up with their soul group and loved ones on the other side. Some people refer to this plane as "heaven", a place that is not up in the air, but in another dimension right in front of us that we can't see.

Whenever I do a reading for someone, it generally starts with a communicator coming in for that person. It may be the person's relative who has passed over to the other side or a guide that they are working with at the time. My own loving guides, White Feather, my main guide or my gatekeeper, Red Hawk and Margaret help me as well. I also work with a plethora of other brilliant guides who are all part of my team of spirit helpers.

If I am communicating with someone the client knew who has passed over, I usually get what is called "proof of survival", and so they know who I am talking to. This involves details identifying the spirit who has crossed over, including their gender, name, age, how they passed, what they looked like, where they lived and their relationship to the client. I am sometimes given messages or information that the person in spirit wants them to know. There are no secrets in the spirit world; they know everything we have been up to and usually have something to say, as they are eternally linked to us with our love.

As an immortal soul, when a person dies they automatically leave their body and float above in the room or place where they have died. With the commencement of death, their loving guide they were born with comes in straight away and they are swept up and carried far away from the earth and taken to what we call the "source". This is also called the "light" or the "other side"; it is similar to earth but a brighter and vaster space. Once they arrive with their guide they are met with others from their own soul group, their council, or wise ones, and are taken to spirit hospital, to receive healing, and make contact with loved ones still on the earth plane.

On the other hand, earth-bound spirits or lost souls do not cross over and are stuck and confused in the astral. Often they do not know where they are or how they got there. In most cases they are also not aware that they are actually dead. They are usually too scared or timid and do not understand what is happening to them.

There may be several reasons why they have not crossed over and the causes can be some of the following:
- A fatal accident or sudden death.
- A case of suicide as often when souls do this they are in such turmoil and may be too scared of the consequences, not believing there is a place for everyone in heaven.
- A case of mental illness where they were either afraid of death, or had committed a bad act and been afraid of what will happen to them.

- Religious or other beliefs where they may have behaved so badly in their life they fear death and certain circumstances.
- An obsessive love or greed for the material world, lust and attachment to earthly possessions.
- An unresolved conflict with their loved ones or family.
- Where they are fear based and may not believe in the possibility an afterlife. Or they may have behaved badly and believe in hell and think they will end up there. I know for a fact that there is no hell and that it was invented by the Christian church to control the masses.

Earth-bound spirit can wander around lost and confused until they are rescued by either a trained medium and sent into the light, or by their own guide, but that can take time. These spirits can be found all over the place, especially where large groups of people congregate. These may be places such as hospitals, churches, football stadiums, jails police stations, shopping centres and railroad stations.

It is not often you will find a lost soul in a lonely house, unless they have accidentally died there or lived there for a while and the home is familiar. Such spirits can sometimes follow people home and become a pest because of the disharmony they bring into the home.

To move them on can be very taxing and draining work and most mediums like to work in pairs to do so because of the energy expenditure.

If you have a lost soul in your house it is likely you will have a few issues. Some of the problems you will encounter may be one of the following examples.

- Your home will feel ice cold and unpleasant in certain areas and no matter what you do, the energy will be heavy and uncomfortable to live in.
- Most of the family living there will frequently pick up colds or flu or may develop unexplained illnesses.

- There may be continual fights, arguments or disagreements because of the imbalance of the energy in the house.
- It will be almost impossible to sell or make changes to the house because there will be constant delays.
- There may have unexplained or ongoing problems with electricity or water for no obvious reasons.
- There may be unusual sounds, things disappearing, strange smells and constant confusion.

If by chance you have an earth-bound spirit in your home, you are bound to have many problems as well. When anybody rings me, I often tell them to burn sage in the home every day for seven days and see what happens as this generally weakens the spirit and they may go. They can be persistent and may not want to leave in which case it may be wise to call for professional assistance as this dark and heavy energy can be sucking your own energy and making life miserable.

People often say they have been woken up in the middle of the night by the doorbell and when they open the door nobody is there. This is a sign that such a spirit is active. One client I know took two years to renovate her house because her earth-bound spirit did not like all the noise and changes and did not want her there. He was an old man who owned a lot of the land in the area when he was alive, so I had to lift the disruptive energy off the contract of the house as well. As soon as I sent him off to the light, she was able to finish her whole house without any more problems and all the workmen turned up with without any more delays.

Whenever I clean a house or rescue an earth-bound spirit I encase the whole house in a purple light, then go inside, find the spirit and send it off to the light. I always take my time at this, as the spirit can often be really scared so I might hear a little whimper. Sometimes I check inside cupboards and under things in case they are hiding from me. Afterwards I sage or smudge the house to rid it of any negative energy, allowing the house to breathe again. Then I go to all the doorways and place a tiny amount of oil in the opening so to what I call "seal the house" so no other spirit can ever enter. When I am finished I play one of my crystal bowls to realign the house to its original energy.

One of the few times I have ever had a problem with a spirit rescue was when the spirit was Aboriginal. He was being a nuisance and was keeping a young girl up all night by constantly moving things around the home. She was frightened to death and had no chance of ever getting any sleep. After I saged the house with gum leaves, the only way I could get my spirit friend to leave was to call on the Elder of his tribe to come and take the spirit into the light and out of the home. Once I had done this, the spirit left and never came back.

Case study 1—Stella

A quiet unassuming woman with a gentle, humble energy, Stella was a regular student in my psychic development classes and a gifted healer. We met at a healing centre on the North Coast, when I was working out there doing readings and healings and she expressed her desire to come and join one of the groups I was running as she was interested in learning about energy. I welcomed her into the group and everything was going really well until about a year later when she started to have marital problems. Her energy started to shift and she became very sensitive and more aware of things and energy around her.

Her home situation was looking rocky and because she was becoming clearer and beginning to open up more she was starting to become unsettled. It was becoming obvious her own personal life did not serve her. Occasionally she would open up and everyone in the group had a sense that things were not right at home. It was also obvious her relationship with her husband was under pressure and deteriorating. This upset her deeply as she was divorced and this was her second marriage.

Often when you do any type of spiritual work on yourself or personal self development your energy and whole life will change for the better. It is very common for dramatic changes to happen, as everything that does not serve you any longer, including relationships, will simply fade from your life and will no longer be important.

Another important aspect is that when you sit in a circle there are bound to be no secrets as everyone is usually aware of what is going on in each other's life. You must keep it to yourself and be discreet. As time went on, Stella started to "freak out" in class and it was obvious to all of us in the circle that she was extremely unhappy. As the weeks went on she started to bring her personal problems into our group.

Stella also was becoming less grounded and more paranoid and started talking gibberish, wanting everyone's attention. As group leader I tried to speak to her several times about her behaviour as it was disruptive and she became more irritating and attention seeking. She began to become fearful of the simplest of things, such as healing and would question everything we had always done in a menacing, malicious way. She also began to boast about her healing work and say how powerful she was. Stella soon became so full of herself that I felt her energy not stable and compatible to the rest of the group. I asked her to leave and take time out to work on herself and her unsuccessful marriage, which I felt was really the problem.

After a few weeks, fed up and at his wits end, Stella called me for help. Everything was out of control in her life and she was beginning to fall to pieces and I could sense she was in a really bad way and needed assistance. She soon told me that she was being kept awake all night by supernatural "beings" that she claimed would not leave her alone. She had not had a proper night's sleep for weeks and said she felt like his world was being ripped from under her.

She also complained that she was broke all the time, because her husband, who she was not talking to any longer, had left them in great financial difficulty. He was from India and was drawing money out of their account on a daily basis and sending large sums to his family without her permission. Stella found this not only very distressing but dishonest and was angry that her husband was taking advantage of their savings. Because of her poor health, they were now in a bad financial situation and she blamed this on the bad spirits running amok in his house and keeping her up all night.

Deciding to investigate the paranormal matter at hand, I rang my partner Bill who I always work with in spirit rescues and asked him to meet me at Stella's house. Bill also sits in the group, and was not surprised that Stella had contacted us. We both felt something was definitely happening to Stella and wanted to get to the bottom of it.

As soon as we arrived at her home, Bill and I both felt sick in the stomach and sensed something negative was going on. We both started to get a severe headache and quickly began to protect ourselves with white light. As soon as we did this, I began to burp, which is always a sure indicator for me that spirits are present. The two-storey, run down house was in total disarray with clutter and mess everywhere. It almost seemed incredible that people actually lived in such a place.

The energy felt completely out of balance, sad and depressing. As soon as we entered the property we could feel a "heaviness" looming over us like a dark, miserable cloud that was hard to shake off.

Energetically this was not a good situation, as everything felt so strained and tense like a war zone, almost to point it was hard to think. The energy was also what I can only describe as "electric" all around us, giving us good indication that there were probably several earth-bound spirits trapped on the property. As Bill and I scanned the energy outside the home, we quickly placed a purple bubble around the whole home so no earth-bound spirits could escape while we worked inside the property.

When we finished doing this, Stella, walking besides us, told us that her husband's relatives lived in the top storey of the house and the husband, a very angry man, screamed at the top of his lungs all the time, due to stress.

Apparently, he was unemployed and was suffering a great deal of financial hardship as well. Both families were desperate to sell the home but for some reason could not find the energy to clean the mess up all around them. Why they had neglected and let the place get so run down was incredible to comprehend but not for us to judge. We just wanted to do our work and go.

I was not surprised as there were so many disharmonies everywhere and everything felt so tense and uptight.

Once we entered Stella's part of the home we discovered, to our astonishment, more of her husband's relatives living in other rooms. It was easy to see and we were beginning to see and get more of a picture of what was going on. Having a quick giggle to himself, Bill quietly saw the humour in the situation and turned around to me and whispered softly in my ear about how the place reminded him of the sitcom *Little Britain*, and its character Ting Tong, the lady from Thailand, who stuffs her relatives in the kitchen cupboard, supposedly without her husband ever knowing what was going on under his nose.

I almost choked with laugher, which was good because it made me relax and not get too caught up with the energy which was playing havoc with my nerves.

After about 20 minutes and feeling as if we were being watched by prying invisible eyes, both spirit and human, Bill and I finished scanning the house psychically. We had discovered what is called "a portal", or large dimensional tear or inter-dimensional opening in one of the bedrooms which was the main reason which was causing most of the problems in the home. The energy in the room was freezing and the portal was, in our understanding, creating havoc for spirits to come and go as they pleased which was affecting the balance and harmony of the home both upstairs and down.

As soon as we told Stella this information, she agreed that this was indeed the spot in the house where most of the spirit visitations were actually taking place and where she felt she was having the most problems at night.

The portal, we explained to Stella was a problem and had to be closed down so the home could heal as it was not natural, was creating chaos and more importantly, allowing unwanted spirits which were not welcomed, to come and go as they pleased.

No sooner had we repaired the dimensional tear with white light and closed down the leaking energy, my ears began to ache painfully and to buzz loudly. Within seconds, two spirits appeared in the room and stood by Bill and me. One appeared as an old man and the other was a female energy, probably his wife. The female spirit seemed scared but the male energy was extremely fierce and angry. Suddenly the whole room changed in temperature, and I could feel "prickly energy" like electricity in the air making all my hairs stand up on my arms. Stepping forward, I asked who the spirits were and what they wanted.

The male told me his name and how he and his wife had lived in the house for as long as they could remember. He asked what we were doing there and it was obvious to me that he had no idea that he was dead. He remembered being sick and dying there but nothing else. The man spirit also wanted to know who the noisy people living in his house were and about the screaming man who lived upstairs. Before I could answer, I was pushed across the room and landed on the bed which was on the opposite side of the room. As soon as this happened, Bill stepped forward and, without wasting any time, brought down the white light. As soon as this was done, we held hands, said the Lord's Prayer several times and proceeded to talk to the spirits gently, telling them that they were dead and to open their eyes and to go into the light so they could cross over and go home. Within a few moments, we felt them leave and the temperature in the room changed back to normal. All that was left were little grey dots that eventually disappeared too. The healing had taken place and their own guides had come and helped them cross over. Once the couple entered into the light, I heard a big thank you and goodbye and knew that everything would be all right.

A few weeks later, Stella came to visit me at the shop where I was reading, and told me how much better she felt, and that there had been no disturbances of any sort any longer. The relationships in the home had improved and everything had been restored back to normal. Stella and her husband had decided to spend more time together and build on their relationship. The last I heard was that she was happy and is still continuing with her healing work.

Case study 2—George

George had been married to his wife, Jillian, for a very long time. They were both doctors and came to Australia from Europe, when they were young. George worked as a surgeon and was to set up a practice, straight away with great success. Unfortunately, Jillian after giving birth to their two children later developed some type of depression which very sadly developed into a type of schizophrenia. Over the years, her personality changed dramatically and she not only became house-bound but was also forgetful, confused and unhappy and made everyone's life miserable.

George rang me and asked if I could clear his house. Although Jillian had been dead for some time he could still feel her energy was around. He had moved on in his life, and had met a new woman but things were starting to disappear from his house and he was sure that Jillian, although in spirit, was not happy with his new arrangement. He was convinced she had come back to haunt him and was jealous and angry that he was in love with another woman.

As soon as I arrived, I encased the house in a purple and gold bubble of light to ensure any lost spirits would not be able to escape which is the usual procedure. Walking in the front door I felt Jillian's presence sitting on a chair, next to her husband. As I tuned into the spirit energy, I could feel she had difficulty breathing when she died and she showed me, in my mind's eye, what had happened to her.

When she was sick, her husband had taken her to the hospital. This was the first time she had left her home since she had become housebound and ill. She was terrified when she later died in the emergency section of a heart attack, so instead of leaving with her spirit guide and crossing over into the light, she decided to go back home and jumped back into the car with her husband. She went on to tell me since the onset of her mental illness she had been terrified of leaving the house and spent most of her time in her bed. (This was later confirmed by her husband who nodded and cried in agreement when I told him what she had said.)

Walking into her bedroom, I saw her lying under the covers in her bed where she spent most of her time when she was alive and unwell. The energy in the room was toxic, heavy, sad and depressing. It would have been almost impossible for anyone to want to sleep in there and I noticed the family dog starting to bark when I moved into the room. Animals always have an inner sixth sense to what is going on in the spirit world and

I am convinced they can see spirits walking around the place. Moving gently closer so as not to scare her, I brought down a portal of light and told her to open her eyes and explained to her that she was dead. I went on to tell her, in a loving and compassionate voice, that she no longer belonged here and that it was time to cross over and go home to where all her loved ones were waiting for her in spirit.

Once I explained this, she seemed willing to go, hesitated for about a minute and jumped swiftly into the light and said goodbye. This made me realise she was ready. Sometimes, if lost souls are really scared, you can hear them whimper and you have to talk to them very lovingly and gently to coax them to leave. Sometimes you have to be patient as this can take time. I knew Jillian was happy to go because she had such a miserable and lonely life. As she left, I heard her ask me if I would tell her husband and children that she loved them and she was sorry for all the pain that she had caused.

As soon as Jillian was gone, the family dog which had been waiting patiently by the door started running around barking. Moving around, I cleansed her room with grandfather sage and energetically cleared out all the stale and negative energy from the rest of the house that had gathered up over the years of her illness. I also instructed her husband, George to sage the house for seven days as a precaution; he was terrified she would come back even though I reassured him it would not happen. Then I went to all the doorways of the house and sealed the energy with some special oil I had made up which consisted of olive oil, garlic and sage. This acts as a deterrent for any other unwanted spirits or negative influences that may want to move in.

After doing this the house felt very calm and relaxed for probably the first time in ages, as all the old energy that had saturated the house for years had finally been shifted into portals of light I had set up energetically in the corners of the rooms.

Saying goodbye, I hugged my client goodbye, patted the dog and wished them both a happy life. Smiling happily, he thanked me warmly and closed the door behind him.

Case study 3— Spirit rescue in the prison officers' home

One day Bill, my partner in spirit rescue, and I were called out to a large house in the Liverpool area in south-western Sydney. Bill is usually in charge of healing energies or lay lines and it is my job to do the spirit rescue. We work well as a team and it is always good to have back-up as you never known what can happen. The family were having problems with earth-bound spirits that were keeping them awake at night. Furniture was being moved around in the middle of the night and the daughter was too scared to sleep in her room as she felt something kept rocking her bed all night as it vibrated on its own accord while she tried to sleep.

As soon as we arrived, we protected ourselves quickly with white light, sealed the house and started scanning the energy for earth-bound spirits.

Once we stepped inside we could feel the house was ice cold. Leanne, the owner, was stressed and unhappy and explained that no matter how hard she tried to warm it, there was no change. She told us about the constant family fights, many colds and sickness in the family, furniture being moved around when they were sleeping and the death of all her beloved pets, which very sadly was totally unexplainable.

She had tried everything in her power to rid herself of this problem but she was convinced the house was cursed, haunted and something evil was in it. Others, including a priest had come to help but nothing seemed to work. She begged us to do something and we told her we would try our best.

As I walked slowly through the house with Bill, we scanned each room and found spirit people nearly in every room. It was like a hotel for earth-bound spirits that had nothing better to do with their time. No wonder the family had no peace. In each room we brought down a column of light and asked the different spirits to cross over. The process took us well over an hour, by which time we were becoming tired and weary as the work was taking its toll and we were using quite lot of energy and I could gradually feel myself becoming tired.

In all, that day, we freed 11 spirits. It would have to be a record for a house in the suburbs, I would have thought. Also Leanne and her daughter had a couple of attachments in their own energy fields or aura, which were quickly dealt with and healed.

Over a cup of tea and biscuits, which was greatly appreciated, she told us later how her daughter, ever since she was a baby, was terrified to sleep in her own room. The young girl always felt some type of spirit presence and found it almost impossible to sleep in there alone unless she had a light on all night, which seemed to work for a while. She was now in her early twenties and nothing had changed except the bed, which these days was beginning to rock non-stop whenever the light was off and her furniture was being moved around as well. I told her I was not surprised as her room, for some reason, had to be the worst in the house, as the energy there was really heavy. In that room alone, I removed four earthbound spirits. Why they picked his room I can't tell you but I can understand how the poor girl must have suffered all those years.

As we drank our tea, Leanne went on to tell us the heartache of losing some of her pets to mysterious illnesses over the years. She was convinced that it was due to the energy in the house. As she talked, I wondered why there was so much negative energy in the house, and asked Leanne what she did for a living. She told me that she worked for the prison service and her husband worked at a psychiatric hospital.

As soon as she said this it all started to make sense.

Psychiatric hospitals are full of negative energy, and murders and deaths a common occurrence in prisons. Often, people may unconsciously "sweep" or "pick up" earth-bound spirits from these places without even knowing they are doing so. It was no wonder the home was a mess as they must have been bringing spirits home for quite a while and not knowing it!

After we had cleared the house, and smudged it thoroughly with sage, we told her to continue doing this for a week. I then quickly showed Leanne and her partner how to protect themselves with white light when they went to work. I also showed them how to make an energetic grid of light over the entrance to the house to stop any earth-bound spirits from entering.

I then "sealed" the home with my oil as a secondary measure and showed them how to do this in the future if needed ... This would deter any incoming spirits who may have followed Leanne and her partner from work and they would not be allowed in.

Outside the house Bill healed the earth energy and ley lines to balance the home from all the stress and trauma from the past.

Finally, the family were well on their way to a normal and peaceful life.

Healing lost souls in the aura or spirits or entities attached to the aura

Besides the home, we can sometimes have spirits or entities which may attach themselves to our aura or energy field. This happens when we have a break, or hole, in our energy field and can sometimes manifest as a type of depression. Over the years I have seen and felt many attachments in people's energies fields with my shamanistic spiritual healing and hypnotherapy and have successfully been able to remove them. This work is called releasing unwanted spirits or attachments from the aura.

To have a break or tear in the aura, in my opinion can be caused by a few of the following events.
- A general anaesthetic.
- Car accident or sudden shock or trauma.
- Excessive and long-term drug or alcohol intake.
- Sexual, mental, or psychical abuse.
- Long-term illness.
- Continuing use of heavy medication as in prescription drugs.

For more information, I recommend one of the pioneers on the subject, Dr William J Baldwin, who wrote *Healing Lost, Souls: releasing unwanted spirits from your energy field.*

Case study 1—Ted

Ted had been looking after his mother while she was dying until she passed over. She had been terrified of leaving her son and did not want to die. After she was buried, he remained sad and fragile for a couple of years. Many people thought him to be depressed, because it was as if his life force had been sucked out of him. He had tried anti-depressants but nothing seemed to work. Ted was unemployed and felt something was wrong with him but he could not understand exactly what it was.

When he walked into the healing centre, I could see his energy was very low, as his aura was shrunken and dark, and looked to be very thin around his body. He looked pale and tired. As I began to heal him energetically, I could see that he had what I call an attachment in his aura, which turned out to be his mother. Quickly I removed her energy from his aura, and sent her straight into the light. Instead of crossing over she had attached herself to him like a parasite, draining all the energy out of his body.

When the healing was finally over, I told him what I thought was going on in his life and what had happened energetically to him. He totally understood as there was never a day went by when he did not think of his mother. After the healing, he looked like a different person and was full of energy. No longer overshadowed by his mother, his eyes were brighter and he said he felt much better. He told me he was glad that she was gone, so he could now get on with his own life that had seemed to disappear.

Case study 2—Samantha

Samantha came for a reading and was having trouble with an old boyfriend. He was married and had promised to leave his wife for 10 years, but nothing had happened. She had also fallen pregnant on several occasions and had several terminations. This had been a very unpleasant and emotional experience on her part, and she was feeling depressed about the whole saga.

She had spent time with a counsellor and had worked out what to do with her life, but still felt unwell so she came to me for a spiritual healing. On first appearance, I could see that she was overweight, was a heavy smoker and, even though she had finally finished with her lover over six months ago, she was very fragile and found it hard to feel positive or find anything remotely good in her life.

As I examined the energy around her aura I felt that it was shrunken and heavy and I could feel a slight break in the front. I felt this by a slight breeze in one area of her body and this is an indication that there is aura damage. She seemed to be carrying a lot of weight, especially around her shoulders. She said she felt depressed and was unable to enjoy her life or move forwards. I suggested that we cut the ties and disengage her from her ex-lover as I could feel his energy still around her. This would not only help her but would help him as well to move forward energetically. After I regressed her, and cut the ties with her ex, I took her further down into trance and we arrived at what I call "the white room". This is a place where I take clients to see if they have any entities or unwanted spirits in their energy field.

Once there I located a male spirit energy that did not belong in the person's aura. I quickly told him he was dead and that he needed to go to the light. Once I did this the spirit left my client and said she felt lighter. After the session, I explained to her she may have picked up her "lost soul" attachment when she had a termination as the agony, stress and the anaesthetic may have been the cause of the hole in her aura.

Six weeks later she rang me and told me how wonderful she felt. She had lost weight, had given up smoking and was totally over her ex. She felt like she was finally in control of her life again and was ready to move on. The healing that we had done together had obviously helped her in whatever she may have needed. She also told me she had found a good counsellor, as I suggested, helping her with any other problems that may arise in the future. She now had the confidence to live a full life again.

Case study 3—Tracey

Tracey was a client of mine who felt lost most of her life. She had spent a small fortune trying to get better and had done the rounds of nearly every psychotherapist and therapist in town.

Tracey had been trying to get well for a while but had never discovered why she felt so bad all her life. She was now convinced that she was never going to get well and that she must have had either an incurable disease of some sort or was plain unlucky and had a curse on her. Initially, I was very sad that this was the case and wondered what I could do to help her, considering that she had already been everywhere else. Keeping my mind open, I suggested that she ring for an appointment. At the time I was working at several centres around town and it was relatively easy to do this. As time went on, I started to think that she was a time-waster as she cancelled two appointments and did not turn up to the third. I thought I would never hear from her again.

Meanwhile, one of her friends was determined to get help for her. She had spent a lot of time with Tracey and felt that there was something terribly wrong as she was beside herself with stress and worry and unable to move on.

Monday was one of my busiest days in a long time, and it was just before Christmas. The phone was ringing full throttle with clients wanting last minute help with flower essences, healings, readings and hypnotherapy sessions. Some clients had even flown in from Melbourne to see me, so I knew I would be busy as everyone had booked well in advance. Just as I had finished work for the day the phone started ringing and when I picked it up, I heard it was Tracey.

She seemed very nervous and kept apologising, pleading for me to see her and begging me for an appointment. At first I was annoyed as I was busy and had no time for people to muck me around but I could hear from her voice that the woman was at an all-time low. The voice in my head told me to give her a chance, as she was genuine, so I told her to make another time after Christmas as I was so busy. After talking to her a while, I sensed she needed to see me that day so I decided to break my own rules and boundaries and told her to come after 6pm after I had finished for the day. I was curious to see if there was any way I could help her as she seemed so desperate. The other thing I was aware of was that as most of us know in the healing professions, Christmas can be a bad time for many as it stirs up people's energy, throwing them into a healing crisis.

As soon as she walked into the room, she rushed over and hugged me for seeing her. I was a bit taken aback as my nose is incredibly sensitive and I could smell a slight smell of alcohol on her breath. Annoyed and wondering what I had got myself in for, I informed her cordially that I couldn't help her as she had been drinking and it wasn't ethical. Normally I would have pressed the eject button and sent her on her way, but my guides said to give her another chance. Being an ex-registered nurse, I was used to dealing with difficult patients and wasn't afraid to stand my ground.

I felt there was indeed something terribly wrong as on first glance her aura was incredibly shrunken and her energy was dark, prickly and low. She wasn't drunk, and had probably scoffed a quick drink to calm her nerves as she seemed on edge. After all, she was coming to see a "healer" who was supposed to remove curses and whatever else she had imagined in her head. She had also never met me before and most likely did not realise that I looked like any other housewife in the suburbs. Her imagination must have been on overdrive and she was probably expecting to see me with a big hairy wart on my chin, a motorised broomstick in the cupboard, and with a goat head cooking in a cauldron on the hearth.

Plopping herself down wearily, she looked me up and down and stared wide-eyed at my red hair and Charlie Brown pants.

As she scanned the room looking for something weird, I nearly burst out laughing because I could see what she was thinking. She must have put herself through a terrible panic just to come and see me and had realised how silly she had been when she had seen how normal I appeared.

Taking a deep breath, she started crying softly and began to tell me everything that had happened to her. The poor woman was in such a state it was no wonder she had freaked out before and hadn't had the courage to come and see me. Once I offered her a cup of tea, she soon started to relax and began to tell me everything that was troubling her.

She was 35 years old, and had never been able to feel any emotion or love of any sort and felt she was a misfit and a miserable soul. She felt empty, sad and lonely but could not figure out why or give a simple reason. Her childhood had been the same as far back as she could remember. It was as if she always had a dark shadow over her. Her whole existence was one of isolation as she always felt she had no connection with others, even though she was once married. All her relationships, as well as her last, with a bikie, went belly-up and ending badly. For years she had visited various psychiatrists and other professionals who didn't know how to help her but charged her large amounts of money then filed her in the too-hard basket.

Scanning her energy and aura with my hands, I realised straight away it was cracked and had a large hole in it. I could feel a cool breeze on the palm of my hands and realised she must have had this for quite a while. Instinctively I felt that Tracey wasn't mad at all, but had an attachment or spirit entity living in her like a vampire sucking all her energy. It was in fact a large parasite was firmly planted in her emotional body.

The entity, or attachment, had its own feelings and agendas and had completely overtaken Tracey's being, embedding its own needs and feelings into Tracey for years and years. It was the spirit of an old man who had died on the earth plane, and had jumped into Tracey's energy when she came out of her mother's birth canal. The entity had probably died in the hospital and did not want to "pass over", so becoming earth-bound in her energy. Tracey didn't stand a chance. No wonder she thought she was mad when she was actually living somebody else's life.

Once I tapped into what was going on, the parasite or entity was scared and did not want to leave at first. Asking for Tracey's assistance, together we told it that it no longer had permission to live in her energy field, and it had to go into the light for healing.

After several attempts and futile arguments with the thing, and help from my loving guides and spiritual friends, we slowly removed the entity and sent it packing into the vortex of light I had created with my guides. The entity put up a good fight, and left with a howling scream but was carried straight into the light through my body.

From her birth, Tracey's whole life had been that of an unwilling host to something alien. As soon as the healing was complete, Tracey started laughing and said she felt lighter and relieved as soon as she felt the "thing" leave. Almost immediately she could feel a remarkable difference in her energy. The darkness she had carried and felt most of her life was no longer there and she felt energised and clearer. The heaviness in her head was gone and her eyes felt clearer and more focused. For years when nobody could help her and treated her like she was mad, she had felt like she was going crazy and perhaps had been "cursed", or not of this world. It was also impossible for her as a young girl to feel anything for her own family as she had always felt disconnected.

After she had settled down, I regressed her through hypnotherapy to let her see her own aura so she could see the new and beautiful new colours glowing out of her. I also suggested a few positive affirmations to help move her forward with her life.

At first her aura had been dark and compacted but after bringing healing light into her energy field, it changed to a brighter colour and expanded widely so it was strong and certainly clear of any attachments and breaks in the energy field. She was able to see for herself that there was nothing attached to her energy field and all traces of the spirit were gone. Her only complaint was why she had to wait 35 years to find somebody that could help in this way. It was sad that this was the case, but sometimes these kinds of things happen in life and we will never get an explanation why this is so.

My reply was she had never sought help from a spiritual healer. That is why I always say it is important to mix conventional medicine with alternative as they go hand in hand. Why she had to wait so long may have been part of her contract on earth or perhaps she was just unlucky. That was one question I couldn't help her with but I am sure this all had to do with her own spiritual contract or karma.

Are curses real?

I have heard many psychics and others say there are no such thing as curses. I wish it was true but I have experienced this phenomenon at first hand. If I was to ask why I was affected, I can only say I was meant to experience it so I could help other people in the same situation. One thing is for sure, it is all fear based, no matter what you believe in. Placing somebody's name in the freezer is cursing them and is not healing as there is no resolution or forgiveness involved. All you are doing is freezing the problem and bringing disharmony and imbalance into your life by not moving on.

For years I did this when things were not going my way. I had no idea what I was doing but one thing I know for sure is that my problems never went away.

I had a life-changing experience when my ex sister-in-law, who was often saying terrible things about me behind my back, annoyed me so much I stuck her name in the freezer. The next time I saw her, she told me she had an enlarged tumour in her throat. Shocked to the core that I had perhaps caused this, I ran home and defrosted her name and swore never to do this again. A couple of weeks later I heard that her tumour had disappeared. Also I was not setting an example for my own two daughters, as I discovered all their teachers' names were in the freezer as well.

Here are some examples of so-called curses. Many years ago when I was a young nurse in training in the medical ward, we would do the round with the sister, ward doctor and specialist.

We would all stand around the bed staring down at the patient with the curtains closed, listening to the specialist talking to his patient. It was the same scenario played over and over to patients who had a so-called "incurable" disease. The patient was always told that they only had a certain amount of time to live (often it would be a couple of months, if they were lucky), and then they were told it would be best for all concerned if they could get their lives in order.

Once they were told this there was never a patient who survived a day over what was predicted, or what they were told. It seemed to me as if they never had a chance and had been given a death sentence. Often upset, because I felt it was wrong, I would discuss this with my other nurse colleagues, but it was out of our control and in the hands of the higher powers in the hospital system.

Even though I loved nursing, I was once told that I must always remember that nurses are dispensable. Shortly after that statement, I finally left the system and never worked as a trained nurse again.

Recipe for releasing negative energy, curses or dark energy

I mix crushed garlic and grandfather sage together in a quarter of bottle of pure olive oil. Then I place a dab on the client's third eye, and both wrists. Lighting a white candle, I stand behind the client and place both my hands on their shoulders. Holding my crucifix in my left hand, I say the Lord's Prayer and ask for God's assistance. I call on the Holy Spirit to remove any negative energy, any negative curses, outworn contracts, or any unwanted attachments to leave the client's energy field at once and go into the light for healing. I repeat this three times.

I then ask that the dark energy go into the light for healing and transmutation. All this only takes about five minutes, and then it is finished. You will feel lightness in your client and a slight energy shift. It is very subtle, but this is how spirit works.

I also use this mixture to seal houses I have cleared after I remove unwanted spirits or have done a spirit rescue. This is done by placing a tiny amount on top of all the doorways of the home. After you have done this you light a candle, say the Lord's Prayer and form a circle with two to three people (which opens a portal of light energy) and ask the negative or bad energy to leave. As I have stated there are different degrees of curses and psychic attack but generally they are treated in the same way.

Negative thought forms and earthbound energies and souls are all treated with the white light and sent into the light. Simply burning sage in a house will work wonders as it weakens the negative energy, and I generally ask the client to do this for a week or so. I also tell them to place my oil mixture on the tops of their doorways in and out of the house, light a candle and call on the light to remove the negative energy form the home.

Stick to these guidelines and you should be fine. If you have further trouble, then call a professional medium who is trained in this type of work. Always trust your own judgement, as well, because sometimes people cannot do what they say they can.

Case study 1—Sibiu's story

As a young girl growing up in a small country town full of migrants from all over the world, I was subjected to many beliefs and cultures. One of my dearest friends, Sibiu was a young Turkish girl who used to read my cards once a month. She had two gorgeous little children, two lovely girls and was married to a Greek guy called Tommy. If you know your history this is not perhaps a good match, as they are both politically different from one another and may have problems in the family as they are from different cultures.

Even though they loved each other and were happily married, Tommy's mother hated her daughter-in-law with a vengeance. So much so that she was always going to the local witch doctor down the road and buying curses to try to get rid of her. Whenever the mother-in-law came into Sibiu's house, she would hide all these little dolls when she thought her daughter-in-law wasn't looking and all hell would break loose. She would cunningly stick them all over the place in and around the outside of the home, or wherever she could get to in such a short time.

Straight away and without fail Sibiu would get sick or start to argue with her husband for silly reasons. When she hunted around and checked the house she would always find one of these awful little parcels stashed and hidden in the most obscure places. When she first told me about this, I only laughed as I found it all a bit far out and crazy. Before she would throw them into the bin, she would always show me and tell me about her continuing problems with her mother-in-law. I couldn't get my head around it as it seemed so unbelievable. Why would anyone in their right mind want to harm another person, especially family and a mother with two children? I never quite understood what she was talking about until it happened to me.

Every night after I finished working afternoon shift at the hospital, I would come home and hop into bed exhausted but I found it impossible to go to sleep. Night after night, I felt like something dark and sinister was watching me, hidden somewhere in the room. I even swore I saw some type of psychic snake on the top of my cupboard. When I turned all the lights on, nothing was there but my feeling remained. The energy in my home was so dark and foreboding that it used to make me shake and send shivers down my body. I tried to tell some of the nurses at work and ask them for some advice, but nobody knew what I was talking about and they even suggested I go and talk to the psychiatrist. But after a semester with him as a tutor, we all thought I was better off to work it out myself.

I must have saged the room a hundred times to get rid of the negative energy and felt it was not an earth-bound spirit as I would have been able to send it into the light. Nothing seemed to make any difference and nothing seemed to be working in my life. I was with another no-hoper muso boyfriend, and it was really hard for me to earn and save money. As soon as I was paid, the money was gone. I was unable to move ahead and I felt I was stuck and powerless to do anything.

In tears I went to Sibiu's house and begged her for help. In my eyes she was like a wise old woman who knew everything there was to know about the supernatural. I also felt intuitively she could probably help me and when I explained what was happening in my life, she totally understood. I apologised for my poor behaviour in not believing her with the mother-in-law saga as I am the type of person who has to experience things first-hand as my rational mind still thinks the whole concept of curses seems so ridiculous.

Sibiu told me not to worry about anything as she would take me to her Turkish doctor, who lived in Sydney. I had a curse on me, she said, shaking her head in sadness, and he would remove it for me. After my experience with the Turkish doctor, which felt like being in a movie called *The Outer Limits*, I now believe curses are real. The good news is that you can also get rid of them.

They are basically black magic but remember white light or white magic is far more powerful and much stronger as it comes from the source of love.

Whenever I feel afraid, or need protection, I visualise white light all around me. I used it as a child when I went to sleep to stop spirits and I still use it to this day. It is pure loving energy that is connected to the source. Whenever I have a client who thinks they have been cursed, I tell them that they have come to the right person and I do understand and it will be removed straight away. Any bad luck they may be carrying around will be relinquished if it has been placed on them by another person. I am not talking about karma here.

Case study 2—Julie

Julie was a client who was recommended to me by a friend for a spiritual healing. When she first walked into my office, I saw she was extremely physically thin and pale, as if she had been suffering from some type of eating disorder. On closer examination I could also see that her energetic field and aura appeared dark and weak and was very close to her body. It was not the typical aura you would see in a person of such a young age. Above her head, around what we call the crown chakra, or energy centre above the body, she had a dark brown energy that signals depression or constant worry.

She said she had been suffering from some type of mystery illness for the last two years that left her weak and tired all the time. She had felt this way for years but no-one had been able to solve the mystery of the illness. She had become more and more despondent and was also seeing a psychotherapist, but was not improving as she was depressed and crying constantly. Her mother, who was at her wit's end and extremely worried about her daughter's condition, sent her all over the place to different doctors and specialists, but nothing they ever did seemed to help. By the time she had come to me she was ready to give up as she had had enough and just wanted to get on with her life.

Sitting her down, and helping her relax, I gently asked her what had happened. Julie told me about a man from overseas she was involved with around the time she first got sick. She began an affair with him when he was married but, after about a year, he left his wife for her. Soon afterwards, he took her on a trip and told her of his new job in Pakistan and his plans to take her over there to live with him as he was so in love with her and wanted them to be together.

She was horrified at the mere idea and had no intention of going there to live with him as she didn't like the heat and resented his jealous outbursts and his possessive behaviour. The more time she spent with him the more she realised what he was really like. Julie was a young free-spirited woman who was used to doing what she wanted. She had been planning to end the relationship for a while but was too afraid to tell him. A life with him was out of the question after she learnt he was a control freak, and his insecurity and loud outbursts were starting to make her life a misery.

Once she confessed to how she really felt, he became really nasty and started to show his true colours. Losing his temper, he angrily berated her about her immature behaviour and the way she had embarrassed him at the markets that morning.

Apparently she had been really rude to a beggar they had met and he convinced her that he had seen the beggar look at her in a funny way and that she had probably been cursed.

His outburst of rage continued because he told her how he had noticed that none of the locals in the market place liked her. He was certain that she would now be dammed for all eternity and be alone forever. Once she had left him, he said she would never find another man to love her and would live with the consequences.

After they broke up, she tried desperately not to believe his cruel words but they never left her mind. She was convinced she was cursed and her life gradually fell apart. Not only did she become tired and depleted of energy but she was terrified of relationships and always felt something evil was watching everything she did or trying to get her.

After the healing, Julie said she felt a lot better and no longer felt fearful. I told her I had removed any negative energy from her body and that she had nothing to worry about any longer. It was time for her to now move on and not worry about her ex or the past. As far as I was concerned there was nothing bad around her energy field. Upon leaving she thanked me for helping her and promised she would get on with her life and see all of this as just a learning experience.

Case study 3—Sienna's story

Sienna first came to me for a reading one day with her cousin, Mary. She was a small pale European woman in her 30s. She had a terrible life in her country, and was abused verbally and beaten black and blue by her first husband. As she had a small child she left, frightened for her life, and came to Australia to live with her cousins to get away from her tyrant of a husband and his terrible mother. She was nervous and shy and life to her was hard.

As I tuned into her energies I could sense she had been cursed as she had a small shrunken aura that was very dark. Even though she had escaped and moved away from her tormentor, her life was still the same in many ways, as there was no sense of happiness in her confined life.

Instead her life on a daily basis was full of fear and dread, as if she was still living with her husband.

Sienna had very little money and worked in a factory to support herself and her daughter. She had always dreamed of working in an office as a secretary, but did not have the confidence or skills to do so. She was basically just surviving for her daughter and her livelihood, which was sad to see. She knew she had been cursed as her mother-in-law told her she had done this when she threatened to leave her son and take the daughter away. She was angry with herself because she said her own mother had warned her not to marry him and she knew deep down that the relationship was wrong but she was in love and fell pregnant very fast.

Within minutes of removing the negative energy from her aura and sending it into the light, her energy quickly shifted in a big way and she no longer appeared weak, tired and downtrodden. Her round wrinkled gentle face softened and she started to sit up straight with a new type of confidence. She commented that she was starting to feel different, just like she was before she was married. She knew that it was time for her to make changes in her life because when she was younger she was always a strong character who did what she wanted.

As I spread the tarot cards for her, I told her she would indeed be making changes and I could see that she would be working in a small office within a year. I also saw another marriage for her, with more love coming into her life. She was so happy and full of optimism, that she hugged me and thanked me for helping her, with tears of joy running down her face. I was just pleased

I could help her and told her it was time to take her power back and to live her life in accordance to her life's plan. She no longer had any more setbacks. I also made up a bottle of flower essences to take twice a day, including Lichen, Angelsword, Sundew, Fringed Violet and Walnut.

Psychic attack

When I first started opening up energetically and starting to learn about energy I was often what I call "psychically attacked". I would wake up in the middle of the night and feel somebody or something pressing down on me, or trying to suffocate me, all at once. I would wake up screaming and scaring the life out of my poor husband who would jump out of the bed thinking someone was trying to kill him. It was like having some type of really scary nightmare except I could feel myself being strangled.

When I looked around the room I could see there was no spirits in the room but I could certainly feel a nasty energy around me. This would leave me frightened and terrified and it would take me hours to get back to sleep because so much would be going on in my head as I wondered what was going on. Whenever I had these psychic attacks, the bad feeling would also take ages to go away and I would kick myself for not putting any white light or energy around the room for protection.

My husband suffered as well and would complain bitterly the next day because he found it really hard to go back to sleep as well and was worried about how he was going to cope at work . I didn't blame him for feeling that way because the last thing you want is to be woken by someone screaming loudly in your ear in the dead of the night. No amount of vitamin B is going to help nerves that are shattered and raw. Lack of sleep is not a good thing so we watched a lot of late night television in those days.

My meditation teacher said she couldn't give me any real answers as it had never happened to her and perhaps I needed to work on myself and lift my vibration as it was probably at a very low rate. I knew this wasn't true, as most of the people I was sitting with in the group still had the same problems even after 10 years. They were not moving on and dealing with their own situations. Our group may have been about love and light, and they were lovely ladies with hearts of gold, but whenever we had coffee later they would all start bitching and talking about the same old problems. An analogy that always makes me laugh is that most people can't see anything beyond the hole in the donut. In other words, it is always easy to see other people's stuff but really hard to see your own.

I didn't accept my teacher's answer to my problem as it did not feel right and deep down I knew that spirit was trying to teach me something. I soon learnt that these episodes are called psychic attacks and are a build-up of negative energy that was in my room. The next day I meditated and my guides told me who was sending me this nasty energy so I would burn sage, or sweep the room with white light, and the energy would immediately disappear. I then would imagine the person and put them in a pink bubble of love and ask for their forgiveness. If the energy was really bad I would use a clear quartz crystal terminator and direct the crystal towards it. I would not send it back to the person it came from but would direct it into the light of consciousness or back to source for healing.

If I had sent this negative energy back to the sender, I would ride on a broomstick, wear a tall pointy hat and a dark cloak and have a couple of big warts on my face by now. I would also probably be really unhappy, living in a world of darkness and misery, full of suspicion and paranoia.

I once attended a meditation class for years where I had an unpleasant connection with another so-called spiritual woman in the group. I sensed this was probably a past life connection and felt intuitively that no matter what I did or said, she did not like me and never would. I soon gave up trying to be friendly, and just ignored her, but every time I saw her I would leave the group with an awful feeling of being drained.

She was what I call a psychic vampire. Sure enough, every time I attended the class, the same thing would happen. I would leave feeling so drained and tired that I would have to go to bed, even in the middle of the day. It was obvious she did not want me there and I could literally feel invisible knives in my back and pain in my solar plexus. I still have no idea how she did this, but it worked pretty well.

Spiritual people should know better so, not wanting to be around her energy, I decided it was time for me to go. My guide White Feather told me the group was the wrong energy for me anyway and I had learnt all I could and to move on. Not long after I soon started my own groups and have never looked back.

Sometimes when we have had fall-outs, bad connections, or altercations with people or simply not on the same wavelength anymore, people can still send us negative energy or thought forms. We often know who that person is because you can generally feel their energy around you. To stop any "psychic attack" or negative connection, as we are all energy, it is best to throw away any so-called gifts or things that the person may have given you from the relationship so that you break the connection. If you don't want to throw them away and want to keep them, or have trouble with letting these things go, at least sage them thoroughly.

This is usually easy to do and once you have sent them love and released them from "their contract" with you, the energy will slowly dissipate. I always sage my home as well, just as a precaution, whenever I have negative people around. Say you have a really bad relationship with your mother- or father-in-law, or somebody that comes into your space and makes you feel bad, they will often unconsciously mark your territory with their negative energy.

I also have an energy grid at the front door to stop negative people from bringing in their load, and once a week I put energy or light around my home to stop intruders or negative energy from coming in. In our busy lives we often forget to do this, but I always make a conscious effort as I am so aware how energy works and how people forget about personal boundaries.

Another thing I do is when I am feeling really low on energy or drained is to recall my energy back. Often, when I used to come home from the day shift at the hospital, I would feel so drained and tired I could hardly walk. Everybody in the house, including the cats, used to hide from me because they knew what a bad mood I would be in. Lying on my bed I would call back all my energy that had been taken during the shift. Slowly, after a good cup of tea, I could feel my energy return and I would be ready to enjoy the evening with my family.

Meditation for clearing and shielding your energy field

Find a quiet place or go to your sacred space and light a candle.

Sitting up nice and straight, slowly breathe in and out three times deeply to release any blocked energy.

Now gently visualise yourself starting to bring healing energy up from the earth star into your base chakra.

As you do this, feel it moving around your body and now begin to blow out any negative energy out through your mouth with your breath.

Continue this process, moving slowly upwards, making sure you continue to breathe out, releasing as you continue up through all your chakras: beginning with base (red), sacral (orange), solar plexus (yellow), heart (green), throat (blue), third eye (indigo), crown (purple), and transpersonal point (white).

As you do this, feel all your chakras in gentle alignment.

Now expand your energy ten centimetres from your body. Then, take your energy field out to the size of the room, out to the world, the universe, and outer dimensions.

When you have done this know that you are one with everything in the universe and ask for all your soul energy that has been taken from you to come back.

When you have done this, pull your energy back close to your body and feel your awareness in your heart.

Now gently wrap yourself like a beautiful cocoon of light with white light, then purple light and following with a sheaf of golden energy which washes all over you.

When you are ready to come back, feel all your energy in your heart chakra and open your eyes.

Animals

Ever since I can remember I have always had a pet. Our beloved pets, like our children, are innocent and must always be protected from harm's way. They are here as companions, are part of our family and, more importantly, also teach us all about unconditional love.

I have always loved cats, and have had the pleasure of owning one ever since I can remember. As a child, whenever I saw spirits in the house I noticed my cat would also see the same thing. Often it would hiss or just stare in the direction of where I thought the spirit was in the room. Many of us have experienced the same thing and I have heard many people remark how they think their dog or cat is psychic.

Many years ago, I used to sit in a circle called the angel circle. It was run by a lovely minister called Peter who worked there. Each week we would talk about angels, healing and spirituality and meditate. The people who went were all very spiritual and I got to meet many like-minded people. I also got to meet Peter's dog and one-eyed cat, who wandered in and out of the hall whenever we had our meetings. I think they were attracted to the calming, healing energy.

This is very common as one of my cats, Charlie, a yellow Burmese, would always meow constantly whenever I did healings. As soon as I finally opened the door to my healing room, he would run in as fast as his legs would carry him, jump on the client and proceed to give whoever was laying on the table a little healing massage with his paws. Luckily, I had some lovely understanding clients in those days who didn't mind the interference from my over-zealous healing cat. They just thought it was hysterical when they saw how determined he was to get in the room.

One day after the angel service, Peter took me aside and asked me if I would have a look at his dog Penny. She was an elderly Alsatian, which had developed a rather large tumour in her abdominal region and was due to have an operation in the next couple of days. The whole family were beside themselves with worry, as the dog had been part of the family for many years.

Laying the dog down on a blanket, I gently placed my hands on her stomach and psychically tuned into her cells and energy. After about 20 minutes, I lifted my hands off the dog's stomach, closed down my energy and turned to Peter who was sitting patiently beside me.

"Peter, are you and your family going overseas soon?" I asked rather quietly.

"Why yes," he replied, with an odd look on his face.

"What has that got to do with the tumour?" he asked, perplexed by my question.

"What I am actually getting is that you have all been talking to each other about your trip and the dog has been listening. She is scared she will be left behind with nobody to look after her and does not understand what is going on. You need to reassure her you are coming back and she will be well looked after.

"Her tumour is benign, and not cancerous, but I feel she has grown it for attention as she is terrified she is no longer wanted. As far as she is concerned, she is going to be abandoned. Haven't you realised that every time you talk about your family trip, she hears everything you say. I think you have to learn to spell," I laughed.

"That is totally unbelievable," laughed Peter, relieved that his dog was not going to die. "Who would ever have thought that? We're not going to leave you Penny! We have a lovely lady coming in who is going to spoil you to death and take you for long walks till we get back, OK?"

After the operation Peter rang and thanked me for my advice. "You were right, the tumour was benign and the dog is going to be fine. And, by the way, we tell Penny every day what is going on so she will no longer fret and she seems a lot happier."

"Funny about that," I laughed, putting down the phone. It always amazes me how we learn something new every day.

Animal spirits

Throughout my years as a psychic medium, I have served in many spiritual churches around Sydney and Queensland. This has been a great learning experience that has helped me grow as a medium. You get to work with large crowds that pull you along to the next level and you also help many people who have lost loved ones with proof of survival. Connecting to your loved ones is by far the greatest type of healing as it proves time and time again that our loved ones are always with us, and that life as a soul is eternal. I have always enjoyed this work as the energy can be exhilarating. You also get to meet many different people from all walks of life and there's never a dull moment.

Luckily, my earlier life working as an actor on the stage and television helped prepare me for my life's work. It taught me not to be self-conscious, to enjoy what I am doing and how to connect to the audience. But stepping into a club instead of a church can be quite different as the crowd often does not know what to expect, and you need to educate them. This makes you work even harder, as you are aware that often people have never experienced this type of work before or let alone ever been to a medium. Also, these people have often paid money to see you, so you have to be on your toes! Often when I have worked in these clubs I am completely exhausted by the end of the night and all I want to do is go home, unwind and go to bed.

Spirit people are not the only energy we work with. Often it is common to make contact with a loved spirit animal or pet.

Sometimes I will see an animal or bird fly or run across the room or be sitting quietly next to someone in the audience. I have seen dogs, cats, birds and horses that have all crossed over to spirit and have been asked more than once by clients if I could find out how their beloved pet is going and if they can give me some confirmation that their pet is now safe.

I have also worked with animals or pets with spiritual healing. Years ago when I was at a Spiritualist Church, I saw a beautiful black and white cat sitting next to a lady in the audience. It was sitting quietly cleaning itself, not really paying me any attention, occasionally looking up as it cleaned itself, and being very aloof and snobby. Walking over to the lady, I started to describe the cat. I told her it was black and white, was a female and looked very elegant. As the cat was sitting next to her, I assumed it was hers, but the lady insisted otherwise. I found this to be very frustrating as I was convinced that the cat belonged to her. She even went on to tell me how she disliked cats immensely, and preferred dogs as cats always gave her allergic reactions which made her sneeze. Looking closer at the cat, I realised that she was correct as the cat actually belonged to me. It was my beloved cat Sammy who had passed three months earlier when I had to have her put down as she had developed cancer. It had been very traumatic as she was part of our family for many years and we all missed her.

Laughing happily, I told everybody my mistake and, when the service was over, I rushed home to tell my husband what I had seen. "Get a beer out of the fridge," he said, not removing his eyes from the television. Football has always been one of his greatest passions so I suppose he believed me. But it didn't matter as I was thrilled and relieved she had let me know that she was OK. Animal spirits come through as they are connected to our love and want to let us know that they are safe and well and we no longer need to grieve for them.

Another time in the same church, I saw a large white horse standing at the back. I started to think that spirit was giving me a run of animals so I just went with it. Nobody could place the horse, of course, until the animal telepathically gave me the street name where it lived. Finally, a hand went up and a small lady said she had lived across the road from a horse in that street. I said thank you and as I faced her, straight away I was telepathically given information about her daughter. "Your daughter is having problems with her studies and she is very frustrated at the moment," I said.

"Yes that is correct," answered the woman.

"Well, I am being told that you need to give Sylvia a bit of space as you are always on her back and she is completely frustrated. No matter what you do, she is not listening to you."

"Yes, that is correct. But how do you know this?" answered the woman.

I went on to tell her that I was getting all my information from the horse in spirit. As it had nothing to do but stand around all day and eat grass, it was aware of what was going on as it used to watch the house all the time and saw who came and who went. The crowd roared with laughter and were amazed that the horse knew so much. The horse even went on to say how much he loved Sylvia as she had been very kind to him and had even given him apples to eat. She always made an effort to say hello and smile at the horse when she was going to school. In this way, they had become good friends over the years.

When you do this work all the time, nothing ever amazes you in the end and these are the stories that you love to remember.

Psychic children

I have always had a soft spot for children and much of the voluntary work I do is to raise money for kids with terminal diseases. Nothing touches me more than to do a reading for a parent who has lost a child.

As we go through the changes on the planet, more and more children are being born that are different. Some of these children have what we call Rainbow, Indigo and Crystal energies. Doreen Virtue and an angel intuitive is an expert in this field and has written several books over the years, on the subject.

Rainbow: These children are entirely fearless and she calls them little avatars. She goes on to claim that they are only here to give and already are at their spiritual peak.

They are also known as the "Star children" by some.

Crystal children: deeply gifted individuals with deep soulful eyes and a soft calling energy. I have seen many of these children and one of my daughters is one. She is extremely sensitive, very intuitive and when she was small did not speak until she was three years old.

Indigo children: being born an Indigo child myself, I understand how it feels to be different. Indigo children are usually old souls, are very driven, stubborn and seem to answer to a higher calling. They also have a purple halo around the top of their heads in their aura.

I myself am what is termed "Indigo" and am able to use my psychic abilities and mediumship to give accurate readings. My ability is what I can only describe, like an antennae or a transmission, to receive answers to anything I want, usually for myself, friends or clients.

Looking back at my own childhood, life would certainly have been easier if I had more support in my life. My parents had no idea of what I was talking about, as my gift was not passed on. They could not help me in any way except to allow me to keep the light on all night which made me feel safe and it deterred wandering spirits.

Children who are psychic or are able to "see spirit", in my eyes are what I call close to God. Some children have extraordinary abilities and this is becoming even more common. Some can even talk to trees and animals or see colours around people's energy fields or auras. Many of these gifts are also brought in from past lives as well and the child is able to remember certain things. They are so in touch with their own power, if only they are shown how to use it. Often they do understand their abilities but are left feeling vulnerable, prone to anxiety and powerless because of the fear factor.

An example of this is children who often talk of certain things that are not in their current lives, or what they could not know possibly anything about.

When I was small I always used to talk about living in a cold country and having to make a fire. My mother always used to ask me what I was talking about. Years later I was drawn to Norway and could speak the language within six weeks.

As parents we must learn to listen to what they have to say and to believe them, even though it may seem extraordinary. In their eyes, what they see is real and is often the case. We need to teach them that they will be okay if they talk to us about these matters.

With psychic children, I suggest teaching them a white light exercise. This protection works as white energy is always stronger than dark as it is connected to the Christ consciousness or source, unconditional love in other words. There is nothing on the planet that is stronger. I use it all the time around my bed when I sleep, and in my home, and with my children. You always have 100 per cent activation and protection.

Dark energy or dark magic on the other hand is a denser type of energy that works faster, but does not last. It always has ramifications and in my own opinions is not advisable to use at all. What goes around comes around. I don't understand why people get involved with this type of energy.

Activating white light energy for children

Gently close your eyes and imagine white energy of pure love pouring in through the top of your head and coming down into your body.

You may begin to feel a warm sensation or type of tingling on your skin.

Imagine yourself gently wrapping this pure energy or light around your entire body. This will last for as long as you want throughout the day.

When you go to sleep at night, mentally wrap it around your bed and room so that nothing can penetrate its energy.

Whenever you are out, or are around toxic people, imagine the white light coming out of your finger.

Use it to protect your loved ones, and anything you want, including yourself.

Points to remember with psychic children

Always make the time to listen to your child and most importantly, tell them you believe them no matter what.

Let them know that they have nothing to fear and are in control of any situation as spirits cannot hurt them but fear can.

Watch their diet for hidden sugars as these are not helpful for their wellbeing. Too much sugar in the blood will make them overactive and it will be difficult for them to concentrate and focus.

Encourage them to learn to meditate with a tape or CD when they go to sleep and let them have a night light on so they are not afraid of the dark or, more to the point, what is in it.

Find a meditation class that they can join with other children and learn to listen to their guides and own inner voice.

Allow them to select a crystal themselves or place a rose quartz crystal by their beds as it generates loving energy.

Get them involved in some type of martial arts such as tai chi, qigong or yoga as this will help centre and ground their energies.

Teach your psychic child to harness their abilities and learn to focus them in positive directions.

And, remember, the most important thing of all is to always believe your children.

Lessons from spirit

Often when I am in a deep sleep and dreaming, I will feel as if I am in a school or classroom situation on the other side and I am getting lessons from a higher being and there are many obstacles in my way. Later, when I have done the tests I am told in a loving way in the dream state that I have done well, or that there will be more lessons again later when they feel I am ready to learn more. Even when I meditate, which I do every day, I receive instructions and messages from loving guides and spirits. We are never alone; all we have to do is ask spirit for help and it will be given.

When I am sick, I meditate and take myself over to the spirit hospital, a place in my imagination full of pure light energy and love. I lay myself down on a slab of clear quartz and can feel the spirit doctors working on my subtle etheric bodies. When I wake up I feel tired, but within a few days feel re-energised and healthy again.

One of my favourite teachers, Verna Yater, who is now in spirit, always used to say that if you want the spirit doctors to work on you while you sleep, you need white sheets.

Spiritual lesson and contracts

Throughout my journey so far, I have come to realise that spirit often gives us so-called situations or tests or to see if we have understood the lesson we are supposed to learn here on Earth. I have always seen our planet as an enormous stage where we play out these different roles. Often these tests repeat until we have understood the lesson. These experiences are not what I would call pleasant, in fact, they can be heart breaking and extremely worrying. Once we see what we are creating, we move to a higher vibration, clear out our chakras or energy centres, and do not have to go through the lesson again. Many of our blocks are carried through from past lives and may continue to repeat themselves, until we have learnt to simply move on.

All healing, as I understand it, is about facing our fears or the dark side of ourselves and surrendering with unconditional love and forgiveness. I have tried many types of healing and the most powerful would have to be FORGIVENESS on every level. You don't have to actually like the person, but once you have forgiven them you are cutting the energy connection between you and you can heal.

Case study—Kelly

Kelly was the close friend of my friend Josh from England. They met and both worked in many healing centres together throughout the years and often spent their spare time talking about their families and mutual acquaintances.

Kelly was tired of her job and really wanted to be like the other mediums and dreamt of one day doing the work herself.

Most professional healers and mediums spend years developing and working on themselves in groups, as training and studying all types of therapies and metaphysics in colleges or groups is an integral part of the work. Eventually most of these hard working souls learn how to work with their guides in meditation, so they have a good understanding of how spirit works.

Josh was a very kind generous person who understood how his friend felt and encouraged Kelly continually to undergo training or a counselling course to help her with her medium ship as it was essential for her to have some understanding about the fundamentals the work entailed.

When you are working for the public, in general, it is a huge responsibility as you can have a significant impact on your client's welfare and life. As a medium, you are working with people who have lost loved ones and are grieving so you must have people skills. This type of work can also be terribly taxing and you have to be psychically strong and healthy as the work we do is not for the faint-hearted.

In my time as a nurse, I learnt how to work with the general public in service. Without this training I would never have been able to do the work I do today. Over the years I have seen and met so many so-called psychics who have never done any work on themselves, let alone studied any healing modalities. Because of this they find it very difficult and don't do the job properly They are usually the type who may have lost themselves and have no compassion for anyone in their lives except themselves. These misguided people will use everything in their power to get what they want by pretending to be your friend or whatever suits them on the day, just so they can get some kind of recognition. Once they have got what they want, they will ride on your coat-tails and grab everything they can from you just so they can make their way up the ladder of success or to get their needs met. Once they achieve this, there is no more room in their world for any type of friendship. You will never see them again as they will be into bigger and better things. They may get where they want to go but at a cost with miserable personal lives and constant relationship problems because nothing will ever work out.

I put this down to the ways of spirit or the law of karma, because what goes around comes around, as the saying goes. These types have no concept of spirit energy and at the end of the day will learn the hard way as we are here on Planet Earth to learn our lessons.

As the years went on, Josh lost contact with Kelly for a while and was surprised when he bumped into her again while doing volunteer work at one of the spiritualist churches in Sydney. As it turned out, Josh was working as a medium on the day and the minister had asked him if he minded sharing the platform with a new young medium, none other than Kelly. Josh was overjoyed to see his good friend again and was more than happy to lend a helping hand but was soon confused over Kelly's rather odd behaviour.

Once the congregation arrived, Kelly wouldn't even look Josh in the eyes, and kept running off to the toilet complaining that she did not feel comfortable. She seemed to feel threatened that she would not get any messages because Josh, who was helping her, kept taking all the messages. Once you start to work on the platform for spirit, it is imperative that you stay there to hold the energy as it takes time to build up. Each time Kelly ran off, the energy she and Josh had built to try and get the "link" with spirit would go down.

Feeling embarrassed, Josh just carried on and ignored Kelly's poor behaviour as he understood she was just feeling insecure. He went on to assure her lovingly that he was just there to do the work, and not get in her way as she was just doing her job and wanted to help her. As far as Josh was concerned he was only there on the day to receive messages from spirits who had crossed over and to give proof of survival and messages to the loved ones who were sitting and waiting in the church.

When Josh told me this I wondered why he bothered to be friends with Kelly and wondered if this was some type of lesson he was perhaps going through. I was soon horrified and appalled with what happened later to my naive and very dear friend.

A couple of years later both mediums were brought together again by fate. This time they were both working as readers, but on different days. Putting the past behind him Josh again felt sorry for Kelly as she was again broke and out of work. Josh had grown quite successful over the years and finding humility in his heart asked Kelly if she wanted to work together so he could help her get on her feet.

Everything went well for a while until jealousy reared its ugly head again. Kelly was not happy that her so called good friend and business partner was doing far better than her. As far as she was concerned it was not fair that Josh, as talented as he was, and far better trained from years of study, should get all the clients.

Josh felt this but could not understand Kelly's way of thinking and kept thinking his friend's insecurity would eventually settle and she would be able to grow within her own right.

Sadly, it did not take long before fate stepped in and Josh learnt the hard way again. Originally from England, Josh was called home because a family member was dying of cancer. While he was gone, Kelly, showing her true colours, took over all the work they had built up together in last year. When Josh found out he was utterly devastated and rocked to the core.

Understandably, he felt deeply betrayed by his "friend" and could not understand why it had happened, but at the end of the day he was more disappointed in himself for not listening to his own intuition that had been trying to warn him from the beginning. Spirit had long been telling him he needed to work by himself as part of his lesson here in this lifetime. He needed to believe in himself and truly remember who he was as a soul.

In reality Kelly was in fact one of the best teachers Josh could ever have asked for.

Not long after a similar type of person came into Josh's life. She was even from the same place in Queensland as Kelly, had the same colour hair, and spoke of similar family problems. The similarities between the two women were uncanny. Josh helped the lady get work for a while but it soon became evident that she was a "poor me" energy like Kelly and no matter what was done for her, it was not enough. Josh finally realised that he was repeating the same type of pattern of trying to rescue people.

He had just been taught an enormous lesson by his so-called friend, in spiritual energy.

Josh learnt the hard way that it is always best to just stand back and let the poor me's of the world work out their problems for themselves, so they can find their own empowerment. By doing everything for them, he was actually taking their energy away.

As I have said many times before, life is about lessons and learning. When one door shuts, another will close, but as my good friend White feather always says: "The door has to be shut first before the person in question gets it."

Hopefully, Kelly's karma will be understood by her one day, if it already hasn't because as the old saying goes, what goes around comes around.

Case study 2—Naughty Cleo

Cleo was a good friend who I met in my early development days. She was a colourful, attractive character from England and we both worked as mediums and healers in a new age centre. She was an excellent medium and, over the years, we have sometimes worked together doing spirit demonstrations and spirit rescues in homes around Sydney.

She, unbeknown to me, was unhappily married and had been having affairs on and off for years, often getting away with it. I had no idea of her extra-marital affairs until I was confronted by one of her spurned conquests one day.

We had never discussed our private lives, as our relationship was purely professional and our work exhausting anyway, so when one of her boyfriends turned up angry and upset on my doorstep, I got quite a shock.

He went on to tell me all about their sordid affair, and how Cleo would not leave her husband for him. Why he came to me, I have no idea but it really annoyed me as I had no interest in hearing anything about it. I had no idea Cleo was a "Casanova" type and to be quite honest felt embarrassed to say the least. It was no wonder she looked tired and worn out every time I saw her.

It was obvious to see that the jilted boyfriend was extremely upset and way out of balance, traumatised by the fact that his lover was not going to leave her husband. He was sweating profusely and panting and behaving oddly. His eyes were glazed over and bulging strangely and he kept muttering to himself. Using my counselling skills from my nursing days in psychiatric wards, I was able to calm and settle him down. He was starting to scare me and I began to think of all the ways I would tell Cleo off when and if I ever saw her again.

I insisted that I knew nothing of her private life, which was true, and just stood and listened to him rant, which is what you are supposed to do when somebody is so upset and highly agitated. If anything, I was worried he would try and kill himself. All the while, I could not help but think why the hell he would want to get involved with a married woman, with children that still lived at home, in the first place and what was he doing at my front door. He took no notice of the little advice I gave him, and to my relief finally left when he had calmed himself down and gained his composure.

Instead of going home, as I had asked him to do and calming down, he did the rounds of all the other people he thought knew Cleo and sat out the front of their homes in his car, ringing them up on his mobile and telling them all ridiculous lies and fantasies.

I don't know how many people rang me afterwards, complaining of his audacity to think he had the right to behave like this. He was obviously hurting very much and was still in love with Cleo, even though his love was not returned. His distorted lies and negativity overcame him, as he continued on his destructive rampage throughout the night. There is nothing like a man being spurned, as the saying goes.

Ringing Cleo the next day I was furious and told her about the situation she had created. She, of course, became angry and wanted nothing to do with him. She told me that he had driven over to her place as well and was parked outside her home all night waiting to talk to her. I told her it was her responsibility to deal with him and if she did not want to see him face to face, to try talking to hid higher self first with my Bubble of Forgiveness technique. I often use this myself if I have problems with people and cannot resolve an issue. She told me she would and I wished her all the best, after telling her not to bring her love problems ever into my life again.

Bubble of forgiveness exercise

Find a quiet place where you can be alone for a while and light a candle. Gently close your eyes and breathe deeply in and out three times, releasing any stress or negative emotion from your mind and body. As you relax, feel all the tensions of the day leaving your body.

You will now begin to feel lighter and more relaxed, as you drift deeper and deeper into relaxation.

In your mind's eye, visualise a beautiful pure pink bubble of forgiveness. Now put yourself inside and then the other person.

Now begin a dialogue with them by telling them you are sorry and ask for their forgiveness.

Wait for a response. (If they do not say anything, repeat again what you have said.) Now ask them gently, to forgive you.

When they have listened to what you have to say, ask them if they would like to say something as well.

After you get a response, tell them that you now release all negative energy and karma and that the contract between you is finished.

Then, with their permission, send them healing and love.

If they say no, don't send it.

When you have finished, send the bubble, after you have filled it with a beautiful green energy and light, to the source for healing and transmutation and open your eyes.

When you do this exercise, which is actually talking to the person's higher-self, it may take a while and you may have to do it a couple of times before the other person is ready to give you any dialogue, but remember, with persistence, miracles do happen.

Auras and their colours

When a person comes to see me, the first thing I might do is open up and scan their energy and I am able to get a lot of information. This is called reading the aura and I only do this with permission and would never just cold read anyone I saw on a bus or wherever as it would be breaking the universal law of spirit. It never ceases to amaze me how much you can see in people aura's or energy fields, like a kaleidoscope of vast energy and colour. I am also able to see or sense the guide standing next to the client and any loved ones who may be standing behind them.

My own guide stands at my left and if I tilt my head slightly, I am able to ask any question as I have clear communication. It took me years when I was younger to realise that not everybody can do this as I found it so easy. The only time it doesn't work is when I am over-emotional and or stressed and my emotional body blocks everything. Usually, I just switch it on and I have a direct line to the spirit world as it acts like a rather long antennae.

Often I can see if people have a lot of stress or worry as you can see a big brown blob or dark mass right above their head. I remember once I was doing a course and I could not block out my auric vision of the big brown blob of energy above the teacher's head. I did not say anything but I will always remember the incident.

If you tilt your head backwards and half close your eyes, you can see that the aura is a subtle energy that surrounds all living things and inanimate objects as well. It is often described as being like a subtle electrical or magnetic energy that radiates from human beings, animals, plants, stones, machines, buildings, household objects and most anything else that you can think of.

Everyone can learn to see auras. It just takes patience and practice. With time, you will be able to see the many beautiful colours that radiate from the body, and if you are keen, you can even see the outline of your guides or guardian angels.

Auras can vary in texture, size, quality, feel and colour in relation to the vibrational nature of each individual. We all have a basic vibration rate that fluctuates from moment to moment as we change and develop. The size of the aura depends on the person's state of health, energy levels, moods, thought patterns and underlying spiritual purpose.

The best way to see somebody's aura is with the dimmer switch on against a pale wall. The first thing you will see is what we call the etheric field of the aura which is a white body of energy around the person as it is quite easy to see.

Affirmations for auric vision

Over the years I have developed easy affirmations to use with my healing work. Here are a few of them.

"I ask spirit to help me and give me permission and assistance to see auras. I ask only to work for the person's highest self in love and light."

"As I have now received permission from my client, I open myself up to my highest good to be able to see and experience colour in the aura."

"I am now ready and give myself permission to develop a powerful healing relationship with sheer light and colour as I know I can only do good for my client."

"I ask my higher self to effectively and sensitively interpret the colour, mass and quality of aura I am seeing."

"I am the Christ consciousness within. I am a clear and perfect channel of light and love as I now ask for my healing guide to come forward and help me with my important work and inner vision."

Interpreting the aura

These are colours I have seen in many people's energy fields or auras.

They are from my own experience only which I have developed over the years. Other people's interpretations may be different from my own and vary in colour.

Clear bright aura: a healthy, happy vibrant person. The bigger the aura, the healthier they are.

Muddy, or brown: unhealthy, indicates negativity or emotional turmoil, perhaps sickness.

On appearance and on closer examination the aura is usually weak, thin and shrunken. I have seen this appear above the crown chakra when somebody is really stressed or suffering from a type of depression.

Red: may indicate anger, selfishness, hate, a quick temper, power and energy. Alternatively, red can indicate vitality, ambition and raw sexual power.

I have seen flashes of this around the head, stomach and hip area.

Orange: sensuality and sexuality, pleasure, exercise, creativity, motivation, warmth, passion, balancing, recovery from illness, pride. Sometimes I can relate this to past life trauma as well.

Yellow: intellectual activity, power of the mind, higher intelligence of the body, study. I have seen a lot of this above the solar plexus area.

Green: balance, harmony, calmness, love, compassion, growth, healing abilities. I once saw a student with a green guide that was an angel. It stood on his right side and was working with him with his healing work. The student went on to be a very successful healer.

Blues: communication, expression, detachment, inspiration and information. Can also indicate new learning for the client.

Turquoise: new age colour, positive spiritual growth, new opportunities opening for spiritual learning.
Amazingly beautiful colour.

Indigo: intuition, natural psychic ability and awareness, spiritual abilities. I have seen a lot of this over the years in students that are opening up to their latent psychic abilities.

Lavender: divine, master energy, softness, playfulness.

Violet: wisdom, pathway to enlightenment, the bridge between the mind and the higher mind, the bridge from the higher mind to the collective consciousness.

Pink: unconditional love, warmth, tenderness, modesty, gentleness, innocence, healing, empathic, selfless love, timid or shy.

Gold: higher self, brilliance, prosperity, spiritual radiance, higher creativity, in alignment with a master guide's energy such as Jesus or the ascended masters.

I have been blessed to have seen this in a few people who have been wonderful teachers for me.

Silver: versatility, high energy, constant change, shape-shifter. I have seen this with "star" people and sometimes carry this energy or vibration when I am working with one of my guides "Three of One".

Black: depression, wisps of sadness, evil, malice, sinister, low life force, possible entity attachment. You can generally know this colour is in the aura as soon as the person walks into the room as it comes with what I can only call a "heaviness feeling."

Grey: narrow minded, stuck in past with emotions, conservative, depressed, low life force energy, fear.

When there is no aura, the spirit is usually ready to leave the body.

With practice and an open mind and heart, the pathway of discovery is always opened for the student who works with unconditional love and quality and energy of spirit. As you practise seeing these colours in the aura you will discover a vast number of different shades of varied colour, flash right in front of your eyes as if by magic. This experience will open up your healing abilities and the more you practise it may later on help you as a diagnostic tool with your healing work.

We must always have permission from the client or the client's higher self before commencing any work.

Note: This type of work does not take the place of your own medical doctor.

Exercise

Stand client against a white wall not too brightly lit.

Scan auric field and notice qualities and characteristics, such as size, shape and strength.

Ask the client to slowly count to 40 (with a happy feeling) this expands the aura.

Now look for the white energy around the outside of the body. It will look fuzzy at first, but with practice on lowering the eyes as if you are looking down, it will become easier.

When you can see this, continue breathing slowly and feel yourself tuning into their energy.

When you have done this you will see flashes of colour.

Work around the head first, then continue going down to the shoulders and lower body.

Ask them to think of a happy thought to increase their energy size as they breathe in and out. To decrease the energy field ask them to think of a sad event and this will almost make the aura shrink or disappear.

Often you will "see" the outline of their guides, relatives or angels standing next to them. My guide stands on my left side, but for others this may be different. The more you practise, the more you will see.

Five-day living in the present exercise

Day one:

Lie down or sit quietly for a couple of moments and identify as many different sounds as possible. Be open during the day to identify different noises that you hear. This opens up the ear chakras in your ears and will help if you want to develop your clairaudience or clear hearing.

Day two:

Look at the ceiling and the walls. Identify as many colours as possible and, during your day, stop and look at them again. This will help you open up to seeing different colours in people's energy fields.

Day three:

Become aware of smell. Do not be judgemental but just acknowledge that it exists. This will come in and help you later in your mediumship. E.g. quite often I can tell if the spirit has smoked or wore a different type of perfume or scent when they were alive by the smell. This awareness will build the more you practise.

Day four:

Open up your senses more, and become aware of touch and texture whether it's smooth or rough, cold or hot, or so on.

Day five:

Now become aware of taste. Be aware of all the ingredients.

Do not mix the exercises. By doing this simple practice you will become not only more aware of what is around you but more sensitive as well to your surroundings. Because of our busy lives we forget to daydream or live simply in the NOW.

Flower essences

When I lived in Trondheim in Norway many years ago, I worked as a nurse at the local hospital. Around the same time, I was approached by a good friend of mine from Germany called Arthur. He was a doctor of natural medicine and was working in the town. I had met him at a local soup kitchen where we were both doing volunteer work for the homeless. We both were politically minded with similar interests and got on really well. He had the same type of humour as me and his energy was very familiar. He also ran a meditation group with his wife, and I always felt he was like a spiritual brother to me. His wife was lovely and very gentle natured but was happy to stay at home while we were busy involved in many different things.

Knowing my passion for alternative therapies, Arthur asked me if I would be interested in working as his assistant. He said he would train me in Bach flowers, iridology and reflexology. As I was already trained in medicine, and knew my anatomy and physiology, the work would be perfect for me. Overjoyed, I accepted his offer and started to study with him. I loved the work and he was so easy to be with I am certain we have had many past lives before.

Unfortunately, it was never going to go far, because when I contacted the authorities about my decision to leave the hospital, I was refused permission to work with him and instead was sent back to the hospital where I already had a contract. If I wanted to stay in the country I had no other choice but to work at the hospital. It was easy for Arthur to work in his own practice as his wife was a Norwegian citizen, giving him the same status. I was sad about this at first but not for long. A new door of opportunity was opening for me with music and was beginning to take up a lot of my time.

I still studied the flower essences, and have always been inspired by the great work of Dr Bach, an Englishman and the founder of the essences last century. He was truly an incredible talented man in his time and was able to heal many people with his amazing essences. His vision was simple. He believed that good health was the result of emotional, spiritual and mental harmony.

I believe that God provides everything that we need in life in the beauty and nature that surrounds us. We have been given the flowers in nature, not only to feel good when we see them but to use as medicine as well.

Flower essences work on a vibrational level on the emotional body of the aura and over time help clear all negative emotions from the aura, thus stopping disease. They are able to give us the courage and strength to clear any blocks so we can access our higher self, or what we call our inner wisdom. By doing this we are also able to know our innate higher purpose and follow our true heart's desire by fulfilling not only our hopes but our dreams.

One of my teachers used to say, three months of Bach flowers is equivalent to 10 years of psychotherapy. I couldn't agree more as I have used them not only on myself and family but all my clients as well with wonderful results. In conjunction with modern, conventional medicine today, they are indeed complementary.

I have been using all types of flower essences from all over the world now for many years and find they are an essential part of my life and practice. I have a great understanding of the flower essences and how they work and have made many essences for myself over the years whenever I go into the bush. The Australian bush is magnificent and has the most incredible variety of flowers full of beauty and strength and very spiritual as well.

My husband and I love to go bush walking and will often go deep into the bush to see many of these special flowers. He always acts as my assistant and carries all my little bottles for me on his back if I decide to make an essence. Most of the time we just spend walking around and taking in the magic and tranquillity the bush has to offer as nature is such an important aspect of our lives.

Case study

About eight years ago, my friend Rianna asked me if I wanted to come with her to a three-day course in the mountains run by a teacher who worked with the Australian Bush Flower Essences. I was keen as I have always wanted to make an essence from the Pink Flannel Flower that is supposed to grow in that region. It is a beautiful essence that connects to unconditional love and joy.

I couldn't wait to work with the energy that was all around us. On the first morning, as soon as the sun was up, we all ate breakfast and were sent out into the bush by our teacher to work with a flower. We had to chose one, open up to its energy or what we call essence, talk to it, and discover its healing qualities. We later had to bring it back to the house and make an essence which would be bottled.

All I could think about was finding my favourite flower. I couldn't wait for the experience as it was something that I had dreamed about for ages As far as I knew it only grew in this region and was difficult to find but I was confident that I would have no problems.

This would also be an easy exercise for me because as far as I can remember I have always been able to "hear" flowers talking and have a feel for the bush. As we walked into the thick scrub, I was excited. Rianna and I soon decided to separate so we could go our own way. Once we had done this we would open up, find our flower and get to work with connecting to it with a meditation. This was sacred work and had to be taken seriously. Hanging around with Rianna would just make me laugh as we could never stop chatting about everything we were into.

I must have walked for what seemed like hours, going around and around in circles, searching for my beloved flower. I was starting to feel tired and extremely disappointed as all I could see was the dreaded Mountain Devil flower, a spiky red flower that works on anger and hatred, all around me. There seemed to be hundreds of them scattered everywhere among the bush, as far as the eye could see. I had never in my entire lifetime seen so many flowers in one place before but no way was I going to work with a flower I did not like it as it did not interest me in the slightest.

Unfortunately for me, everywhere I went, around every corner I turned, I could see nothing but the Mountain Devil flowers staring back and me and bobbing up and down as if they were waving to me. They were everywhere and I could almost hear their squeals of delight wanting me to join them and work with them for the day.

As they deal with hatred, anger, grudges and suspiciousness they were definitely not going to be on my agenda. They have a very similar energy to what Holly is in the Bach Flower essences.

However, I was fighting with my brother at the time, which was really unusual as we have always been great friends and he is a terrific guy and wonderful family man. Both of us thought we were right and were not talking to each other. We were meeting up with my parents the next day to drive up the coast to join my sister and the rest of our family as our cousin Jan had died and we were going to her untimely funeral the next day. Cousin Jan had been battling cancer for months and had died that week. Every time I thought of the battle she had been through I could not stop crying, but at least she was safe now and living and doing her healing in spirit. Her long battle was over and she was no longer in pain.

As I walked through the bush, all I could think about was the stupid argument I had had with my brother. I would have to sit in the back of my parent's car for six hours, and not say anything. If I did, all my buttons would be pushed and I would probably end up saying something stupid and explode with anger and I would feel like a fool and regret it later.

My parents would be mortified, and I would end up looking like the bad guy and feel ashamed for rocking the boat for the rest of the year. Our parents have always treated us equally and loved us unconditionally but also made the point that we should never argue and get on no matter what. For some reason, the mere thought of this drove me crazy, as I have always had to say my truth because I was born with a big mouth. Suddenly I became really angry. I could not believe where this was coming from as I had no idea that my brother really bugged me so much. Every time I thought of him, however, I felt I would explode with rage and tell him off for being such an idiot.

The emotion that was building up in my mind was becoming so strong and all-consuming that I started to weep uncontrollably. It must have been buried so deeply within for so many years and may even have been a past life issue. All I wanted to do was scream my head off and beat my fists into the ground with sheer rage.

Deciding that I'd had enough, I turned to go back and started to run as fast as I could, as far away from the horrible red flowers that seemed to be scratching me and surrounding me everywhere

I went, playing cruel games with my mind. As I ran around a corner, I fell over a tuft of grass and landed in a thick bush of spiky Mountain Devil flowers. The bright red flowers stuck into my face and eyes and its brittle prickly leaves scratched my face and arms. I could taste dirt in my mouth and my face was full of leaves, flowers and mud. Stunned, I could not get my head around what was happening so I just surrendered and worked with the flower after all. It seemed I had no choice in the matter as the flowers had me trapped and up for ransom.

I sensed this was happening for a reason so I decided then and there to go with it. I knew intuitively that I was not going to get out of the bush until I did anyway, so shakily I poured my clean water into my glass bowl, and carefully cut one of the red flowers off the bush so not to touch or bruise it and let it drop into the bottom of my glass bowl. No sooner than this was done, nagging thoughts of sweet bitterness and hatred swept through my mind, not only about my brother, my family even me. I became consumed with thoughts of how bloody unfair life was and how I was always treated like the black sheep of the family and how dare people treat me like I was a deranged weirdo. I started to imagine that I must have been adopted as I was so different from the rest of the family. I didn't even have the same blood group as them. My mother used to say all my problems had come from being dropped on the floor at birth when I came out of the birth canal because I was so difficult and over-sensitive.

The dreadful mind talk went on relentlessly for what seemed liked hours. I was now lying in the foetal position, completely consumed by the emotions that looping around in my poor head. "I will never talk to them again," I swore, lying wracked in pain from all the emotions going through my mind, body and soul.

Angry thoughts of hate and rebellion continued to fill me in waves and I shook with frustration as I wept like a baby who had lost its mother for what seemed like hours.

No matter how hard I tried to reconcile my terrible thoughts, the flower seemed to bring everything up to the surface and I found it was impossible to make peace with myself.

Unable to go on, I weakly started to crawl out of the bushland then stood up and started to make the long trek back to my room in the house. If anybody had been watching they might have thought I was a madwoman who had been let loose in the bush. As far as I was concerned, my bed was the only place I would find peace and I would go back and try and work it out somehow. I was drained and my head ached so much it was hard to walk.

I made my way back to the house, which was deserted. Clutching the bowl with the flower in it, I made my way to my room. I must have looked a sight as my eyes were running and swollen, I ached all over and I had scratches and dirt all over me. Leaves were sticking out of my clothes and hair. Hobbling in pain, feeling defeated and lost, I fell exhausted down on the bed and cried like a baby, feeling terribly sorry for myself and my lot in life.

Suddenly, my teacher walked quietly into the room and asked, "What are you doing here Kerrie? You should be in the bush." She sat down on the bed, gently stroking my head.

"Leave me alone," I cried not wanting to be disturbed.

"What's going on?" she asked. "You shouldn't be here you should be back out in the bush, working on your flower with the others. Nobody has returned yet as it is not time."

Hardly daring to look at her, I tried to explain to her what the terrible flower was doing to me.

"The flower doesn't understand me and there is no way I can explain to it what I want to say," I wailed. "It won't listen to me and will not give me a break. I hate it, and that stupid flower hates me too."

"Get up now and get back into the bush straight away and make sure you put yourself back in your body," she said sternly, not wanting to hear anymore of my poor me story. "Pay attention to me, Kerrie, because it is important. You are actually standing outside your physical body and you need to ground yourself and finish what you started," she said patiently.

Before I even had time to think about what she was saying, I dragged myself from my bed and started making my way out of the room.

"Hurry," she said. "You need to finish what you started and you will feel better afterwards. Go now."

Something in her voice made me realise that I had no other choice but do exactly what she said. Remembering her instructions I dried my wet and tired eyes, sniffed loudly and made my way back into the heavy bushland with the flower still in the bowl grasped tightly in my hands. As I marched back into the bush I was determined to finish what I had started. I had no choice. This was some type of lesson and I had to finish it. For some reason I had opened up Pandora's Box and even though everything seemed out of control, I had to deal with it to learn the lesson.

Harsh criticism is always difficult for me and most of us to deal with in life. Whether it is from people or friends you love, you just have to learn from it and just carry on, no matter how hurtful it is at the time. You have to learn to let go even though you might not understand what it is all about in the first place. Often people get stuck in their lives and get jealous of others so instead of looking at their own stuff they prefer to blame others and not take responsibility.

After a while, my journey with the flower soon took me to a clearing, one I hadn't seen before, even though I had walked the same way before. I decided that I would make a little sacred alter out of twigs and stones in the bush and say sorry to the flower that represented my issues, and every person I loved and had upset or was rude to: my brother, my sister, my family, friends, old lovers, my cat for kicking it off the bed the day before when it did a wee on my pillow, and everyone in the whole wide world for that matter, and lastly myself.

I thanked and blessed the flower for showing me the deep emotion that I must have had stored and buried deep inside me for so long and needed to transmute. As I lay on my belly, digging a little grave for the flower deep into the earth with my hands, I thanked the flower once more and sent it healing, love, light and the deepest respect I could conjure from my heart and soul.

As soon as I did this I felt an enormous weight lift. My heart started thumping so hard like it wanted to break out into a song and dance. Laughing hysterically like a mad woman from deep within my belly, I rolled around on the ground, delirious with happiness. I felt like I was the happiest and luckiest woman alive on the planet. The black cloud of gloom and doom was gone, miraculously disappearing into nothingness. I was on a total high.

Waves of exhilaration swept over me and I started to sing loudly to all the surrounding bush, birds and insects around me. Luckily for me, there was nobody else to witness me singing badly at the top of my voice. Anybody watching might have called the police because a madwoman was loose in the bush.

All I could feel was joy, forgiveness and love towards my brother, my family, everyone. My brother wasn't perfect, but then again neither was I. Why should the world revolve around me and what I thought? Everybody is different and sometimes people come into your life to challenge you, and to teach you things about yourself you might not want to know at the time, but at the end of the day, it is all about lessons.

Everything seemed so surreal and beautiful and bright, even though at the back of my mind I knew the long day was coming to and end as I could feel the cold creeping in.

Still lying on my back on the ground, my merriment was suddenly interrupted by a giant lizard, the size of a big snake that came out of nowhere. Making its way towards my head, I slowly stopped singing and turned just in time to stare right into its eyes. Glistening in the light, the lizard's eyes appeared very round, large and yellow. Mesmerised I stared back, not daring to move a muscle in case I would break the moment and even if I had tried, I couldn't move anyway. As it crawled closer towards me, it slowly made its way right up to my face, flashing its tongue. Other smaller lizards followed and slowly began to form a circle around me.

Great, I thought, first the flower now I am going to be eaten by these reptiles, nearly bursting out laughing. Taking a deep breath to calm myself, I could now hear its voice telepathically in my head. There was no logic in anything up to this point, so I made a conscious effort to stop thinking and just open up psychically to what was happening. After all I was always talking to dead people, plants and animals so why not listen to a lizard. It was telling me something that I have heard many times before: "Remember who you are and what you have to do. You are not alone. There are many here as well who will help you with your work."

A loud bird call in the distance brought me back to reality. Distracted, I turned my head to see what the bird was doing, and stared into the bush but could see nothing. When I turned back to face the lizard, the energy had shifted and I was alone. All the lizards had disappeared to wherever they had come from.

Jumping to my feet and full of energy once again, I brushed myself down, removed all the twigs from my hair and clothes and decided that it was time to go. It was starting to get late and the light was fading rapidly. Shivering, and hugging myself from the cold, I couldn't wait to get back to tell the others what had happened.

They probably wouldn't believe me anyway, but it was a great story and worth the effort to tell. I felt on top of the world and started to giggle again. I suddenly started to feel like the character Alice, from *Alice in Wonderland*, one of my all-time favourite stories.

After dinner, Rianna and I decided to grab a few of the girls to go and watch the sun set. It had been a long day and we all wanted to catch up and discuss our stories. When I told everyone what had happened to me in the bush, they all laughed so much that they had to tell me stop so they wouldn't wet themselves. I don't know if they believed me of course but it did not matter as it was my own experience. Anyway everybody, including the teacher, howled with laughter for ages, and told me off a couple of times as they all nearly choked on the delicious food we had prepared for the night.

I still sometimes think of the lizard, the flower and the valuable lesson on how powerful and magical these amazing flower essences really are. The trouble is that every time now I see a Mountain Devil flower when I am out in the bush, I make a conscious effort to go the other way but first give it a quick wink.

Angels

This is a simple prayer I use when working with my favourite angel in my healing work. I use all four Archangels in my practice and always call in the Archangel Michael whenever I am doing spirit rescue.

THE ARCHANGEL URIEL
Uriel, the Angel of change and transmutation,
Tells us it is time to be who we really are,
Time to move on,
Time to let go,
Enjoy the fruits around us,
Enjoy the process,
As you grow to new heights, of wisdom and love,
Let the journey begin,
Rejoice with every step,
Trust now, feel support,
Smell the roses, feel the breeze, see the sun and clouds above your heads,
Feel the earth under your feet.
Truly see what you have inside you,
Oh wondrous Uriel, angel of fire and transmutation …

Angel oil recipe
3 drops frangipani essential oil
2 drops clary sage essential oil

5 drops rose essential oil

2 drops lavender essential oil

1 drop black pepper

Place all these aromatherapy essences into a carrier oil and place a few drops mixed with water into a burner, spray bottle or just simply rub on the side of your head, whenever you want to feel angels present in your healing work and life.

People I meet often ask me if I believe in angels and whether I have ever met one. I have to say yes, because I have done so on many occasions. Here are two of my favourite stories so you can judge for yourself.

Case study 1—Saved by the light

When I was overseas in my early 20s, I was travelling from Morocco back to Spain by ferry. While visiting one of the small farms in the mountains of Ketama I was given a present, which I later found out when I unwrapped it was an illegal substance from my kind host, Abdul. I knew this to be illegal in my country, but being young and stupid I decided to keep it and take it out of the country, not a good thing if I was caught. All the while I knew it was wrong and I could not stop thinking of that terrible movie called *Midnight Express*. My mind kept playing the same scene in my head, where the main character is imprisoned in a Turkish jail.

As I have always been a very high-maintenance female, I couldn't live without waxing or getting my toes painted every week, or ever seeing my loved ones again. My travelling companion at the time, who was probably just as naive as me, insisted that I would be fine and that nothing would happen.

My intuition told me otherwise, of course, and from experience I knew just to listen and simply trust whatever came up for me, as upstairs was never wrong, no matter how many times I tested them. After a while, this is how you learn to live your life and no matter what anybody else says you are always right. That familiar bad feeling is never going to just simply go away until you give in and listen to it.

Unable to contain myself any longer and starting to panic, I nervously got up from my seat in the ship's cabin, and told my friend that I was going to get some fresh air upstairs on the deck. I started praying and asking for guidance. The feelings and emotions I was experiencing were really starting to make me feel quite sick. No sooner than I had done this, than I saw a vision of Jesus dressed in a white robe and looking like an angel. Taken aback, I nearly fainted because I hadn't expected anything like this so fast and right in front of me.

As I stared in shock at the apparition or angel, it looked back at me silently with a stern expression. I kept getting the message, "no, no, no!"

I felt relieved as my nagging intuition had me in a corner, and I knew that it was right. Instantly, I reached into my shoe, grabbed the illegal substance that was making me feel terrible and tossed it wildly into the sea. Spinning around behind me, I heard a strange noise, and saw the apparition of Jesus slowly melting away, until it was gone.

A sense of utter relief washed over me instantly. The host and his family seemed so nice. I could not believe that they would do this to me. No way was I going to be locked away in a dirty rat-infested cell for the rest of my life. Exhausted from fear, I dropped to my knees and thanked God for all the support I was given on that fateful day. Something of a small miracle had just occurred, right in front of me. I felt so humbled that I was being looked after, and it proved to me that I was loved and everything would be fine.

Once the boat pulled into port, I thought it was very strange how I was the only female who was pulled out of the line going into Customs and given a full body search as I got off the boat from Morocco. The whole thing was obviously a set-up. Why was I the only person pulled out of the line at customs?

I shook uncontrollably and could not stop thinking how they probably had done this to many young tourists beforehand. I was only 20, had no real experience of the world and had just spent the last three years studying. They must have seen me coming. It was a humiliating experience as I was completely stripped naked and searched by a burly foreign policewoman who prodded and poked at me until she was convinced she would find nothing.

Whenever I have needed help with anything in my life, I have always prayed and asked for assistance from spirit. No matter what the odds are you will always receive help, no matter what the request is. You just have to remember to give thanks afterwards and believe in the feelings that you are experiencing. To ignore them could have been life changing for me and if I had not listened to spirit on the day, I am sure my life would have ended then. I am grateful for my divine intervention.

What are angels and what do they do?

Angels are universal beings who are here to help us on Earth. They act as messengers, protectors and guardians and can come in the form of visions, intuition, knowing and dreams. I have always believed in angels and have often asked them for help for as long as I can remember and also use them in healings.

They can often test us as well. Once I was up at the local station, trying to get a train into the city. It was a hot summer day and all I could think about was having a cold drink and getting on the train as fast as I possibly could. There was no one at the station, which was rather odd, and only a little bit of shade that I tried to squeeze under. As I stood there, all alone, a man came over and started to talk to me. He smelt of rotten food and was really dirty. He looked really haggard and when he spoke his brown teeth gleamed in the light. I could see by just looking at him, he was homeless.

He was asking me for money so he could get a drink and I reached into my pocket and gave him all my change, which probably amounted to about 20 dollars. As soon as I handed this over to him, he smiled the most beautiful smile and all my hairs on my body stood on end. Turning quickly away in embarrassment, I was just about to remember my manners and thank him as well but he had suddenly disappeared. The station platform was bare and there was not a single person in sight. It would have been impossible for anyone to disappear as quickly as that. My guides told me he was an angel and that I was being "tested". Whether or not I passed I cannot tell you as I never saw him again.

I have also learnt that angels teach us so many things and these include the following lessons.

- Not to take life so seriously; laugh more as creativity comes from humour and letting go of the small stuff.
- Life is precious and beautiful like all the colours in nature.
- We need to be aware to bring more joy and play into our lives.
- To trust and love ourselves unconditionally.
- Angels will only assist when asked; they never intervene.

To recognize the presence of angels is mostly through the senses. You may hear bells chime, singing or smell sweet perfumed flowers like jasmine or, in my experience, roses. Their energy is always soft, subtle and gentle.

Here are some examples of how to call on angels to help you!

"Angel of new job opportunity please come and assist me when now I am ready for new work."

I don't know how many times I have asked for that one and I still do. I know if I ask, I will always be helped. Part of the angels' work is to help us, which they love doing.

"Angel of protection please help me find the strength I have within me to do what I need to do …"

(I always use *WHITE LIGHT* to protect myself if I am walking down the street late at night, whenever I need protection or help. You can also use it for keeping your loved ones safe, and protecting your car and home.)

"Angel of finances, please help me find a way to help pay off my bills."

These are just a few examples of how to ask the angels for help. When you start to incorporate angels into your life, you will never look back and will wonder how you survived without them.

Case study—Believing in miracles

When I left my first husband in Norway, after an abusive marriage, I found it difficult to survive financially. I had just arrived back in Australia with my small daughter and had nothing but a bass guitar and a broken-down stroller in tow. I was penniless but I still had my gorgeous daughter and all my dreams of becoming a good musician or, better still, playing with some really cool people in different bands. Leaving all my worldly possessions behind, I just wanted to make a new start. I always remained optimistic and was happy just to feel free without having to hide or look out for my ex. He was quite dangerous and destructive with his drinking problems and once I got on that plane it was an enormous relief.

My parents helped me a lot in the beginning and then I was left to work it out for myself. When you are so poor you have to grill Spam for dinner, it is something that you never forget. I may have had a fabulous figure in those days but being at the bottom of the financial food chain is a degrading experience and one I do not want to ever experience again. You get treated like a second-hand citizen and there is nothing worse than living on charity as it eats away all your self-respect. It was a valuable lesson, though, as it taught me to believe in myself and made me focus on what I wanted to do with my life.

Education is one of the fundamental requirements for anyone to grow as a soul and I was so grateful that spirit soon provided that for me in a big way. The money I received as a single mother was not enough to live on so I enrolled in university to study drama and music, which I went on to do for many years with great success. The government in those days gave you a small income as an incentive to study, so I thought it would help take my mind off the situation I had just escaped. It was also a sign that I should take the time to study as there were no jobs for registered nurses in the country hospitals where I lived on the South Coast. I couldn't even get a job in the cancer clinic, one place where most people don't want to work.

Every time I felt like giving up, as some days were really hard, I would find the angels always provided me with some extra money. I would just have to think of extra cash and I would receive it in the most bizarre ways. One day I was walking along the street when I found a 100 dollar bill. Money seemed to come from the most unusual places. I even had a long-lost aunt who died in England at the time and left me a small inheritance. Another time, out of the blue someone returned money I had lent them years before. The more I believed that I would be looked after, my faith became stronger and money would just pour in whenever I needed it. This episode in my life taught me to be a better person, and also to trust and know that I will be OK, no matter how bad times may be. When you believe in the power of spirit, you are always looked after, no matter what. Remember, all you have to do is ask for their assistance and thank them afterwards.

One of my most favourite angels, even though they are all fabulous, is Archangel Michael. I have had the pleasure to work with this being many times throughout my life, not only in my healings with clients, but also to help me get over things on a personal level. He is what I call the bouncer boy of the angels. He, alongside Uriel, Gabriel and Raphael, is an integral part of the team I call on when working with lost souls in the aura or spirit rescue, which has always been a part of my work

Angel meditation

Find yourself a quiet space and breathe deeply three times to centre yourself.

Feel yourself relaxing as you slowly breathe in and out. Visualise the colours of the chakras: red, orange, yellow, green, blue, indigo and violet. Imagine you have come to a most beautiful garden, a place of peace, tranquillity and unconditional love.

Sit down a bed of soft green moss as you continue to breathe in a relaxed manner. Feel yourself fill with light and love, and know that you are completely centred.

Focusing your intention begin to call in the Archangels. Call upon the Archangel Michael, the big bouncer of the angels. Ask him to present himself to you. As you do so, let go of any fear and distrust in your higher self. Let go of any negative emotions that may block your spiritual sight. Feel his loving energy as he stands next to you. Call on the Archangel Gabriel, so that you receive wisdom and love required to evolve to a higher good. Feel his loving energy as he stands next to you.

Call on Archangel Raphael, for all that is hidden is now known as my intuition. I now have clarity of vision. Feel his loving energy as he stands next to you.

Call on Archangel Uriel. Allow light and wisdom to shine down on you. Feel his love as he stands next to you.

Now it is time to call upon your guardian angel. Is it male or female or androgynous? What does your angel feel like? Is there a message or gift for you? Feel your loving angel's energy.

Ask now for a healing and ask that any negative energy or unwanted cords be cut out of your aura and body and anything else that you no longer need in your life.

Now it is time to say goodbye until the next time you want to call upon your angel again for love and support. Thank the Archangels for being present.

Fairies

Angels and fairies go hand in hand as they are here to help us.

I have always loved fairies from a very early age perhaps because they are magical creatures and nature is an important part of our life. Whenever I swam in the sea I always saw myself as a mermaid. One part of nature we are not familiar with is the elementals. The elementals, or nature spirits, work hand in hand with our loving and busy angels. The only thing that is required from these beings is respect for our environment.

The four elemental types of fairies
Undines
Using your imagination, visualise these beautiful water spirits as graceful little creatures that live around rocky pools in nature. They have strong personalities and are often called fairies. They are shape shifters which mean that they can change into any shape or form at the blink of an eye.

Sylphs
These beings are air or wind spirits that are full of ideas and inspiration such as butterflies, dragonflies and other winged creatures.

Salamanders
These are fire spirits such as fireflies and so on.

Earth spirits

These are the gnomes, goblins, pixies and elves, the beings connected to Mother Earth.

With so much pollution and rubbish on our planet, the elementals have to work overtime. We can help them by being careful with our rubbish, recycling our waste goods and stop putting pollutants in our water systems.

In one of my channelling sessions, I was quite surprised to meet a tiny fairy called Erin who lives in my garden. She is a very proud being, with tiny wings and a big personality. She told me, in the trance, about her contempt for humans who litter the bush with used coffee cups, rubbish and their uneducated ways of not respecting the nature around them. Sadly, there are many people like that today. She told me she loved my garden with all the flowers, wind chimes and buddas because they created a lot of peace in my yard. Whenever I have hired gardeners to work in my garden, they always comment on the energy they can feel around my home.

Fairy gardens are lovely for children and well as the inner child within us all.

If ever you want to make contact with the nature spirits, open your mind and take a walk in the bush. Besides feeling refreshed and content, afterwards, look around you and you might discover there is really another world out there.

Healing with nature spirits

Whenever you feel run down, depressed, tired, ungrounded or simply out of sorts, take a long walk in nature and let the nature spirits do their work. By connecting to this powerful energy, you will not only feel rested, peaceful and happy again, but your aura will be cleansed of any impurities and back into balance. Your wellbeing will increase tenfold. Even taking a few minutes of your time to watch a sunset, sit under or hug a tree, to lie on the grass or swim in the sea is healing. Letting the wind blow on your face and through your hair is healing. Feeling the warm sun caress your body is healing. Surrender your problems to the angels and the source and know that everything will be taken care of.

A visit to the Kimberleys

My husband Andrew and I travelled with friends on a holiday to the Kimberleys. We flew by small plane and helicopter to remote Kimberley Camp as we were interested in seeing some ancient rock art in the area and doing a bit of fishing. Now I know why they call it the last frontier. The energy is wild and pristine as there are hardly any humans living in that part of the world. Instead it is governed by a vast wilderness that spans thousands of miles, abounding in vegetation, fish, crocodiles, wild birds and waterways.

My husband and I camped in a tent next to a very large boab tree which had one flower on it which was unusual for the time of year as we were told it usually flowers in the wet season which is in September and October. One of my dreams has always been to make an essence from this magnificent tree as boab is one of the most powerful bush flower essences you can use for releasing negative karma and old family patterns from generations.

While I was sleeping in my tent I could feel the presence of a spirit watching me. It unnerved me at first, but I just relaxed, put some white light around myself and the tent, and kept watching the stars, trying really not to think too much about it. All I could sense was that the spirit watching me was an Aboriginal. After a couple of days, I knew there were many spirits visiting this place as we came across quite a few sacred burial grounds in the area. There were no earth-bound spirits, however, only visiting ones.

On one of the last days we decided to fly by helicopter again, as driving is impossible, to a location with the most ancient rock art in the area. We were to meet with somebody from the National Parks and Alex, an Aboriginal man, who would explain the history of the art we were seeing.

On our arrival, I started casually talking to Alex, who is an artist. He is a kind and spiritual man who was interested in my work as a medium because he had lost his daughter in a tragic accident a few years ago. Before I had a chance to really start talking to him, my husband rushed up and handed me a wild flower which he had found behind a rock. As soon as he handed me the flower I could feel Alex's daughter coming in and she started to give me messages which I gave to her father with his consent.

Alex couldn't believe his eyes. The flower my husband gave to me was called Kimberley Rose. His daughter's name was spelt Kimberley Rose after the wild Kimberley Rose flower.

I went on to tell him that she had died in a car accident and went pretty fast over to the over side. There were other messages as well, but these were personal.

After our chance meeting, I briefly told him about my experience in the tent back at Kimberley Camp and how scared I had been. He told me he also had a similar experience as he had stayed in the same tent before. He said it was the "Jillinya", who is a spirit woman. There were many painting of her work in the rock art in the camp, so she had a strong presence and I am sure many who have travelled to that remote place have felt her energy. After returning to Sydney, he sent me her story by email. We have remained friends ever since. He also gave me permission to take these photos so this story can be told.

Alex's story

Jillinya is a spirit woman, a mermaid who comes from the salt water. She travels from the ocean to the mainland; looking for men I'm told.

As I said … Jimmy continued, I had a mystical experience with her on the 4th December 2007 when I was lying in my bed awake but eyes closed, and I could sense someone looking at me. I opened my eyes and she was looking at me. She tried to do something to me by locking my eyes shut as I was lying there, rolling my head from side to side and trying to open my eyes. I could not move my body, and I felt my spirit guide push me in the middle of the back and lift me up out of the bed into a sitting position. As soon as this happened, she disappeared.

I saw with my own eyes a very beautiful woman with black skin, a round face, big eyes and long black matted hair hanging down to her shoulders. It was like looking at a ghost that was superimposed in a movie, if you know what I mean. Anyway the story goes that if you want a wife you can grab the Jillinya. What you have to do is lie there in waiting when you can sense her approaching; you have to be very still.

As she is in spirit form, you need to take a knife and cut beneath her feet very quickly as she is floating next to you. I'm told this will cut the cord that connects her to something, I really can't say what. You will then see blood dripping on the ground. This is when she is manifesting from spirit form into physical form. You have to grab her and tie her up and whip and beat her and flog her until she starts to cry and howl and you will see tears coming from her eyes.

She is then yours to be your wife. You have to teach her to talk and do all the things that you want her to do but you must not let her go near the river or any rock pools because if she sees her reflection in the water, she will vanish back to the sea. You have to keep her away until she forgets where she is from.

She is depicted on rock art sites all around the north Kimberley coastline and is part of the history and mythology of the Mitchell Plateau traditional owners.

I am told that the old people did have Jillinyas as wives. A lot of the younger Aboriginal men, when travelling in these parts of the country, are afraid of Jillinya, as she might grab them and take them. I should have grabbed one myself as I have been single for four years now, he laughed.

Both my husband and I sat in awe as he finished his story.

I could not help but feel afterward how wonderful the spirit world works, by this chance meeting with this amazing man and his beloved daughter in spirit. I smiled to myself afterwards and was happy to think that I had managed to connect my friend to his daughter and the fact that she was able to get a message of love across. She must have been feeling his grief and loneliness and wanted to help him in any way she could. The fact that she told him he would soon meet a new woman and they would have a child brought tears to his eyes. I only hope and pray that he now finds the peace he has been searching for since her death.

Dreams

People often ask me if their dreams are important. They are your connection to your super-consciousness and your higher self. Taking note of your dreams will clarify what is going on in your life and can, in some cases, be predictive.

I sometimes have clients who are able to predict through their dreams but they are a bit afraid if it comes true.

I always say that if spirit gives you something you don't want, then please ask them to take it away.

Usually spirit will not give you situations you cannot handle. Release the fear and the world is your oyster. To have any type of psychic ability is a gift that we can all use as it not only helps you in life, it keeps you safe and out of harm's way.

Being psychic from such an early age, I was always having dreams and knew when things were going to happen. Often in the dream state I can feel and hear my guides teaching me things. I feel we get many spiritual lessons while we are sleeping and often go out of our bodies and travel to other dimensions and places to learn as well. Spirits also use the dream state to heal us on all our different energy levels. The dream state is also a place used by people who have passed over to make contact with their loved ones. People often tell me they dreamed of their late mother last night, or felt their old dog licking their face in their dreams.

A simple way to remember your dreams is to keep a journal and a pen next to the bed and before you get up in the morning, write down everything you can remember, down to the tiniest detail, including colours and numbers. Before I go to sleep I always ask my guides to help me remember what I dream. Also buy yourself a good dream book to help with interpretations but the most important detail of all is to trust your intuition.

When I was younger I was always very sporty and my father used to train me in running around the local oval. My biggest dream was to be the junior champion of the school, as my best friend Lea, who lived across the road, was a runner and told me how easy it was. I learnt from an early age that having goals helped you focus.

Every night I had a recurring dream where I could see myself running and winning the gold cup. It put a lot of pressure on me but I made it happen in the end through sheer determination.

Finally the day I had been dreaming about arrived and I won the race. I remember feeling incredibly high and what I can only describe as over the moon.

I could not believe I had actually won and was given the trophy! My dream had become reality and all my inspirations and goals had finally come true.

You can also have bad dreams as well. When I was younger I often dreamed about my first husband who was always unfaithful. When he finally arrived home from his night of passion, in the dead of night, I would wake up and ask him who he had been with. I would go on to shock him by describing the strange woman in great detail, (though I can laugh about it now). Spirit would always give me the girl's name, what she looked like and other useful information I could use against his lies. The poor guy never had a chance to defend himself as I was always right. He would look at me shocked and guilty as hell that I knew everything he had been up to that night.

After a while, I had no interest in knowing such details about him and asked spirit to take that gift away as I did not want it. After I left him, I never dreamed other dreams like that again.

Favourite case studies

Kathryn's story

Kathryn was a slender woman in her 60s who came for a reading to make contact with her son who had passed away from cancer. He was only 30 years old when he died and unhappy as he was still a young man in the prime of his life. She was heartbroken, like anybody in her situation, and just wanted to know about her son Andrew.

To lose a child and someone so young would have to be one of the worst situations a parent must go through. I should know as I have sat with many people who have suffered the same fate. No matter how hard I try, it always affects me as my heart always goes out to them. As soon as she sat down, I could feel a very strong male presence come in. It was Andrew, who was just as anxious to get into contact with her as if he had been waiting for her to arrive. He was so excited that he never stopped talking in my ear throughout the whole very emotional session. He was angry that he had to go, but once he had passed over and received healing on the other side he accepted his early death.

He chattered so much it was hard for me to keep up with him, as I relayed the messages back to his mother, who sat on the edge of her chair, smiling happily with tears in her eyes. He just wanted to let his mum know that he was fine, and not to worry, that he was doing well. He missed his family terribly but he had come to understand that it was his time. He also seemed to know everything that his mother was up to in her life. Overwhelmed, his mother couldn't believe her ears and kept telling me jokingly that she had never heard him talk so much, as when he was alive he never had much to say, being a quiet, reserved young man.

Unfortunately, I have also had situations with other clients that don't go as smoothly as that. Sometimes I will make contact with a loved one in spirit, and they have nothing much to say at all or the spirit that they want to contact will not come through. They may end up with an uncle or somebody else they don't want to talk to. This can be really upsetting for everyone involved because, as you can imagine, the client will usually have many questions to ask. If you have a bad communicator, even your guides can't help you. Sometimes I think the spirit must be so busy on the other side they just don't have time to stay and have a chat.

I once did a show where a young woman, who was sitting with all her family, asked me if I could get in contact with her mother. As soon as she finished speaking, an elderly woman come through in spirit and stood next to her. She went on to tell me very feebly that she had recently died and had only been gone for three weeks. She then went on to say that she was a very religious woman, showing me a picture of Mary in my mind's eye, and that she had died from a long illness which was cancer.

She said she was very sick for a very long time. She had nothing much to say at all except to let her family know that she was around and how much she loved them all. She also went on to thank them for the splendid funeral and was happy that so many people were there. As I relayed the message to her family I could suddenly hear beautiful music of *Ave Maria* in my ears.

When I told the family what I could hear, they all nodded and said that was her favourite song and it was played at her funeral. There wasn't a dry eye in the audience. After the show the same people who I did the reading for complained to a friend in the audience that I did not give them enough information and that all Italians have the song *Ave Maria* at their funerals.

I have never been to an Italian funeral in my life. I was upset as people do not understand how hard the medium and the deceased relative have to work to even get a message across. I was put on the spot and they were lucky that she came through as fast as she did as she wasn't lined up with the rest of the spirit people my guides had.

To me the message was so clear and so full of love. As far as I was concerned the family were lucky that she could get through as she must have used a lot of energy to get her message across to the grieving family. When I do these shows there are a lot of people in the audience just dying to get a chance to have a reading or make contact with their loved one on the other side as not everyone will receive a message on the night. Then again, sometimes one message can be for many people in the audience because that is the way spirit works. Looking back, I can understand their frustration as they were still grieving, as their beloved mother had only just died in the last three weeks. From my experience, a person needs a good six months to get over a death.

The elderly woman in spirit, whose name was Maria, made a tremendous effort to get through to let them know that she was OK. I can only hope that they will one day understand that. Once you pass over to the other side and meet your guide and loved ones from your soul group, you receive healing and higher beings or guardians, called the council or wise ones, review your life's lessons or contract with you.

People who have problems with their loved ones while on planet earth often don't get to understand what the relationship was all about until they have passed over and are back in the spirit world. Once they have been to the spiritual council and had their lives reviewed for them from another perspective they are able to understand a lot more of themselves as immortal souls and are ready to move on.

When this happens, often the spirit will come through and say they are sorry, which can be an enormous relief and healing for the client.

Janet's story

Janet was a frail, thin middle-aged woman who came to one of my Rainbow Shows. The Rainbow Show is an educational vehicle to raise awareness and teach people about spirit. All the money I make at these events goes directly to the Children's Hospital. It may not be much, but I have always believed that a little bit of love can go a long way. I have always worked as a volunteer in some capacity, because in many ways I have been so blessed, so I like to help others. When you truly work for spirit you are always guided to give something back in some small way.

I could see by just looking at Janet that she was what I call one of the many battlers in life that found it really hard to just survive in her daily life. Her face was like a canvas, full of deep pain lines etched all over it. As I tuned into her I could feel she was a wounded soul, as her sadness and her energy were extremely low and depleted. She had such a sad defeated look about her that you could not help but see she had lived a very difficult life.

As soon as I came to her, I felt the presence of an elderly man around her who came through telling me that his name was Tom and that he was her father. The link I had with him was exceptionally strong and I just knew that he must have used a lot of energy to come through and had been probably waiting to get in contact and give a message for a long time. Often when spirit wants to get a message across, or get in contact with you, they will set up these so-called meetings.

Janet had never been to a medium before and while she was a bit nervous and did not know what to expect, she booked herself in anyway because she felt the need to do so. When she saw the advertisement for the Rainbow Show, she jumped at the opportunity to come. Janet's dad then went on to tell me that when he was alive, he was a terrible alcoholic and abused not only her mother but Janet as well.

Janet agreed with this and just shook her head. He then went on to say that he was a terrible father who never appreciated what he had in life. Not once had he ever given them any time or shown any love or respect to his family. He felt it was his fault that Janet had ended up the way she was as he had not ever shown her any kindness or affection. He then went on to tell me that she had married a man who treated her in the same way. He said he was unhappy with her situation and wanted her to know that it was not too late and that she needed to get help.

In my mind's eyes he showed me how her husband beat her black and blue. He kept urging me to tell her to have some confidence and move on and not to be a doormat any longer. She had been mentally and physically abused her whole life and he felt it was his fault as he had never taught her about self-respect and boundaries. Finally he begged for her forgiveness and told her that she was still his little girl and that he loved her. As Janet silently cried and wiped her eyes there was not a dry eye in the audience. As I looked around I wondered if there were other people like Janet in the audience, because sometimes when a message comes through as strong as this, it can be meant for others who have a similar situation in their lives.

Normally I would not say so much, but this message really needed to get across to Janet and any anyone else in that situation. I felt intuitively that I was being asked by my guides to just give what I was getting as this was something that Janet really needed to hear to help her move on. I just had to trust in the process. Before he left he asked me to tell her once again that he loved her and said to say hello to her mum.

I never saw Janet again after the show. Spirit had helped her father come through to give Janet the opportunity to heal and get her back on her feet. It was time for her to move forward. This is just one of the small miracles I see on a daily basis called divine intervention. It was spirit's way of showing her that we all have choices in life, and it is up to us to take a chance with our lives if we want to bring more balance and harmony into it. I only hope and pray that she took the opportunity to do so.

If she was expecting to see someone in spirit at the show, I am sure it wasn't her father. To get a message from spirit like that in my eyes is what keeps me going. If I can help make a difference in somebody's life in any way as a medium, then I have done my job well.

Everything helps in the grieving process and often forgiveness is the key to all healing. This may surprise some people because they think that their loved one will never get it and will stay the same but I am here to say, fortunately, this is not the case.

I never planned to be a psychic medium it just turned out that way. I had other ideas and dreams, and certainly resisted it for years, but obviously I must have chosen this work on some higher spiritual plane. I put it down to the spiritual contract I signed up for while I was living on the other side before I was born.

I am not what you call extraordinary, far from it, but I do have gifts that I was born with that can help people. My life to date is certainly interesting to say the least and not what most people around me would call normal. Ever since I was little I always knew that my life's work would be of service, which is to work for spirit. Not that I ever really wanted it that way, it was a just a simple knowing from deep within that I had certain abilities. That is probably why I was a nurse in the earlier part of my life because I felt my life's plan was to help people in whatever way I could. I have always been compassionate but nursing also teaches you about discipline and organisation.

My life to date has been one of learning on a deep soul level. When I sleep at night or meditate, I can feel my guides working on me in the dream state. It is a very subtle experience, but I often find that later I seem to know how to do certain things. It is as if I have been what I call "downloaded" or given certain information that will help me with my healing work and my everyday life. I am just so grateful to spirit that I have been given this gift.

Life is also about lessons and learning. A certain theme will present itself continuously until I have got it and moved on. Sometimes this can be frustrating or painful but when you let it go, and learn the spiritual lesson everything just flows much more easily and seems to expand. Life becomes better and more exciting. The people you meet along the way on your journey just seem to pull you along, taking you to the next stage or level.

The more you think you know, the more you don't as life is continually changing, full of tests, as spirit teaches you about energy and the afterlife. Setting goals and knowing that I can achieve them inspires me to keep going. Spirit is always with us; we are never alone. Each day is different and exciting as the spirit world is always full of surprises and miracles. What truly inspires me every day is that the work I do results in someone, somewhere, changing their future.

There are also many wonderful and talented people out there working for spirit but there are also a lot who don't have any real skills. I should know because I have worked with a few. Use discretion when choosing a reputable healer or medium. I always go by recommendations myself. Working for spirit becomes your life's work and you do not have time for anything else. There is also an enormous responsibility that comes with the job.

Many people go unrewarded for their efforts and the job they do, but they do their work so well and so effortlessly and so full of love. I call these special people earth angels or light workers.

My work is also about empowerment, and teaching people that they have the power within themselves to change their destiny, as in reality nothing is final or completely mapped out. It all depends entirely on the individual on how they see themselves and if they are willing to learn from their own lessons and experiences.

I really believe by taking personal responsibility for our lives we can create miracles in the way we think. If our emotions and feelings are cluttered we can draw negative experiences to us. If we feel good about ourselves and continually work on ourselves our life becomes much easier as we draw experiences to us to learn. After all, don't they say earth is a big stage where we play out these experiences?

Sally-Anne's story

Sally-Anne was a client who had sat in one of my development circles, and had come for spiritual healings and flower remedies over the years. Later, she became a good friend, who shared many great moments with me. Through past life regression we saw that we once lived as Vikings together in the longboats.

Sally-Anne was a tall attractive single mother with two children. She had come from a dysfunctional family, like most of us, involving alcohol. Her childhood had been hard because she not only lost her mother when she was really young, but her brother as well. She had very low self-esteem that she hid incredibly well under a veil of good humour.

Whenever we sat in a meditation, all her spirit relatives that had passed over to the other side would come through with lots of love, information, funny stories or warnings. Her mother came through from the spirit world many times and always sent her love and encouragement. She would tell her how proud she was of her, and how well she had done in her life just as a mother would.

I was always telling her also that she would be moving away from Sydney as I could see her living in the countryside with horses and mountains. Every time I was around her, I could see and feel green pastures and clear skies all around her energy.

Finally Sally-Anne moved to Cairns to be with her lover. It was sad to see her go, and I reluctantly helped her pack up her house but I had been warned by my guides for ages that she would move so I was not surprised when she finally did. She had met and fallen deeply in love with a man she had known from childhood. I did not have a good feeling about this at all. But it was her choice and there was nothing I could do about it no matter how hard I tried to talk any sense into her. Every time I tried to talk to her about my concerns, she had no time to listen as the sexual attraction was far too strong.

Once she moved to Cairns he soon changed. She began to find out that he didn't have much time for her as he was too involved with his local football club, drinking with friends and working tirelessly in his own thriving business.

After a long conversation on the phone one night, she told me in confidence that he said he did not love her. Sally-Anne was devastated and tried everything she could to keep him. She still slept with him and jumped every time the phone rang, or whenever he wanted to see her. It was hard for her in the end to even go to his house as he still had all his dead wife's clothes in the wardrobe and they were sleeping in the same bed. I must say I was not surprised when I heard all of this. My fears were becoming reality.

Before she went, she brought him around to meet me. I always go by first impressions, and I was not impressed. He was handsome and very proud, but with no manners and just plain rude. He certainly wasn't my type, as I do not go for rugged men but, as they say, whatever turns you on! Anyway, he was her boyfriend and not mine!

It took almost two years of heart-breaking long phone conversations before she finally came to the conclusion he wasn't the one. After listening to her problems for hours on end, and her seeing a counsellor, I was finally able to convince her to leave him. She had been humiliated and abused too many times. She was tired, suffering from depression and had lost touch with her life. She had lost all her Viking power, and her self-esteem, which wasn't healthy in the first place, was at an all-time low.

I suggested I would fly up to Cairns and do a cutting of the ties, and a past life regression to find out what spiritual contract she had with him. In the session, I took her back to one of the strongest past lives she had with him, as they had shared many lives together.

He was a cruel Egyptian landowner who had many slaves that he treated like cattle. To Sally-Anne's horror, she was one of his slaves and workers that he owned and he in turn treated her very badly. He was selfish, constantly belittling her and demanding more in return. She had children with him and they were treated in the same manner.

She could see all the similar qualities in him from this past life. Nothing had changed. She soon realised very quickly why he couldn't love her. The regression gave a lot of insight into their relationship about why he would never take her anywhere or introduce her as his girlfriend.

None of his friends liked her either, thinking she was difficult and highly strung. They were all similar to him and liked the same things as him whereas she had nothing in common with any of them.

Sally-Anne was ready to move on. The past life not only gave her clarity, but it also taught her the importance of her own self worth. It was also a lesson about boundaries and about lust, which is not love. About two years later, after licking her wounds, she met another man similar to her but she was still not satisfied. After treating him quite badly, she broke up with him as well and is still looking for her Mr Right.

She is much stronger now but knows herself better after that lesson because she knows who she is as a person and what she can expect in a relationship. If she wants to find somebody as a soul mate she needs to start to love herself first, then she won't have any more problems.

Jenny's story

Jenny was having an affair with a married man, who was a sex addict. After tuning into her energy I told her because of her own abuse when she was younger, she was attracting this type of energy into her life. We tried to cut him off but she wasn't ready, as she thought she was still in love with him and wanted to give it a go. The second visit, much later, was more successful. She had come to the conclusion that he wasn't going to change, and was sick of the continual merry-go-round of abusive relationships that had filled her life. Firstly, I scanned her aura psychically with my guides, looking for any entities or lost souls that may have attached themselves to her energy field. Sure enough, she had a large crack down the front of her aura as I could feel the cool breeze on my hands.

I asked the usual questions, had she had any shock, traumas, taken loads of drugs, or been in any accidents, trying to find out how she had this massive tear in her aura. Her eyes widened, and she told me how she had been involved in a terrible accident at work. She had been run over by a forklift and had been hospitalised for months. The next part was easy as I swiftly removed a lost soul, or parasite, that had buried itself in her energy field and sent it to the light. Instantly she felt the energy change. Then I repaired the aura, first imaging to stitch it with spiritual cotton, and then filling it with white light until it bounced out, healthy again.

When we have damage to our aura, it is easy for psychic debris to get in. This in turn can cause a lot of damage, especially to the emotional body, as these parasites have their own agenda. Next we cut the ties with the core issue in her life. She had been raped when she was four, and had never had a loving relationship with anyone. Her life was lonely and sad. Gradually we managed to heal all the people who had hurt her in her life, and give her closure. After the session had finished I sent her home with a hug and lots of remedies I had made up for her and other instructions. Walking out the door, she turned to me and smiled. The look on her face was priceless. She looked like a young woman again, one who was ready to take on the world.

Bruce's story

A couple of years ago, my good friend Bruce became very sick. His cancer had come back, and he wasn't the least bit impressed. We had become good friends from the moment we met as we were both odd to most people. He was the only gay in the village, and I was the crazy lady who not only talked to spirits but was weird. We were both wicked.

He was always kind to my cats and we both laughed when my old girl Sammy moved in next door to live with him until the day she died. Her name was even changed to Princess and she was spoilt rotten. He tried everything possible to get better, because he had beaten cancer before but this time nothing worked, and the cancer beat him in the end. All I could think of was that it was perhaps his time. He was terrified at first, then angry, and finally too weak to care. As his cancer became more and more aggressive he was sent off the hospital so he could get the best care. I promised that I would visit him daily and give him healings, to help him with his transition.

Each day as I sat by the bed quietly giving him healing, I could hear family members in spirit all chatting away in the room. It was almost as if they were all popping in to catch up with each other and welcome him home again. Sometimes I would even tell them to shush as I couldn't concentrate on the healing I was giving him. I could even hear somebody in spirit playing the piano. It was like a big party, with every one of his relatives having a good old chinwag.

When he would awaken, as towards the end of his illness he would sleep most of the day, I would ask him, "Bruce do you know so and so?" He would look up at my face, from his pillows all stacked on top of each other and politely smile and say, "Well yes, Kerrie, but they have been dead for years, and boy oh boy, she was a bossy old thing!"

He seemed pleased that he was not alone and was rather amused that all his family were starting to pop in. His face looked serene, and the old familiar glint in his eye had returned. He was no longer afraid; his pain was under control and he had come to terms with what was going on. He was tired and had had enough and just wanted to leave without any fuss. He had triumphed over his illness and made peace with himself.

Sitting by his bed I would just laugh and continue with my job of hands-on healing, which made him feel better in his body. The warmth from my hands was very comforting and helped him feel slightly more comfortable and relaxed.

Sadly, Bruce being an old queen, was not accepted by a lot of people in his life socially, and ended up being quite lonely. He had very few friends, except for me, my family and my cats, who adored him. Most of his immediate family had all passed over to the other side. As each day passed, his life became another story. His room was beginning to fill with so many spirit people, it was not funny. It was soon looking and feeling like busy Pitt Street mall in the middle of Sydney. All the spirit people were coming to pay their respects and were getting ready for his journey home. My job of helping him pass over was coming to an end.

On the last day I saw him he was unconscious and I could see a purple energy above his head. It was like his spirit was already making its way out of his body through the crown chakra at the top of his head. This was something I have never witnessed first-hand before, even though I had looked after many dying people when I was a nurse. I feel spirit wanted me to see this, so I would have a better understanding of death on a personal level.

The next time I saw Bruce he was lying proudly in his coffin, dressed in a very smart suit and surrounded by all his spirit relatives. After the funeral, which was very moving, I didn't feel his energy around me for a while and then one day, while meditating, I heard his voice call out from spirit for the first time.

"Kerrie, its Bruce here. How are you?" I wasn't the least bit surprised because I was waiting for him to drop in! "Just to let you know that Mum and I are together again and everything is fine."

"That's good Bruce," I replied in my thoughts. "I am glad that you are fine. Miss you darling …" Without another word and any further messages he went as fast as he had arrived. I guess he had a lot of catching up to do with all his family.

He had crossed over safely, was doing well and was with his beloved mother who he adored. They had made a quick trip over to see how the sale of the house was going, popped in to see me and were off. Everything else was fine. As for the rest of us, we were all left to pick up the pieces. He would be greatly missed by one and all, especially his boyfriend and love of his life, Martin.

Love always finds a way

Tuesday is normally my walking day with my good friend Effy. She is a great friend and we always manage to have a good laugh while exercising, talking and getting fit. As we walk, we talk and often share our life's stories, even though we live in completely different worlds. We usually fit between seven and 10 kilometres, and I find this exercise extremely important, as it is very good grounding for the type of work I do. (Also keeps off the weight!)

This day turned out to be different. It started with an early morning phone call on my message bank from a woman called Roberta. She wanted me to help her find a medium in Queensland for her sister, as her niece had died.

After my day out with Effy even though I was tired and aching all over from the big work-out, I decided to get in contact with the woman who had rang earlier in the day, and try and help her.

Ringing her back I suddenly sensed a little girl in spirit, standing next to me. "Is the little girl seven, has she got light hair, and has she died of cancer?" I gently asked the shocked woman on the phone.

"Yes, that's right," gasped the woman, totally bewildered. "Have you got her with you now?"

"Seems to be the case," I answered, bemused at how fast the little girl had come in from the early morning. "She has been hanging around me all day. She is quite a little chatterbox. She told me all about herself, how she loves music and dancing, especially Madonna, (probably all little girls love her) and how she hates to wear shoes."

The woman on the other end of the phone was silent for a moment, and then asked me if I could please ring her sister in Queensland and tell her that I had made contact with her daughter. "Oh, I am not sure at the moment, because I feel sick and I am coming down with a cold. Maybe another time." I coughed over the line. Hearing her desperate sigh, and noticing the little girl in spirit had no intention of leaving until she got a message through to her mother, I quickly apologised and agreed. Putting the phone down, I lit a candle (like I always do for spirit) and waited patiently for an hour for the mother to ring.

The little girl in spirit was delighted and started to talk non-stop, dancing around the room. If anything she was the most determined spirit child I have ever witnessed in my working life as a medium! Finally the woman from Queensland rang. As soon as I introduced myself, the little girl started to give survival evidence and messages via me to her poor grieving mother over the phone. The little girl was concerned how grief-stricken her mother was, and she even informed me that there was going to be a new baby born.

Slowly the woman started to cry and began to tell me how hard the pain was of losing her seven-year-old daughter, as she loved her so much. They were not only best friends but got on like sisters. After trying to pull myself together as well, I told the woman the little girl had said that she was coming back again, to live another life on earth and not to worry. I informed the woman her daughter was from her own soul group and they would always be connected with love.

After talking to the woman for about half an hour, my energy started to become really flat and I was slowly losing the link with the little girl. I couldn't believe my ears with what came next. "I just wish I could find some way to contact her again, as I miss her so much."

The woman was so deep in grief she did not for one second understand the miracle that was happening to her.

"Can't you understand what is going on here," I gently replied. "Your daughter in spirit has found a medium that not only does not live in the same state as you, but has got in contact with you to get her message of love across. That, my dear, is proof that not only is love eternal, but this is a miracle."

The woman was silent for a while and gently began to cry again. Her brave little girl Anna, from the other side, had found a way to make contact with her mother. This, in itself, would help her mother on the road to healing she so greatly needed.

On the anniversary of Anna's death, exactly one year later, Anna's mother rang me once again. She told me she was eight weeks pregnant, and asked if she could speak to her daughter. Almost immediately Anna came quickly into the room, this time on a swing. Her hair was longer, and she told me she liked it as she always wanted to have long hair. She had grown in the spirit world and was in my room happily chattering away. She had come to pass on more information through her mother's love, so I was able to pass on the information without any problems.

They were both excited about the new baby. It would have been a good hour before I finished speaking to both of them by which time I was completely exhausted. "You know, I wouldn't be surprised if it is Anna who comes back as your next baby," I said as I was saying my last goodbyes.

"That would be wonderful!" laughed Anna's mum.

"Well we will have to wait and see, but whatever the case you have nothing to worry about as you will be having a very healthy baby boy."

About a year later Anna's mum rang me from Queensland. She had just given birth to a beautiful baby boy, as predicted, and was over the moon. She was overwhelmed with her bundle of joy as he was a miracle, according to her doctor, who told her it would be just about impossible to have any more children. This type of situation makes you believe that there are no rules in life.

When I asked her to describe the little boy she said he somehow reminded her of Anna every time she looked deep into his eyes. She kept thinking it was her imagination but they looked so familiar. The other odd thing was that the new baby had the same birthmarks on his body as Anna when she was alive. There was one on his wrist which was very visible and one behind the back of his neck. The similarities were incredible. When we discussed this over the phone, I had goosebumps all over my body. When I told her how I felt, she started crying and said she felt the same. It is these scenarios that I draw back on and think about the miracles of life. I only wish all my stories could be so happy.

The developer's tale

Peter is a developer on the North Coast. He may be very wealthy in his own right, but he has a strong social conscience because the work he does improves the lives and living standards of the impoverished in society. He is politically aware in his concept of tithing and I call him an "earth angel" because in my eyes he does everything with integrity and for the highest good of others.

Over many years he and his team of solid workers, whom he looks after well, have been buying dilapidated houses, doing them up and making them habitable for the low-income renters.

A large part of his work involves dealing with problems with various councils, and other unexplainable things that seem to go wrong with his developments for no apparent reason. In some cases this can be put down to having earth-bound spirits in the building that have not passed on. As Peter understands and is aware of the work I do with spirit rescue, he often calls for my services when he has difficult cases. I am a last resort to look at the energy and clear out any problems he may be having on an energetic level.

I have done quite a few jobs for him now over the years and he is not only a fan but a firm believer in the work I do as it usually succeeds and gets him the results he needs to improve the building. For example, a couple of years ago he was having problems with one particular building which was causing him a lot of stress. No matter what he did he never seemed to be able to move forward with his project, and was even having problems with a council representative who went out of his way to stop everything he tried to do. At his wits' end he called me and asked if I would check out the building as he believed that there was spirit activity from the property's history of deaths and murders.

I tuned into the energy of the building by remote viewing, a technique to see psychically with my third eye. I just have to close my eyes and think of something and I can see it quite clearly. The energy around the property was thick and dark. I could sense there were many earth-bound spirits present. They must have been trapped there for years so I knew that I would have my work cut out for me. The house also had a terrible haunting sadness that sent shivers up my spine. There was also some negative energy around the deeds and the contract, so I planned to clear them before I went to the house.

My husband decided he would drive me. On our way I gently closed my eyes, and put a purple and gold bubble around the property to seal it, so no earth-bound spirits could escape till I got there. I also was given a picture in my third eye of an old fashioned horse-drawn carriage and I could hear the sound of horse's hooves on the pavestones. This indicated the house was over 100 years old and probably had problems from then.

I later learnt later from my guide that the house was an old boarding school full of unhappy children. I felt some of the children were treated poorly and which must have been the sadness I picked up.

Before we drove to the old building I asked to see the deeds and contracts of the house which were at Peter's house, around the corner from the property. As I cleared the old energy from the contracts, Peter had told me that since I had rang to confirm that I was coming, all the water in the street had been turned off. It was most peculiar, he said, as they had never had problems before and he wondered if my visit had anything to do with it. Funnily enough, as soon as the contracts were cleared the water came back on. Coincidence or not, that was strange.

Once I reached the building I slowly walked throughout the rooms and could feel the sad energy and history as the place seemed to be aching from the bowels of the house. I decided to open up a big portal of light to release all the earth-bound spirits, as there was so many trapped there it was impossible to do it one by one.

As I opened up psychically, I could hear not only them babbling in my ears, but the sound of crying and many spirits calling out. I also saw spirit children standing in the shadows, fearful and afraid to step forward.

My husband's face was ashen and he looked afraid. He wanted to leave but I told him I needed all the help I could get. Lighting a candle we joined hands and made a circle, which created a portal of light for the trapped spirits to use as a safe passage to leave.

As soon as we began praying and had done this I asked for the spirits to open their eyes and go into the light as it was time to go home. I also told them not to be afraid and said the Lord's Prayer a couple of times.

As the three of us stood there holding hands, I could feel and see spirit energy sweeping up in the circle and out into the cosmos. There must have been over 100 spirits as the healing seemed to take ages. I started to wonder whether news had spread in the spirit world that I was coming as there were so many leaving they must have come from a radius of 10 kilometres around the house. As we stood there clutching hands in the perfect circle we had created, tears ran down my cheeks and I could hear beautiful angelic music in my ears, something I will never forget.

Gradually the heavy energy started to lift and shift and the once-cold room felt less prickly and relaxed. Looking around, we could all sense something had happened as the atmosphere around us was significantly lighter. Looking around, I knew my job was done as the air was clean, I felt lighter and there was the presence of incredible love and life in the room.

Once we had finished, I felt tired and weary. Regaining my energy, I lovingly sealed the house with my oil, so no other earth-bound spirits would make this their home.

Making our way to the car I looked back at the once unhappy house which looked completely different now. Over lunch, Peter told us that he had enjoyed the experience as he had felt the energy and thought the whole thing was quite remarkable. But Andrew said he did not like it one bit and asked me never to take him again as it frightened him. I explained I had to use him as I could not do it by myself as there were far too many spirits present and it was too late to find another medium at such short notice.

Within six weeks, Peter was given approval by the council to start building. There were no further electrical or other problems. As far as I know, the building is complete now and is full of happy residents.

Rina's story

Rina was a lovely Christian Sri Lankan girl I met through working in a shop in Sydney's outer west. She had moved to Australia as a child, but kept her Sri Lankan roots. However, she was cast out from her family after her divorce as this was not tolerated.

As her father was dead, and her mother sick, the eldest brother took over as family head and Rina and her other divorced sister were not only cast out but were cursed by their brother. This was evident by the bad luck they were continually having and the little objects they found round their home that must have been placed there by her warring relatives that lived across the road when they visited.

The first time Rina visited me in one of the centres I was working at, she appeared very bright and was a smart and attractive woman, but as she talked and told me about all her bad luck, I could feel energetically that she was being psychically drained.

As I scanned her energy I could see her aura was dark and heavy and she complained how depressed she felt at her treatment in life. On closer examination I picked up an entity, or attachment, in her aura. Without hesitation, I quickly pulled it out and sent it swiftly into the light, then cleared and balanced her energy field.

After the healing she thanked me and asked if I could come and clear her house as she always felt she was under attack from her brother who lived across the road. Unexplained things would move around her house in the dead of night and she could hear strange noises as well. I explained to her that this was probably an earth-bound spirit trapped in her house, and it would not be a problem to get rid of. I asked her to sage her house with some grandfather sage for a couple of days before I came, as this always weakens the unwanted ghost or spirit.

At her house, I cleared the outer perimeters and put a wall of protection up so her brother's bad spells, curses or whatever would bounce back or go into the light. As I went from room to room, I found four earth-bound spirits and sent them into the light. Soon after she was able to sell her house and move on but, unfortunately, she remains an outcast to some of her family. We might think that this sort of thing does not happen today, but believe me it does. As I grew up in an area heavily populated by migrants, I saw people buying curses from different ehtnic seers or fortune tellers to hurt another or to get rid of a wife or husband. Often due to racial hatred, this behaviour was common.

I was once cursed and had to visit a witch doctor to remove the energy.

This is called psychic attack and I have witnessed this first hand myself. I realise now that this was all part of my learning to work with energy, removing it and sending it to the light.

John and Sarah's story

John and Sarah were a couple in their 60s who had been married for 10 years. John was divorced and from Canada and he had met his second wife Sarah while on holiday in Australia. They fell madly in love and moved in together, often travelling and spending as much time as possible with each other. They must have known that it was not going to last forever, as Sarah soon developed breast cancer which spread throughout her body, going into the bones.

Being the organised and practical Aries that she was, she quickly organised a list of things he had to do when she died. She was worried what would happen to him as they were true soul mates who loved each other dearly. At the suggestion of a friend who knew the couple, John finally came to me about a year later. He was at a loss and did not know what to do with himself. His home was still full of all her clothes and belongings but he couldn't bring himself to get rid of them As soon as he spoke to me in a gentle voice on the phone to make the appointment, I heard the name Sarah called out in spirit and I could hear a spirit woman's voice in my other ear yelling out "Stick to the plan". She repeated this over and over until I gave him the message.

Laughing loudly, he told me that this was indeed his wife and he could not wait to see me. I have never had such a loud message in all my work. This woman was so desperate to help her mate she would do whatever it took.

When he arrived at the sitting, she came through straight away and I felt very emotional as I relayed the messages. She was concerned about him and wanted him to go back to Canada just like they had talked about before she had died. In my mind's eye I pictured a large beautiful lake and a big canoe. This was where John had grown up and wanted to retire to one day. It was a serene place surrounded by a deep forest, and lots of wildlife.

They often talked of retiring to this place, but had not gone there because of Sarah's children.

About two weeks later, John rang to tell me he had cleared everything out of the house and was moving overseas. He knew what he had to do and was grateful for the reading and messages. Sarah had been around him a lot and was grateful to move on and receive healing, knowing her John would be all right.

Sam's story

While working with another medium one night at a club, doing proof of survival, I was instructed by my spirit helpers to go to the back of the room to where a small lady was sitting alone. Usually spirits will just call out names but on this occasion I was told to go to this particular lady who sat with her arm crossed, looking uncomfortable.

When I asked politely if I could come to her and whether she knew anyone called Sam, she yelled out yes and jumped up in her chair.

Straight away I could feel a connection or link radiating out from her energy and within seconds I saw a man in his early 20s standing next to her. As I spoke she was overcome with emotion and tears were falling. I could also understand that she must have been overwhelmed to finally hear that her son had safely crossed over and was now in spirit.

As she started to wipe her eyes, I felt an incredible emotion washing over me as the spirit man moved closer to tell me how he had died. The emotion was so strong that I had to ask the young man in spirit to stand back a little so I could relay the information to his mother, without feeling the cancer he had died of so intensely in my body as it was making me feel nauseous. This was his way of showing me how he had actually died. As I opened up even more, the spirit man began to tell me how he had passed.

"Do you have a son called Sam who passed away from cancer in the stomach region?" I asked, listening very carefully to Sam as he communicated and felt him move closer so I could hear him talking in my ear.

"Yes, that is right," she replied.

Taking a deep breath I continued as I began to feel the energy really build up between the spirit man and myself. "Well he is telling me that he had cancer in his liver and it spread all over his body. He is also saying that before he became sick he was very athletic and liked to play cricket and soccer, because he is now showing me a soccer ball. He is also telling me that he was very angry at the time of his death and constantly complained that he did not want to die and how unfair it all was. He is also saying that the cancer spread to his legs so, in the end, he was in a wheelchair."

Wiping her eyes she continued to nod. "This illness really upset him as he was a very active person and lived life to the fullest. He is also saying that he hated how he had to depend on you even though you said you didn't mind and he is sorry for the way he behaved."

"Yes I understand that," she said, speaking up. "I only loved him and would do what any other mother would do, please tell him that I love him."

He went on to say that his mother had never left his side and for this he was grateful as he was terrified of dying as he had no idea what was going to happen to him. She nursed him throughout his short illness but now missed him terribly. She was now over the moon to receive a message that his spirit had lived on and that he was here to say that he was doing well and not to worry.

The love between the mother and the son was overwhelming and there was not a dry eye in the room. It was hard for me, as the medium, or messenger, as this work is never easy but when you have such strong proof of survival it is the greatest type of healing you can receive.

Fighting back tears I asked my guides for help and healing so as not to break down myself as I was so moved that such a young person had been robbed of their life and at the strong bond between the mother and son that was pure unconditional love. I had to remind myself that it's my job to give the clearest message possible without getting too involved.

About a year later Sam's mother rang me for a private sitting. It was his birthday and she wanted to talk to him. As we spoke, the messages from her son began to come in thick and fast. He must have known about what she was up to and was excited to talk to her again. He had done a lot of healing on the other side, as is the common protocol when you die. His energy was different and he did not seem so angry this time around. He kept telling me it was his birthday as well and could not wait to get in contact with his mum as well as he had so much to tell her.

When she finally arrived on the day, I knew he was waiting for her because I could feel his energy in my small healing room, way before she arrived. After the session she told me how surprised she was at how talkative he was. He had been a quiet person in life and kept things to himself. The happiness on her face was priceless and no longer showed the signs of the grief I had seen on her face the first time we met. The information she had received from her son was helpful as she had a few problems with other family members. He also confirmed how he loved her new house and she was delighted.

It was obvious it was Sam's time to help his mother. His spirit had lived on and all he wanted now was to do as much as he could on the other side to help her. He promised her that he was happy at last and he just wanted her to really enjoy her life as she was always doing so much for so many others. He was no longer angry and said he loved her but was sorry if he had hurt her in any way as this was not his intention. Without her by his bed it would have been impossible for him to cross over as he was so full of fear and dread. Now, he had at last found peace.

Monica's story

Monica was a lovely lady in her forties who had booked in to have a reading. As she walked into the room, I saw an older lady in spirit next to her, and asked if her grandmother had passed. I had a picture of a big-breasted woman, a widow who dressed in black, according to the custom of her country. She lived to a ripe old age, dying of heart and lung problems.

I could feel the breathlessness and pain in my heart as she went on to describe how she had died. Her daughter, Monica's mother, had married and left with her much older husband (Monica's father) to live in Australia. Only two of her children had stayed behind.

In my mind's eye I pictured the old lady, named Eva, sitting next to a bed with a walking frame parked next to it. She had spent much time in a nursing home before she died reminiscing about her past. Her main message was to tell her granddaughter to love herself more and not to worry about things so much. I had the feeling that it was a family habit. Monica's father had passed over too, and Eva said he suffered with depression which had affected the sensitive Monica when she was young as growing up in the family home was hard because of his illness. The grandmother felt this was why Monica held back her own interest and concentrated on everyone else.

After giving Monica a message with the tarot cards, I was able to see she would start a new business and her dreams of working with children would one day become a reality, she just had to believe in herself. This message kept repeating itself through her reading. Later I took her down to her sacred space through hypnosis (a type of very deep meditation), and I was able to contact her guides and introduce them to her. To her surprise, she saw the master Jesus and tears filled her eyes as she was quite overwhelmed. As she was such a compassionate person, I was not surprised to see that she worked with this beautiful energy.

Next a tall guide appeared dressed as an Indian. He introduced himself as Big Bear and she described him as powerful, humble and kind. He was her main guide and had been working with her from birth. After the session Monica was so grateful for all the information I was able to give her.

Her next step, she felt, was to sit in a development group and work on her spiritual growth. I assured her if she did this then her life would improve and her work with the children would be far more beneficial, as she would be sharpening her psychic abilities and senses. The spiritual work would also help her empower herself as well and would be a good tool to use in her personal life.

A visit from the other side by two fathers

One day I received a booking from a woman called Abby who had seen me at one of my Rainbow Shows I held for a children's hospital. Abby had enjoyed the show but wanted a private reading so she could contact her father. She also asked if she could bring her husband, John and their three children. I wondered how I was going to squash them all into my tiny office, so I was a bit nervous.

As soon as they walked into the room I had nothing to worry about. The spirit energy had built up very fast in the room and I could taste the spirit energy in my mouth. Almost immediately Abby's father came in. I could feel chest pain and could tell he had died of a heart attack. It was later confirmed that he had lung cancer as well, which I could feel had also spread down into his stomach and body, but it was his heart that failed him in the end.

Abby's father, Fred, was a gentle, softly spoken man who was over the moon to get in contact with his daughter. She was not able to be with him when he died, as he had lived in South Africa, and she felt guilty about that. He reassured her that it didn't matter that she wasn't there for his death and was even glad, in a way, because he looked as terrible as the disease had wasted him away to half the man that he was. Seeing him in that state would only have upset her terribly. His wife had nursed him to the end and he was extremely grateful for her help and love, even though it had been a burden.

He also said how much he had loved Australia when he visited in the past and went on in great detail about the Barrier Reef. Fred told us, however, that he was also worried about his wife back in England, as she was still grieving for him, even though he had died two years ago. He also knew about the trip Abby was planning for her mother at Christmas time and made a comment about his funeral. He was chuffed at how many people had turned up on the day, not realising how many people he didn't even know had come to pay their respects.

The session began to come to an end as I could feel the link beginning to weaken. Finally he wished her well and sent his love, then said that there was somebody else who wanted to come forward. Suddenly, his mother and grandmother appeared. Everybody had turned up for the occasion and as the link began to fade I could hear spirit names being called out.

After the session with Fred, Abby's husband said that he wanted to get in touch with his father as there had been a lot of mystery surrounding him.

Handing me a photo, I stared at it for a while then began to hear a voice talking to me. The man in question was a soldier and his name was Richard. His personality was completely different from the first spirit father, and he was full of apologies for the way he had treated his son when he was alive. Abby's husband Robert started softly crying as he acknowledged what his father was saying. It felt as if he had waited for this healing his whole life, as he felt he had never been able to live up to his father's expectations.

Richard also went on to talk about his illegitimate son he had with his "other wife" and told his son how they were similar to him. He was sorry about all the mess he had caused between the two families, which John also acknowledged. I could not help thinking how this spirit reminded me of a James Bond type. He certainly must have been a very strong character in life and lived life as he pleased. We all shared a laugh at the end of the session, excited that so many spirits had come through in just one session.

Both John and Abby were pleased and felt they had received a tremendous healing. As they walked through the door thanking me and saying their goodbyes, they looked 10 years younger, happier and in love. I couldn't help but think how beautiful it was to see two people who had been married for 30 years so happy and content. I could see they were certainly soul-mates.

Mike's story

Mike was client of mine in his mid 30s when I met him in the inner city of Sydney. He was a large, robust man with an infectious laugh who always had a good story or joke to tell. He was constantly laughing and playing the clown. All the therapists, including myself, really loved him and looked forward to his visits for his wicked sense of humour. Once you got to know him, though, you could see his happy face was just a cover-up for his loneliness and sadness.

He did not look after his health; his love-life was practically non-existent as he was always chasing and getting involved with the wrong type of woman who just usually used him for his money. No matter how much advice you ever gave him when he came for a healing, he never listened and just grinned like it was a great joke. I would often suggest counselling but he was never interested in doing any work on himself. So his life continued like a merry-go-round of highs and lows and he had no desire in the least to do anything about it.

From an Spanish background, Mike had never married and still lived with his elderly mother and father. He claimed he hated living with his parents and his brother , who was lazy and always complaining.

He said he was desperate to move out and have a family of his own. He was a real daydreamer and all he ever talked about was meeting the woman of his dreams. This, of course, was never going to happen as he was very fixed in his way of thinking and underneath I always felt that he had no desire whatsoever to settle and marry. His social life took first priority and he was forever telling anybody who'd listen about his latest conquest, which was either imaginary or real as nothing ever came of it. If you probed further, he would tell you about all the money he had spent on his new girlfriend, or how he was helping her in some way.

Over time, I became concerned about the real issue, which was his health. If anybody ever said anything or tried to help him, including his local GP who was always prescribing all sorts of drugs, it was just ignored. The energy healing he received on the day was not a cure for all his problems but it certainly helped his emotional body with his self-hatred as he was constantly putting himself down. If he wanted to live a long life he would have to start working on his issues because nobody except himself could really help.

Over time, however, I gradually became disheartened of trying to help him with the healing process so I suggested one day that perhaps it would be better for him to see somebody else as the energy work I was doing on him wasn't making much of a difference any longer. I felt he was wasting not only his money but his and my time as well.

Once I explained my concerns he thanked me for all my time and energy and said he understood. I wished him all the best and did not see him for a while.

About six months later, I nearly fell over backwards one day when he walked into the healing centre for an appointment. To my utter astonishment he was not only double in size, if that was indeed possible because he was already considerably overweight, but a sickly grey colour as well. Energetically his aura was thin, shrunken and weak. He looked drained and tired and appeared energetically to be in a "depressed state'. The poor man seemed forlorn and confused. All his so-called happy energy was gone, as if someone had vacuumed away all his vital life force energy and left behind an empty shell of the man.

Once I got over the initial shock I ushered him into my office and asked him to sit down. As soon as he squeezed himself into the chair, a spirit woman popped into the room and stood next to him. She said she was his maternal grandmother. She wanted to talk to him urgently. Asking her to come closer, so I could hear her clearly, I relayed the messages I was receiving straight back to Mike.

"Mike, I have an elderly lady here in spirit, she is Spanish, from the south of Spain. She is a very proud woman and she is telling me her name is Maria, and she is your grandmother. Is that correct?"

"Yes, that would be her," he said, grinning from ear to ear and sitting up in the chair all excited. "She is always around me as I can feel her when I am not feeling well,"

"Well she is worried about you and is telling me that you have got yourself in a bad situation. She feels you have given up on life and you are too young to sit around and let the world pass you by. Is this correct Mike?" I asked concerned at the state of his health and wondering what he had been up to since I last saw him. Whatever it was, it was not doing him any good.

"That would be right on the money. She always knows what's going on even though she is on the other side. Nothing ever changes does it?" he sighed, looking at me sheepishly.

She then went on to talk about the family and all the fighting that was going on, especially with his brother who was waiting for his parents to die so he could get his hands on the inheritance. Mike was made executor of his parents' will, as his father was gravely ill. This had really upset his brother who believed he would not do the right thing and would take all the money. All the arguing and quarrels were getting him down to such an extent that he no longer desired to live.

He was also heartbroken about his father's ill-health. His grandmother went on to say that Mike would have the last laugh as his brother would have to wait a long time to get his hands on any money. She said his father would pull through, as it was not his time. After the grandmother spoke, her husband came through and said hello. As he went, a pet dog came through and gave his love and greetings. The spirit world was out in force to help poor Mike that day.

As the session slowly began to come to an end, tears of happiness rolled down Mike's cheeks. Beaming from check to check, he thanked me for my help and appeared relieved that everything would be all right.

He also promised that he would go on a diet and stop drinking so he could get his life in order. He seemed happy again and all the heavy energy in his energy field disappeared. Just as he was about to leave, I quickly pulled out my tarot cards and gave him a quick read.

Excited he sat down again and looked intently as he pulled out the cards one by one. As I spread them on the table and was happy to see only positive news. There was nothing bad around him. According to the spread, I could see that within the next six months there would be a romantic interest coming into his life. I told him she was more his age, had two children, but was a really nice lady and she would be good for him.

Rolling his eyes, he laughed and grinned. By the end of the session his energy had expanded and he looked peaceful and serene. It was hard for him to wipe the large smile off his face. His grandmother, whom he had loved very much, had really helped to lift his spirits.

Love is eternal. As for his diet and exercise plan, that remains to be seen.

Love always finds a way

A few years ago, my former mother-in-law from Norway, who I was very close to before she died, decided to bring her family out to Australia to see her grandchild, my eldest daughter Kaja. They planned to come for Christmas and everybody in my family was excited as my ex-parents-in-law and my new husband had never met.

Her middle son, was accompanying them as the rest of the family did not speak a word of English. I knew my husband would hit it off, so to speak, with my ex-brother-in-law as they are both crazy about jazz. I also realised that I would be the one chaperoning the Norwegians around, as Eddie, like a typical single guy, would be hitting the bars and chasing women.

After they arrived, we decided to go to my new mother-in-law's house as it was spacious and perfect for the big day. As the visitors had never spent Christmas in a foreign land before, I told Eddie to pace himself with the food and drink, as it would be excessive, and to try to control his drinking. It turned out to be a sizzling hot day, and everyone was nervous, especially as most were meeting for the first time. As Eddie was sitting next to me, I noticed how he kept accepting all the food and drink that was being offered to him.

Every time I happened to turn my head to see if he was comfortable, his mouth was full of food and alcohol. His English was pretty bad, and he started to tell me in Norwegian that he found it overwhelming to be in charge of his parents where he had to speak English and translate all the time. It was beginning to get him down and he asked me if I could take over, which I was already doing.

Not wanting to be rude, he kept accepting all the plates of food being passed around the table all the while drinking steadily. As the long day went on, he became more and more dishevelled and drunk, and started to sing and jump around. We thought it was funny and did not take much notice of his altered state. So long as he was having a good time, what did it matter as it was Christmas day after all?

When it was time to go, we piled into the two cars, as there was so many of us, said our goodbyes and made our way towards home. Eddie sat in the front of the car I was driving singing and laughing, while my in-laws Anna and Boris were in the back. My husband had taken the others in his car and had sped off as he said he had enough and just wanted to get home and unwind and have a drink or two.

As we began to cross the bridge, Eddie turned to me and said he felt really sick. I explained that I was in the middle of the bridge and it was impossible to pull over as there was so much traffic. His face looked bloated and pale and I knew that any moment he was going to explode.

At first, I couldn't believe his bad timing and then I started to really freak out. Suddenly, Eddie turned towards me and vomited all over me. The stinking, smelling fluid washed over my face and entire body. I could feel it running down my face into my bra and it was making its way into my undies. Tiny little pieces of meat and cake and cream were splattered all over me from head to toe. I started to find it difficult to breathe, and was fearful that I would get some of the vomit in my mouth as it was already up my nose, so I quickly elongated my mouth into a funnel and breathed like I was underwater. It was impossible not to gag and dry retch.

Everybody in the car was screaming and yelling and the smell on that hot day was overwhelming. The car stank of rotten rancid sewerage as the vomit started to thicken and itch on my arms and legs. All I could do was drive and keep in my lane until there was somewhere after the bridge where I would jump in the sea and die.

Sitting in the back seat, Anna was in shock and was becoming more and more hysterical. She kept hitting Eddie on the back of the head and swearing at him in Norwegian. Throughout the chaos, I kept calm and prayed for help. "Dear God, please help me get out of this as I am going to die. I promise to give up cigarettes and swearing, really I will, just find me somewhere where I can pull up and stop," I muttered to myself as the screaming continued around me.

Just as I thought I was going to crash the car, I saw a sign saying "Garage". I could not believe my eyes! As soon as I got off the bridge, I drove into the station, jumped out of the car and ran for the hose.

Soon I had beautiful cool running water gushing all over my body. All the shit and grime and spew of the day were finally washed away. It was one of the best feelings I have ever had. Nobody at the garage said a word. It was if I was invisible and nobody wanted to know or perhaps they just did not want to have anything to do with the crazy woman, who stank like hell as they could smell from way over there.

Years later, sadly Anna passed away peacefully in her home after battling with uterine cancer for a few months. We all cried when we found out as we all loved her. She was so young and agile for her age, it was incredible to find out that she was even sick.

One morning while doing my early meditation I felt her come into my healing room. Looking up and opening my eyes I saw her standing in front of me, laughing in her funny way. "Remember the vomit, I am still angry with Eddie!" she laughed. I was so pleased to see her I had tears in my eyes. I smiled and asked her if she was okay. She went on to tell me that she was good now but she was still worrying about her family as she felt they were still coming to terms with her death. Before I could say anything more she disappeared as quickly as she had come.

When I am out in the garden I can often feel her presence as she loved flowers, nature and the fresh air. Coming from a farming background, these truly made her happy.

Sammy the spirit dog

Louise was a young, shy girl in her 20s who came for a reading one day. She had never been to anyone like me before but was curious though she had no idea what to expect. Most of my work is by referral, so I always know that whoever comes to see me always comes from a good source and the people who do come are open and interested in the work I do. I had met the lady who referred Louise to me. I remembered her name, but could not recollect her in my mind. I see so many people that it is hard to remember who everyone is. I also very seldom remember anything I say as all of the information is channelled or given by spirit.

Inviting her into my office, I quickly made her a cup of tea, excused myself and rushed off to the toilet. I had been working all day and I hadn't even given myself time to eat anything or get ready. As I sat down, I quickly began to tune into her energy and a spirit dog came in and telepathically told me his name was Sammy.

Here we go, I thought, I am going to have a dog as the communicator today.

The one thing I love about this work is that there is never a dull moment and you never know what is going to happen. Spirit just keeps you on your toes and a medium's work is never dull and always a learning experience.

When I finally came out and entered the room I sat down, pushed the recording button and asked her straight out if she knew of a dog called Sammy.

"Why, yes," she replied, looking rather confused, not knowing what to say next or finding any words. "I had a dog called Sammy once, but he got lost and disappeared when I was a kid."

"Was he black and white, with a cream collar and did he lick you all over the face every time you sat and patted him," I asked, staring at the dog in spirit sitting right next to her, continued with the session and the messages. "You also have two brothers that use to play with him as well," I said as she nodded.

"Sammy, who is talking to me in my mind's eye, wants to let you know that one day on one of his early morning walks the reason he did not come back to you was, that there was an accident and he was run over. He was killed straight away. Somebody removed his body off the road and got rid of it. He didn't feel anything so don't get upset, he just wants to you to know that he loves you and he is fine. He comes to visit you all the time in spirit."

Louise started to cry, patting her eyes and nodding her head. "I always wondered what happened to him," she replied smiling sweetly, pausing and revisiting an old memory way back in her mind. "Thank you for that. I have always wanted to know what happened to him as it has always been worrying me my whole life. I've never understood until now."

"Wait, there is more," I went on, as her maternal grandmother had come in and she took over the session with some messages. The old lady in spirit told me about Louise's past bad marriage and the terrible relationship she was in at the moment. Her first husband had betrayed her and she had lost all her confidence so now she was dating a lazy "Pom", who didn't want to have children with her and expected her to wait on him hand and foot.

She said her current boyfriend was "not the one and no good for her." She would be lonely for a while, but would meet another man in about a year's time. She just had to have patience and believe in herself more, as she did before she met her ex-husband. I also saw her moving to a beautiful place by a large river or inland lake where she would be much happier there and her life more in order.

Her spiritual lessons had not been easy, and because she had not listened to her intuition she had been through years of learning things the hard way. I did a healing on her and cut the ties with her husband so she could move on energetically. She felt relieved and was ready to forgive both her ex and current partner, and felt she now had the clarity and insight to move on with her life.

As Louise walked out the door, her whole energy field looked lighter as if she felt she had a new lease on life. Thanking me, she gave me a hug and promised that she would start to get herself together. She no longer felt alone, and was happy she knew her grandmother and dog were together in spirit. As far as she was concerned, things were finally looking up as she now had heaven's help. Louise was ready to accept that help and through her prayers would always be assisted in her life. All she had to do was just ask.

Kylie's story

Kylie was a good-natured, gentle woman in her early 30s, who was happily married to her childhood sweetheart and soul-mate. They had known and been together since early school days and now had three girls. The family was about to move interstate as an opportunity came up with his family for a new beginning in another state.

It would mean a change in work for her husband and a chance for Kylie to study and get into the workforce as she felt stuck in her life and needed the family's support. This would open up a new chapter in their lives and offer wonderful opportunities for the growing family.

With all the change going on around her, Kylie felt it was time for her to try and get into contact with her late father who died under mysterious, unexplained conditions when he was only a small girl. She said she had so many unanswered questions that she needed answered before she could move on. The move had already been organised, but she was apprehensive and anxious about going as she disliked change and was still questioning her father's death.

She was also extremely concerned about her mother, who would miss her as since her father's death she had relied on Kylie for everything. She had to become the "man of the house" and felt responsible for the social welfare of not only her own family but also her mother.

Before she arrived I started to open up energetically to see if I could make contact with any spirits around her. Sometimes I will get names and bits and pieces of information that may help in the session. This can give me a much faster link with spirit. Each medium works in their own way, as we are all individuals. Some like to work with the police in solving murders, for example, while others may have an affinity with working with children who have passed over as they may have lost a child of their own.

I like to have an idea who I will be talking to in the session so I am better prepared and do all types of work if it is needed. I have done murders before, but I have found I am not strong enough to do this work full-time as it is emotionally draining and takes me days to get over. I have always admired the brave mediums that do this work. They should be commended.

As soon as I closed my eyes and tuned psychically into the energy around my client, a spirit man popped into the healing room, talking non-stop. "Stevie told me that he was a friend of Kylie's father's from the "good old days". By the way he spoke, I could see he was a very colourful character and made me chuckle. As we chatted, he told me that he and Kylie's father were both as bad as one another and were wild and woolly teenagers who were always up to no good and looking for trouble. Neither of them finished school, but hung out together and got into all types of mischief, included taking drugs and other socially unacceptable activities. They both spent time in jail, where they became involved with the wrong kind of people, sending them on a destructive path that lead to their downfall.

In my mind's eye, I could see that Stevie had dark, greasy messy hair with bald patches and was well into his 40s before he died. The more I looked at him the clearer he became, until he seemed to be standing in the room right in front of me. He was a bit rough around the edges. He had a few teeth missing and was covered in tattoos and dark patches all over his body. I started to smell cigarette smoke and alcohol and could tell he must have been a big smoker and drinker.

At first I was a bit frightened of his appearance, as he looked creepy and menacing, not someone I would normally associate with let alone take home to mother. After he materialised, he began to look so lifelike that it freaked me out because it seemed he was there in the flesh, looking at me with a big smile on his face. I have not had anything like that happen to me since I was a child when I often saw spirits walking around but did not understand what they wanted. They used to scare me but nobody else could see them. As I got older, my psychic vision seemed to fade as it scared me so much and I could only hear them talking. I have been told by my guides that this is part of my natural development as a medium.

After talking to him for a while I could see that he was a bit of a "softie" when he was alive as he had a gentle, caring personality. He certainly did not come across as sinister as he looked. If I was going to stereotype him I would have to say that he looked a bit like an old friendly bikie who had eaten too much acid in his heyday and had not looked after himself properly. If anything, the spirit man looked like he could do with a good scrub in a hot bath if he was still with us today.

I must admit I was taken aback and couldn't help but wonder what was going to happen next but that's what I love about this work. No session is ever the same and you never know who might appear as the spirit world is always full of surprises. Lucky for me, I have never come across anything too evil or weird that I could not handle. I have great trust in my guide and spirit helpers and know they would never send me anything like that. There are all types of spirits in the spirit world, from all types of walks in life, but we all have to die one day and cross over to get our healing as souls, so in reality we are all the same.

I was amazed at how clearly I could "see" and "hear" the spirit man. Sadly not all spirits in the spirit world are such good communicators. My work is made easier when I have a good clear contact with a spirit communicator and their messages are easier to understand.

He must have made an incredible effort to come through give evidence and have his say. It was pretty obvious to me this meeting was important for Kylie as I was getting so much help from the spirit world. Thanking him for giving me information that would help me with Kylie, I politely asked him to step back and to wait until Kylie arrived. When Kylie walked in the door I told her she had a friend of her dads waiting to talk to her in spirit.

At first Kylie just stood and stared wide-eyed, not knowing what to say or do next. She hesitated as if trying to take it all in and then sat herself on the opposite chair facing me. Clearing my throat, I sipped a glass of water, and continued talking, very aware of how uncomfortable she must have been feeling and trying my best to help her relax so it would all work really well for all of us.

I could see she was very shy and feeling a little bit confused as if she was trying to get her thoughts in order. Her mind seemed full of questions that she was dying to ask me. She was also probably wondering what was going to happen and if she would get the answers to the questios that she had carried with her for most of her life.

By the look on her face I could see she was feeling way out of her comfort zone but was beginning to get excited. After a few minutes her face lit up. "Steve … I know Steve. He was my dad's friend when he was growing up. Mum said they used to hang around together all the time, but I haven't seen him since I was a kid. I didn't even know he was dead!" she said.

"Well he is not of this world any longer and must have passed over to the spirit world without you knowing it. You will probably meet a lot of other spirit people today. You never know what is going to happen and you can never really control who is going to come in." I smiled from the other side of the table stroking one of my cats who had just joined me on the sofa.

She handed me some photos of her father, which I did not look at but laid them on the table in front of us. She told me the sad story of her childhood and how her father had disappeared and apparently killed himself. Kylie had never come to terms with his death and wanted evidence that he was safe in the spirit world. Her father's death had really upset her and she wanted clarity on what the real story was.

She could never understand why her father had done such a thing because he was so full of life and talked about wanting to do so many things. He had also told his daughter that he wanted to give up drugs as it was a waste of a life and he was desperate to go clean.

Even though Kylie's father drifted in and out of her life after he left her mother, Kylie tried to stay in contact with him. She always felt that things were never right but hoped one day he would come to his senses and sort his life out like he always said he would. After the news of his death, Kylie's young life was shattered. Years later she was still heart-broken and had come to me for closure. She had her own family now and was finding it hard to do anything in her life which meant change and making decisions. She put this all down to the fact that she had not made peace with her dad or had the chance to say goodbye. She wanted to know that her dad had found his peace, wherever that was.

As she spoke, I could feel another male energy coming more and more into the room and stand next to me. Without warning, my head became full of heavy and confused emotions. Asking the spirit to stand back, I began to hear a clear male voice in my ear who said his name was Markey. As soon as he said this, I could smell alcohol in the air. The spirit man told me that he was Kylie's father, which Kylie confirmed.

He then went on to describe to me his death, which I relayed word for word to Kylie who sat on the edge of her seat. He told me about the large amount of alcohol and drugs he had consumed before his death.

According to his story he got himself into so much trouble that there was no way in the world he could see a way out. He owed a large amount of money to some bad people who were after him so he decided the only way out was through his own death. This was later confirmed by Kylie who was told the same story by the police. He caught a taxi to the Gap, a notorious suicide area of high cliffs, and threw himself off. Markey said he could not remember the actual death itself but just waking up and finding himself in spirit.

After a slight pause, Kylie's father went on. "I didn't want to die, it was just an accident. If I wasn't so out of it at the time, I could maybe have thought of something else, some other way. I never meant to hurt you all. I am so sorry son. I was too out of control mate, too full of drugs and drink, you know what I mean? Please forgive me, Kylie."

Tears rolling down her face, Kylie sat and cried as she finally understood what had happened that day. Drying her eyes, she looked at me and spoke. "I thought that was the case," she said slowly.

Very gently, I went on with the rest of the messages Kylie's father wanted to say. "He is saying it was just an accident and it was not his intention to die. He was far too young. He was just way out of control and did not know what to do at the time. He keeps saying that he is sorry the way he made the family suffer. He still loves your mum and wants you to tell her so. The other woman at the time of his death was not his soul mate, because he had never stopped loving your mother. He never stopped loving all of you from the moment your mum told him to leave. He understands why she did it then. If he had his time over again, things would have been different. He is saying again that he is so sorry and he loves you."

Markey spoke about the time before his death when he and Kylie had gone camping together and had a really good time. It was the first time they had ever connected as father and daughter and he was really glad that this had happened before he died.

"Your dad also wants to say hello to your mum and sister and to let you know that he is not by himself. He is telling me he is with Stevie, his brother Paul and his grandfather Billy.

"Even though he argued with your mother and they separated he is saying he still loves her as well and that she was his soul mate, if she wants to believe it or not. It all went horribly wrong and he is sorry that he could not fix the relationship. He is saying he did the wrong thing with her as well and he is sorry. Can you tell your mother this as well?" I asked passing on the message.

He then went on to give me more information about what he thought of Kylie's mother's new boyfriend and messages for Kylie's sister, Edie.

As he drifted out, Kylie's grandfather came in as well and gave his approval that his wife, Kylie's grandmother, who was still alive, was happy in her new marriage. He must have been waiting patiently in line for his son to finish before he decided to come in and have his say.

He said that his wife had been lonely after he had passed away from a heart attack and was glad that she had met someone. She was a lot happier that she had somebody to look after her as she had never been alone before. The grandfather then went on to warn Kylie that the bad people his son had gotten involved with were still around and he was happy that she was moving interstate. He suggested that it had been a good idea to change their surname to give them a new start. Kylie agreed with this and said her mother had changed their surname because she was fearful of these people who walked on the dark side of life.

The session was starting to come to an end as I could feel the link becoming weaker and beginning to fade. It was starting to get harder to hear anything. After we had finished, Kylie went on to tell me about her childhood and the wonderful cherished memories. Even though her father had gotten mixed up in a bit of trouble, she still loved him and wished she could have done something to help him. Handing me the photo of her father, I nearly fell over backwards because staring back at me was a most handsome man with blue eyes and blond hair, in the prime of his life!

I could see by the photo that Markey certainly would have been a real charmer, a real ladies man, when he was alive. He may have looked like an angel, but in reality he was a bit of a devil. Looks can be so deceiving. The way he lived his life was quite contrary to what you would assume as he looked so sweet and innocent.

Kylie confirmed this, saying her father was always having affairs with other women and her mother had left him as she was sick of his bad behaviour. His love of the dark side and everything it had to offer was too much of a temptation for him as he could never say no to anything. This in turn unfortunately got him into a lot of trouble because it also attracted all the wrong people that go with that type of lifestyle. He also became heavily involved with drugs and was unable to get out of the vicious circle as he was so addicted. His daughter said he had tried to go straight on many occasions, but it never lasted for long.

As Kylie's father had said, it was an accident because in reality he did not want to die, like most suicides. Only in a very few circumstances has the spirit told me they definitely did not want to be here and that they knew exactly what they were doing. Most spirits I have spoken to have all said they really did not want to die, but they were confused and could not think properly because of some influence they could not deal with at the time of their death. Markey was in terrible trouble, and had "bad" people chasing him for a lot of money. According to him he owed too much money and had no way of paying any of it back as everything in his life had turned to what he called "shit" and everything was totally out of control. He went on to name a few names, which we decided wisely not to remember as I did not want to get involved myself. He also said he saw no other way out but to kill himself because of "what was going down". He didn't want to die but he could see no other way out of his mixed-up situation. It seemed a terrible waste of a life.

Kylie, still with tears in her eyes, just nodded and said she knew that everything that I was picking up was true, as there was a police investigation going on at the time that suggested this was the case, exactly as I had described it. The family thought it best not to do anything about the incident at the time, as they were scared to get involved because of the criminal element.

The last thing Kylie's mother wanted was to be dragged into a mess with her ex that she knew absolutely nothing about. After all, she was a single mother at the time battling to bring up two small children and the last thing she wanted was to get involved in a murder investigation. Markey's death and all the people who were involved remained a mystery and something Kylie had to live with most of her life. It must have been a great burden for her, as it would be for any young kid trying to grow up and not knowing what happened to her father. The police closed the case and nothing much more was done except putting it down to suicide.

With tears still flowing, Kylie thanked me for the session and said she was so happy to at last get in contact with her father and relieved that he was finally in a good place and that he loved her. She was thrilled that her dad now knew she was a mother and accepted the apology that was given to her.

Kylie's father had found peace in the spirit world. He had crossed over safely with his father, who had come to get him, and was surrounded by many people from his own family and soul group.

As she left, I wished Kylie all the best with her new life. She told me that she was excited now and no longer wanted to stay in Sydney. She couldn't wait to get home and tell her husband she was now ready to make the move interstate with his family. She now had the courage and the energy to do so.

The dark, painful shadow of sorrow and grief from the past that had hung over her head like a heavy veil had finally been lifted. She no longer had unanswered questions, or guilt that she couldn't help her dad. She also said that she no longer felt empty and was excited and looking forward to the move. She worried about her mother but she would have to cross that bridge when she came to it. She was now ready to move forward and make the most of her life. She no longer felt sad, and was relieved that her dad had moved on and was safe with his friends and family in spirit.

Part Three

Inspirational Section

How to create your own sacred space for meditation

Meditation is an important tool for our spiritual journey to use in opening our awareness. Not only does it help us focus, so we can do more, by pulling in our energies, it also helps us become much more calm and relaxed. It is a great help on the spiritual path.

Twenty minutes of meditation is equal to four hours of sleep, as we are working on the theta level, a higher vibrational frequency connecting us to our higher self, angels, and loving guides. The more we meditate, the more rewarding life becomes as it helps us go with the flow and not get caught up in all the small stuff. NOTHING is a problem when we learn to connect daily with the Divine Source.

Create a small space in your home just for meditation; a place which is yours, and that feels safe and secure where simply no one can interrupt you. Meditating at the same time each day makes for better results if we want to contact our guides; twice a day would be even better.

Creating your own altar

You can do this anywhere in your home. I have one in my healing room and office and one in my bedroom. Decorate a small table, windowsill or a bench with fresh flowers, pictures, statues, crystals, rocks, shells, feathers, icons, incense burner, candles, or whatever symbolises the divine to you. While you do this be aware on not creating too much clutter by having too many things. Be selective with what you chose. Ask your angels and guides to join you as you create this special and beautiful work of art. Add incense or essential oils for a special aroma when you meditate, if you like.

Harps and flutes also attract loving angels into your sacred space, but bells or any calm relaxing music will do. I have a picture of Jesus on all of my altars, an owl, various pictures of my own favourite masters and fresh flowers.

Creating a sacred space in nature

The bush, beach or a beautiful garden full of flowers and trees is an ideal place to connect to the divine source. Think of a place that is special to you. It may be a beach, a favourite part of the bush you may walk in or even by the side of a lake on a large rock. It may also be one of the most beautiful places in the world you can think of which is close and special to you. Once you have found this place, make a point of visiting it at least once a week as it is healing and you can call back all your power, or energy that has been stolen or given to other people during the time that you have been away.

Once you are here, ask for help from mother nature or the elemental kingdom, tiny nature spirits such as the undines, beautiful water spirits and graceful little creatures that live around rocky pools, winged beings called fairies, air spirits called sylphs who are full of ideas and inspiration, or the salamanders or fire spirits, and lastly the earth nature spirits called gnomes.

You won't believe how energised you feel once you have visited your sacred space and been re-generated.

I once had a friend who always found comfort near the water. Once a week on his days off, he would go and sit at his favourite "sacred" place to simply rest, reflect and contemplate. Whenever I asked him where it was he would just laugh it was a secret and other people were not welcomed!

Creating miracles with the way we think:
Create your own life

Have you ever wondered why things never go right for you? Do you feel stuck in your life? Can't get ahead, always broke and so on? Did you realise you can be your own enemy with the way you think?

Look at your thought patterns:
• I can't.
• I will try.
• Maybe tomorrow.
• I'm not good enough.
• Poor me.
• I've always been like this.
• It's not my fault
• Stop picking on me.
• I can't fit in
• It's not fair
• Why do I always have all the bad luck?

Don't ever let another negative thought enter your head again! They are destructive, dark programs, or old patterns, sabotaging anything that is good in your life. We picked these programs up from childhood. If you believe in miracles and would like to welcome more joy into your life, never ever let another negative thought enter your head again. By simply being aware, you can create more joy and happiness than you ever dreamed possible. Anyone can do it, it's free, and it's easy.

Make a promise to yourself that for the next week or so you will not feel guilty or put blame on yourself for wanting to change the way you live and feel by simply asserting with a positive instead of a negative. This should concern only yourself as you cannot change others. We all have free will and we all need to walk our own path. Why not give yourself a break and take personal responsibility for your own life.

Make a list by writing down every negative word, situation or bad experience you have had in your life up to this date.

Now burn this in a bowl.

When you have done this, bury the ashes in the garden and say a loving prayer, forgiving everything and anyone in your life that has given or caused you this hurtful or painful experience.

Put them in a bubble of love and send them love and healing.

It is now up to you to decide with love what you can and can't do, where you want to live, who you want to have in your life and so on.

Always remember it is simply "okay" to say no. We should all be able to drive our own cars our own way. It is easy to have the power to simply move on and create our own reality

Simple boundaries are always helpful and healthy. Find the power in the word NO.

Mending yourself spiritually
Affirmations

Affirmations are soul food

One of the most important keys for eliminating insecurities and establishing a habit of self-love is the use of affirmations. These really work, especially when done in the mirror so we can see our eyes, which are the windows of the soul. By simply expressing in words what we honestly want and who we want to be, through affirmations we can think ourselves healthier, wealthier, stronger, and more beautiful and more confident.

Try these exercises—whatever our heart desires.

I prefer to do these in the mirror as I look into my eyes which are the windows of my soul.
- "I am a beautiful person and I love you."
- "Every day in every way, I am happy, safe and secure."
- "I always attact loving, happy people who accept me for who I am."

- "I deserve the best always, thank you."
- "I always find myself in the right place at the right time to receive golden opportunities. Golden opportunities come to me always"
- "I see joy and love in everything around me"
- "I now forgive everyone and anything that has ever hurt me"
- "I am always protected and safe with my angels and guides around me"
- "I am always drawn to the right energy people that are on my wave length"
- "I am eternally blessed and thank the God force for all the blessings I have in my life now"

Soon these will become a part of your belief system, and nobody can ever take your belief system away from you ever again as you own it.

Write a letter to the universe

Another effective way to reinforce your affirmations is by writing them down. Address them to God, the Universe, or your angels or spirit guides, whoever you want. Then you may wish to place your request in a "Jesus Box", "Guardian Angel Box" or a "Universal Box" dedicated to the light being of choice. This symbolises surrender and trust that your manifestation is now a reality. By making a commitment, it becomes even stronger. It is an investment in you.

Tithing (energy exchange)

Sharing and giving back to the universe is always a reward. We must remember our friends, our loved ones, and people who aren't as fortunate as us. Caring and sharing brings many spiritual rewards, and it is good karma. What we give back will always come back tenfold. Perhaps you can start to share things in your life you no longer need, make a date with a friend who needs comfort and support or give a small part of your earnings to a charity that needs the help. Whatever you decide is totally up to you. Just be willing to care and share.

Visualise what you want

This is a powerful way to manifest and opens up the creative canvas of your mind and imagination.

Sit quietly, in a comfortable position.

Breathe deeply three times while letting go of any negativity, or disappointment you may be holding in your belief system or mind.

Think of something that you want very much, so long as it is good for your Higher Self.

As you concentrate on what it is that you really want, think of a really happy emotion, holding it in your mind's eye very clearly and precisely.

Now visualise what you want as if it is happening now, holding that happy and good emotion.

Hold this vision for three minutes. You can do this as many times as you like, until you have the desired effect.

Create your own story ... (Be the star of your own show!)

Be the author, star and creator of your dreams. For this, you need to write a story of at least one or two pages long in the present tense about your dream situation. This is how you want your life to be. This simple exercise teaches us about living in the NOW but also helps us see ourselves in the future.

Be careful what you ask for.

Nowadays, with the new energies coming through, and the way energy is moving rapidly to the 5th dimension, you will notice your manifestations happening almost instantaneously, even more reason to ensure that your thoughts are always positive. It is so important to watch our thought patterns. Meditation will help you raise your vibration, keep you grounded and focused and stop you feeling miserable and uncomfortable in your mind and body, through the changes.

Remember at all times to keep your dreams alive and real and not to fall into the pit of helplessness or negativity and old worn out patterns that never got you anywhere anyway. Of course, some dreams will take a bit more time to manifest, as this is only logical as if things were too easy, it would not be so exciting. Nevertheless, you might be pleasantly surprised with what you end up with.

Why not make the world you live in a better place! The world is your oyster if you let it happen.

People often ask me how to manifest things and whether I have any meditations or techniques that are good and actually work.

As I am a great believer in the power of suggestion and visualisation I have plenty of little meditations to share.

I really believe you have to make things happen for yourself. Nobody else is going to do it for you. You are in control of your own destiny and reality.

Years ago I did a workshop with some really great women and we sat and meditated all weekend. One of the meditations that we worked on was called the "Creation Room", which I have used on numerous occasions when I needed something of importance, in my life.

The Creation Room

Sit in a comfortable position.

Gently close your eyes and relax your body.

Take three deep breaths, letting go of any negativity, heaviness or blockages from your body.

Visualise a golden light of love and pure energy radiating around your whole body, making you feel safe, protected, and secure.

See roots or plants coming out of the bottom of your feet and slowly travelling down to the earth star and anchoring your energy there.

Now slowly raising your consciousness and breathing steadily, visualise your energy coming up to a beautiful red colour, then orange, yellow, slowly up to green, to aqua blue, indigo and finally purple, then finally up to the transpersonal point (gold) and feel all your energy points in alignment.

Now imagine you have come to a solid white door, which you slowly open and begin to walk down 12 stairs, counting as you go.

1, 2, 3, 4, 5, 6, 7, 8, 9, 10, 11, 12.

As you reach the bottom step, you now move forward to a long corridor of beautiful golden and purple light, until you come to a large white room, which is a portal of sheer light.

This is your creation room.

As you step into the room, you are welcomed by your own loving guide, who greets you with loving arms.

Feel the love and warmth as you connect with this great loving being. Your guide is here to work with you.

Your loving spirit guide will not only offer you assistance, but love and encouragement as well.

Now it is time have some fun and to decorate your creation room.

Using your incredible imagination, see how creative you really are.

Make this portal of light, whatever size you would like it to be, so long as it is comfortable for you.

Remember to leave the far wall open for the Christ energy and any healing angels, guides, nature and animal spirits to come in as well.

For example, you could colour the walls a soft calming green, a beautiful pink, or a vibrant turquoise or blue.

Add windows that allow you a view of water, clear and calming, or a beautiful lush forest to add power to your healing. There is no limit to what you can do.

Piece by piece decorate your room with your vision of artwork, plants, candles, flowers and other décor you really love.

Don't forget maybe a rug on the floor. The more details and personal touches you give to your room the more real it will seem to you.

Take your time, and make it just perfect for you.

Near the open wall create a large screen with neon light all around it. This is your screen of life.

Next to it stands a clear quartz crystal table. On the table is a large quartz dimensional plug which is connected to the screen of life where you can now manifest your heart's desire by typing in what you want on your computer.

Sit down and write your script but be careful what you ask for.

When you are writing what you want, think of an event that brings up happy emotions to make it even more powerful).

When you have finished the lights around the screen are activated and flash brightly, recording and sending out to the universe your dreams, making them a reality.

After you have finished your script, it is time to visit the healing chamber which is on the right side of your desk. This looks like a simple stained glass shower. Step inside and simply press the green button on the wall.

Now see and feel pure healing loving energy swirling all around you, going deep into your skin and cells.

Now it goes into your mouth, nose, and throat, down into your bloodstream, your lungs, and into all systems of your body, even the skeletal.

Finally, it makes its way into your DNA or blueprint, which holds the memory of your life as an immortal soul.

Feel this pure white energy penetrate your mind and body, entering deep inside you so you feel the beautiful rays cleansing your body, mind, soul and spirit.

When you have finished your healing, simply step out of the chamber. Now feel, how truly wonderful you feel.

Now it is time to leave your creation room, but before you do, your guide points out to you the time travel machine which sits on the other side of the room.

This machine looks like a silver round dome that you just sit inside and can only be used by you.

You can use it to visit anyone, anytime, or simply travel to where you want to go next time you want to come and visit your room.

In a moment I will count to one to ten.

When I have done this, you will awaken and come back into the room.

1, 2, 3, 4, 5, 6, 7, 8, 9,10.

You will awaken, awaken and come back, back into the room.

Meditation to work with your animal spirit guide

When I regress clients down to meet their spiritual guide in a sacred space or garden, I often encourage them to call upon their own animal or bird spirit guide. Once I have called over the loved ones in spirit, the guides and angels, I always ask if they would also like to meet their animal spirit guide as well.

According to shamanistic healing, each animal or bird is a medicine to heal and help us in every way. They are each part of creation and have a distinctive and valid place in the medicine wheel of all that is. These teachings have been handed down by the elders in many indigenous societies.

My own master guide, White Feather, a proud and loving being I work with, has shown me my eagle and owl. Where I live, I am surrounded by owls in the bush, and have a collection of them in all shapes and sizes in my healing office and bedroom. Through meditation we can all learn about our animal guides and get to know them and feel their love. I also love cats and have had many throughout my life. I find that I always have a very strong psychic link with cats, and I can understand them quite easily.

Meditation

Sit in a comfortable position.

Breathing gently in through your nose and out from your mouth, feel all the tension from your body starting to melt away.

Feel your whole body relax, from your head, down your neck, shoulders, arms, abdomen, legs and calves down to your toes.

After you have done this, gently breathe in for the count of four, hold for a count of four, and breathe out for a count of four.

Continue doing this until it becomes easy and natural. This will help you release any further tension, blockages or negative energy you may have stored in your body.

Now feel the earth's energy coming up from the Earth Star directly beneath you, bringing grounding, cleansing and powerful energy up to the base chakra, spleen, solar plexus, heart, throat, third eye, crown, and finally up to the transpersonal point, the energy point just above your crown chakra.

Now feel all your chakras are in complete alignment, like a tight string or bow, at the transpersonal point above your head.

Breathe in and relax.

Now very slowly begin to gently to expand your energy outside the body, pushing any negativity or heaviness out into the universe for healing and transmutation.

When you are ready, bring your energy back and begin to feel it filling inside your heart chakra.

Once you have done this, the energy expands again, until it surrounds you like a cocoon, with pure unconditional love.

Feel the love and warmth wrapping all around you.

As you do this, imagine in your mind's eye it is a warm summer's day and you are walking in a beautiful forest.

It is a perfect day and you have not a worry in the world.

As you slowly make your way through the tall trees and forest you begin to smell the fresh green of the nature all around you.

You feel relaxed and happy and at one with all the beauty from nature that is all around you.

As you relax and continue on your journey, all your senses begin to now open up.

You now can hear the sharp crunching of twigs and leaves under your feet as you walk further and further into the forest.

The air feels fresh and incredibly crisp, and as you breathe it in you can feel it clearing your nostrils and mind.

As you continue even more, you begin to hear the many sounds and varieties of birds, and insects that are all around you.

You now see and hear the call of many birds flying through the forest. As you look around you are surrounded by a canopy of thick beautiful trees.

Soon you come across a clearing that opens up into a beautiful meadow full of many different colours of wildflowers.

Sitting yourself down on the soft grass, you lie down on the ground and feel the warm earth under your body.

The gentle sun shines down filling you with warmth and sunshine.

As you do so you begin to feel even more and more relaxed but your senses are beginning to become sharper. Your mind is relaxed, but alert. Count down, 1, 2, 3, 4, 5, 6, 7, 8, 9, 10.

You now take another deep breath, and you feel completely calm and in control.

In your mind's eye you ask spirit to show you an animal totem that protects you in your daily life.

Your mind now fills the most incredible pictures of many animals, birds, insects and reptiles of all shapes and sizes. They seemed to have been buried in your mind for a very long time.

You study them in great detail as they are all so finely crafted and drawn perfectly in your mind's eye.

The animal or bird or insect that now comes forward is your own spirit guide.

You now feel recognition and a great knowing that is all-consuming and loving.

Know now that this is your power animal. It is an ancient shamanic symbol and its essence and strength will remain with you, even when you are asleep or not aware of it. It will stay with you to help you feel protected and secure as you further develop your psychic skills, and it will help you on your life's journey.

Know that you can call on your power animal for help at any time.
Know that you will always have a deep love connection and bond till you pass into the next life and beyond.
Know that again, that love is eternal.
When you are ready, come back into the room.

Creating a mandala

I sat within a meditation circle of women once a week for over ten years. Many of these wise women were older than me and most had been to see Sai Baba in India. They were a funny lot as they were very conservative in their way, but every single one of them was an old soul and extremely spiritual. I learnt a lot from that group of souls and even though we have all moved on as most of the dear ladies are now living in spirit, I still think of them and thank them for who I am today and what I have learnt.

The group leader, Sharon, a talented astrologer, suggested we make ourselves a mandala once a year, and show it to the class so we could discuss where we were at. I thought it was a splendid idea, and each different drawing I made helped me see where I was heading spiritually and was a beautiful piece of art to collect.

How to make a mandala

A mandala is a Sanskrit word that means circle. Mandalas are symbols of the universe and its energy. Tibetan monks create the archetypal templates to remind us of the cycle of life and death. A mandala has many layers of meaning, be it a cosmic diagram or support for meditation.

We are challenged to express ourselves and see beyond our own definition of art, with its values of innovation.

You can create a personal mandala to reflect on your own life, using colour as your medium and the four elements of nature:

Water: the undine elemental, symbolising love and trust,

Earth: the earth elementals—for introspection and transformation,

Fire: the salamander elementals—to illuminate and clarify, and air for knowledge and wisdom.

Air: the domain of the sylphs, for ideas and inspiration.

With clear intention, we will create an expression of ourselves that will be a reflection of our hopes, dreams and how we see ourselves on a spiritual, mental, physical and emotional level, both now and in the upcoming year.

Drawing and creating your own mandala

Find a quiet place, light a scented candle and play soothing, calming music.

Make yourself as comfortable as possible.

As you prepare and centre yourself, draw a large circle on a sheet of paper.

Using coloured pencils or other materials draw and colour your own symbols or design inside the circle, keeping your thoughts relaxed and happy.

Express yourself and whatever else emerges by just drawing and colouring.

Take your time, do not rush.

Let your imagination flow, and enjoy yourself.

When you have finished, get somebody else to look at it and see what their impression is and what they get out of it.

You will be surprised on how much information comes up about yourself that you may not even be aware of. It is always incredible to see how spirit can work through us. Every year, I draw a mandala and use it as a tool to guide me with my work, and as inspiration to remind me of who I am as a soul. A mandala can also be used with the spring, summer, autumn and winter solstices of each season.

Three examples of mandalas

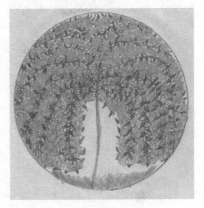

3

The first example was done by an actress. She is a very passionate person and her spirituality is very special to her. Most creative people I have met throughout my life are very psychic and love to express their individuality on the stage of life.

The second mandala was done by a student who makes an effort to create, peace, love, harmony and abundance in her life as these aspects and themes are very important to her. She is a delightful, free spirited individual, who is very grounded and full of joy. She works as a carer and does this with love and compassion. She is a true light worker.

The third mandala is by a woman whose main focus this year is on love and fulfilment of her emotional desires. In her drawing she has the deity Ganesh which signifies change, joy and abundance. The yellow circles are the seven archangels, which are above and below. The pyramid signifies her focus on spirituality. She knows exactly what she is looking for in life and is determined to live her life as she dreams.

This lady works as a fraud investigator and is top of her field.

Why not draw your own mandala and see what you come up with. You may be surprised at the artwork that you create, as it may show you your own inner beauty, light and reflection.

Commonly asked questions

Most people are very curious about the work a medium does and I am always open to helping them understand that our guides are always with us bringing love and support from the spirit world. Our loved ones are always with us in spirit too. Here are common questions that I'm asked on a daily basis.

Are you able to see spirits?

When I was younger I was able to see spirit very clearly as if they were standing in the room. I had no idea what was going on and thought everybody else around me could see and hear the spirit people as well. I soon learnt that this was not the case, so kept my gift a secret as not to be tormented or ridiculed.

Now I see spirit more in my mind's eye and have clear hearing. I am what one would call clairaudient, which means clear hearing. My ear chakras are very open and sensitive and it is easy for me to hear spirits talking, just as if I was speaking on a telephone. Occasionally, the line or link may be fuzzy and I have problems hearing the names. I am also able to have long conversations with my teaching guides through meditation, which is very helpful.

Through my other senses I can feel emotions from the spirit and it is easy for me to know what type of person they were. I have a very strong ability with smell and am often accused of having a sensitive nose, which can be a disadvantage at times.

How can I clear my house of unwanted spirits?

The first thing is to remember is that spirit cannot hurt you but fear can. In most cases the unwanted visitor is more scared of you and may be asking who are these people in my home. These are what we call earth-bound spirits. They did not cross over when they died. I suggest you buy some dried sage and burn it, using the smoke to go around your house.

When you have finished, open up all the windows so you don't suffocate yourself and your family. This will weaken the unwanted spirit and usually they will pack up and leave as they cannot stand the smell. I always suggest doing this for seven days religiously as you will have excellent results.

All you need is some sage, or grandfather sage, which is my favourite. I have also used Australian gum leaves. All you do is place the leaves in a fireproof bowl, light them and smoke the place out. Easy as! Not only will it weaken the unwanted spirit, but it will get rid of any negative energy as well that may have collected in your home. Also make it a practice to open your windows up and have fresh air in your house and let the sunlight in.

If you feel confident light a candle and ask the spirit to go into the light which, in your mind's eye, you bring down in a corner of the home. Be very firm: ask them to open their eyes, tell them they are dead and they need to go home because their loved ones are waiting for them. Their spirit guide will help with this as well as your own. You can ask Archangel Michael to come and assist you as he loves to do this work.

If this does not work the spirit may not want to leave because they are either afraid or they were there first, so you need to consult a professional medium to send the spirit off to the light. I also make up a mixture of grandfather sage, garlic and olive oil and mix it up in an old jar. This looks and smells like something you would put on your roast lamb. Place a few drops on top of all entrances to the house. This will also stop unwanted spirits from coming back in as it seals the home.

For my own home I visualise a grid of white light and place it on the front door. This also stops negative people and unwanted spirits from coming in my home. I re-activate this once a week.

Is it possible to have spirit animals around me and what do they mean?

We all have a master guide, a guardian angel and totem spirit animals or birds around us. In shamanistic healing, each animal or bird is a medicine here to heal and help us in every way. They are each part of creation and have a distinct and valid place in the medicine wheel of all that is. These teachings have been handed down by the elders in many indigenous societies.

I have always been attracted to the indigenous people of the world and have past lives in America as a Native American Indian. I regularly sit in a drumming group and have a vast collection of indigenous artefacts from Australia and overseas. I try as much as possible to spend time or visit in parts of the world which has this energy as I feel I am one with it.

My master guide, White Feather, has shown me my Eagle and my Owl. I have been fascinated by these creatures for a very long time. Of a night, when I am sleeping, I often hear them calling in the night. Through meditation we can all learn about our animal guides and get to know them and feel their love. For more on these, there are many wonderful books written on this subject.

Why do people treat me badly?

My ex brother-in-law Egil asked me this when he was visiting from Norway. I said I wish I knew because I have attracted some not very nice people as my weakness has always been my kindness. Once I feel sorry for someone, I want to rescue them or help them and go out of my way to do everything possible to completely piss them off so they will get so angry they can't stand the sight of me any longer.

When you continually helping someone, you are actually robbing them of their power and they in turn don't learn their lesson. They don't even like being helped, as it feels as if you're taking their own power away from them. To help someone over and over again is not a good thing for everyone involved. I don't know how many times I have done this and it is not easy to stop as it is a bad habit. Just trust your intuition.

Every time I stop listening to my guides, I get into major trouble. I end up feeling like a big stick is hitting me on the head saying, I told you so.

All of us radiate energy, rather like telephone poles. If you have a bad feeling about something or someone, TRUST it as it is always correct. Your first impression is usually the best, after that it gets muddled. We are here on the planet, as on a big stage, learning our lessons and dealing with all our spiritual contracts that we made before we came here.

Why is it that people who do terrible things always get away with it?

Is that really true? I don't think so. It might look like it but in reality they don't. What you give out comes back to you. It is called the LAW OF KARMA. What goes around comes around. It is also about taking personal responsibility for everything that happens in your life. You are the master of your destiny. So get out of the victim role and just move on.

When I lived in Norway, my best girlfriends Gunn and Eileen asked me if I wanted to go to the Molde jazz festival which was many kilometres away, a musical event that is held every year. I was excited to go but was worried about my new kitten that I had found.

A friend said she would look after it so I had no need to worry. While we were at the festival, people I knew stole some food from a shop which we made into a big banquet. I couldn't stop thinking how wrong it was, even though I thoroughly enjoyed the delicious, expensive food.

I had never stolen anything in my life before this and, as a rule; I do not like that kind of thing. I kept thinking something bad was going to happen because I felt really paranoid how I had been involved in the theft. I wanted to go and pay the man in shop but was too scared to because it might involve the police.

My girlfriends told me to shut up and not be so ridiculous but I kept getting the feeling that something bad was going to happen anyway and it would not go away no matter how hard I tried to suppress it. When I got back to town I went to pick up my kitten but was told it was run over. It had escaped from my friend's house and disappeared. They had been calling it for days and eventually found it on the side of the road dead.

Standing over the little grave they had made for it, tears of grief ran down my face. As usual, my feeling had been correct. Why it happened I cannot tell you but I have never been involved with anything like that again.

What is the difference between a twin soul and a soulmate?

How silver-sweet sound lovers' tongues by night, like softest music to attending ears.

William Shakespeare

Soul mates have a different spiritual lineage to you. They come in to help you progress as a soul as they help you with your spiritual development. Once you have met your soul mate you usually have a very happy relationship based on trust, unconditional love and companionship. You both will harmonise and balance your energies and this will stimulate your growth as a spiritual being.

Susan and Mark have been married for almost 27 years and love each other deeply. While they are very different from one another, this seems to keep them together as they find it easy to communicate in a loving way, have great respect for each other's space, know that they are there for each other, and although are often busy with their own interests they take the time to do things together.

Twin souls, on the other hand, have a completely different relationship to this vibration. People who are interested in meeting their twin soul should be aware that these types of relationships can be turbulent because of patterns established during previous incarnations which need to be resolved. Twin soul relationships are generally very difficult as there is too much friction and similarity between the two that causes spiritual growth to stagnate. At the same time, they can also be very healing because working through the conflicts can bring unconditional love.

Isabella was an herbalist who was madly in love with Adam. They shared the same interests and loved each other passionately. Everything was fine until they fought over Adam's commitment issues. It started off with him not being able to sleep in the same bed as her because of an important job he had to go to the next day. He complained that her energy kept him awake so he couldn't sleep properly.

He also had no interests in her long-term friends or in having children and wanted nothing to do with the work she did but was constantly giving her advice on her business. It would take days to get over their terrible fights as both were so badly wounded that they found it difficult to trust each other.

Each time this happened, Isabella became more and more despondent and began to realise that Adam had major issues he either could not or would not discuss with her. Adam, in turn, felt the same way and both of them were left frustrated and angry all the time, not able to make any type of commitment to each other. One minute Isabella could be completely loving and understanding and then she would withdraw from him and not let him do anything for her. In the end, because of their differences, they couldn't live together but also couldn't live without each other.

They both loved each other passionately yet found it really difficult to work through the issues that were continually coming up for them. Unfortunately, they ended up moving away from each other and never saw each other again.

No matter what way you look at it, in my opinion, twin soul relationships are difficult. If you are able to work out your differences and spiritual contracts, good luck.

I have been in a twin soul relationship and also found it difficult at the time. Even though we loved each other dearly, nothing ever worked out and it was just too hard to stay together. An elderly and very wise psychic woman once gave me some very good advice. "If your armour isn't made out of steel, run the other way before you get too involved!"

What happens to you when you die?

When I had my NDE (near death experience) I was only 21 years old. I was on holiday on an island in Greece with my girlfriend and, during a night out someone gave me a substance by mistake which nearly killed me. Beware of strangers bearing gifts! Before I had time to even think, everything around me began to swirl and I remember collapsing and falling to the ground. Having no control I felt myself being pulled and ripped out of my body at an incredible rate. I was blasted like a rocket speeding uncontrollably into space. Time seemed to stand still as everything was dark around me until I was miraculously surrounded by hundreds of lights in the night sky.

The whole experience felt surreal and I knew that I was out of my body as I felt so light and free. I had no idea what was happening, except that I now had images of Jesus and John the Baptist in my head. My mind was racing so fast it was impossible to think as everything around me felt like it was exploding into pure energy.

I felt exhilarated and excited and I had no idea where I was going except the voice inside of me kept telling me that it would soon be all right. It felt like I was being pulled at an incredible rate into some type of vast and incredible consciousness that had no ending. Suddenly, I felt a painful bang inside my body and I was lying in a street surrounded by a sea of strange faces staring down at me. My girlfriend Gunn was at my side, crying and screaming out my name.

Confused and shaken, I was slowly helped up and don't remember the rest except that I couldn't help wondering what John the Baptist and Jesus were doing. I woke up next day in my hotel room with an incredible headache and aching all over. My girlfriend later told me that I had been unconscious and that I had stopped breathing.

Other people have gone further than me and seen the light. I know now from my own experience that when you die, you go straight out of your body at a very fast rate until you are met by your guide and taken over to the other side which is similar to earth but a vast consciousness of colour and love.

When I had my Life Between Lives session, and did training with the Michael Newton Institute I was met by my guide and taken to the spirit hospital, the library where I downloaded much information, and many other places. I have written a whole chapter of this in my book about the afterlife. When I trained with the Michael Newton Institute it helped me understand a lot about what had happened on that night so long ago.

When Cousin Jan died, my mother decided that we should all go to her funeral. My brother would drive my parents up to Sydney, pick me up, and then we would drive up the coast and collect my sister who lived another five hours away. It would be a family get-together with a picnic in between.

I had just finished a course in the Blue Mountains, and they were arriving at 2am to pick me up so we could make our way up the coast. The funeral was mid morning at Crescent Head so we had plenty of time to get there.

Jan, my dear sweet cousin, was only 50 when she died from a melanoma. The cancer was so relentless and aggressive that it killed her in a very short time. We were shocked this could happen to someone who was rarely in the sun because her skin was so fair. We were all very upset and wanted to show our love and support not only to Jan on her day, but to her grieving family as well.

Jan was a lovely quiet girl and we often played together when we were small, as we were the same age. We lost contact as we had gone our own ways and she lived in Sydney and I was down the South Coast.

As we sadly made our way on our long journey, we all reminisced about the good old days when we were younger and told family stories when Jan was still alive. I hadn't seen her for years so it was interesting for me to listen to what she had done with her life and how many children she ended up having.

We all agreed that it was extremely unfair and cruel and unkind that she should die so young and in such tragic circumstances.

When we arrived at the church it was a hot summer's day with not a cloud in the sky. Part of me was expecting lightning and thunder because it would have been a good backdrop for the tragedy that was unfolding as the day went along. The tiny country church was packed with people who must have known and loved her and there wasn't a dry eye at the service.

Sitting next to mum I found it almost impossible stop the tears when Jan's sister's daughter gave the eulogy. Mum and I must have gone through a whole packet of tissues and were crying so loudly that we ended up breathless and exhausted, hysterically gulping for breath. I must have looked a wreck as all my black mascara and kohl was running off my eyes and onto my face and I looked like a wounded warrior. I ended up having red lipstick and black grease all over my face, clothes and arms.

After blowing my nose for the hundredth time, which was becoming redder and sorer by the second, and wiping the tears from my eyes, I looked up at the coffin for the first time. It was small and white and surrounded by beautiful exotic flowers spread all around it. At the foot of the coffin stood Jan, all dressed in white with a beautiful shining light all around her.

Choking back tears I couldn't believe my eyes and kept thinking it was my imagination, but she wouldn't go away and just stood there, very calmly, watching everything around her. She seemed years younger and her face looked different and her long black hair was flowing down her back. Different from the swollen and bald-headed corpse I imagined that was lying in her coffin. Just as I was about to turn away and tell mum what was happening I could hear Jan's voice very loudly in my head. "Tell Mum not to worry and that I am okay. Let the kids know that I love them."

Then she went on even further. "I am here with Dad and Becky (her sister who had died many years before) is here as well." Then as soon as she had said those last words she disappeared into thin air.

Turning to mum I wiped my eyes and breathed a sigh of relief. "You are never going to believe this! I just saw Jan standing next to the coffin and she looked years younger and was all dressed in white."

"What did you say?" asked my mother said drying her eyes and blowing her nose as she turned to look me directly in the face.

"I said I just saw Jan standing next to her coffin."

After a moment of silence she moved closer and whispered into my ear. "That's nice. Before she goes, can you ask you who's next?"

Often when I go to funerals I will see the person who has died standing next to their coffin, watching everything that goes on at the service. Spirits love to attend their own funeral as it is the final goodbye before they cross over.

When I attended my friend Peter's funeral, the same thing happened. Peter and I used to play in a band in the 80s called The Sunday Painters. When you play in a band it takes over your whole life, just like you are married. He was a gifted poet and musician and I was the bass player in the band. We were the main songwriters for a time and used to thrash out ideas and spend a considerable amount of time in each other's company sharing ideas, writing songs and playing music together. It was a glorious time.

We eventually hired a studio, with another guy called Peter, who was in the band and reordered most of the material we had worked on over the last year. He changed one of the songs we had written together without my permission so I became angry and upset and decided to leave the band before the rest of the album was even finished. We had already put down quite a few songs in the studio for the LP and we had finished the single. I didn't care anymore and had lost all interest, so I decided then and there that I had had enough and wanted out.

It wasn't a problem for Peter because he hired another bass player to take my place and the rest is history. I later found out that a lot of people could not understand why I would walk out in the middle of recording an album but it is something that one cannot explain. I was young and restless and just wanted to move on to do other things. I was seriously into acting at the time, and most of my time was spent writing scripts for my course I was trying to finish at university.

Years later I received a phone call from his ex-wife telling me that he had died suddenly in his sleep. Sadly I had lost contact with him over the years as we had other interests and had gone our own way, but the memory of our time together was still fresh in my mind like it was yesterday. As I walked into the funeral home after my drive down from Sydney, I could hear music from the album we had made so long ago coming out of the loudspeakers. Suddenly, *Something to Do*, the song we had argued about so many years ago, came over the loudspeakers and I could hear Peter's wonderful voice booming out triumphantly.

Laughing out loudly, I couldn't believe my ears so I just stood still and clapped my hands. Anybody else who may have been watching might have thought that I was mad with grief. I couldn't help but feel that this was his way for revenge and he was playing an enormous joke on me.

Closing my eyes, tears started to pour down my face, and I smiled and laughed gently to myself and told him in my mind that I missed him and would always remember the great times we had together. When I had finished speaking to him, I walked over to his coffin and there he was standing next to his beloved guitar. He was much skinner than when I had last seen him but looked exactly the same as when we were in our late 20s. He had on his tiny little blue jeans and with his black belt and a white shirt, exactly how he used to dress when I first knew him.

After I got over my shock I realised that this was his way of having a go at me and telling me that we would always be mates. Later on at the wake I walked over and gave his mother my condolences. At first she didn't recognise me as I hadn't seen her in years, then taking a closer look, she wrapped her arms around me lovingly and apologised for not recognising me as I was all grown up.

Next time you go to somebody's funeral, remember to open up all your senses and you may well witness and feel the person you have lost standing at the foot of their coffin in spirit.

Why do children we love so much have to die?

It is absolutely heartbreaking to lose a child and a terrible tragedy for the parents left behind. They go through so much torment, grief and guilt and later may be overwhelmed with thoughts of what else they could have done. The death of a child is something a parent never really gets over and has to live with forever.

My own parents-in-law lost a son, who was a brilliant doctor, to a brain tumour. With his wife, who is also a doctor, they nursed him lovingly until the end so he could stay at home as he wanted. It has been many years since he has passed over but there is not a day that goes by that they do not think of him. His mother now does volunteer work at the children's hospital. She goes and works daily with children who have a terminal illness. I do not know how she does this other than to say that she is a true earth angel, because the love she gives those dear little souls is unconditional. The work she does has helped her move on in her own life. I could never do this type of work myself and when I was a registered nurse I refused to work on the children's ward as it used to upset me too much.

On a spiritual level I have asked my guides this time and time again as it all seems so unfair. I am told it is because they chose this contract as souls before they come down to earth for the experience and spiritual learning.

When I am doing a reading and someone has told me they have had a miscarriage, it is usually the same soul that comes back again to be born again the next time. Often, if they do not come through with the mother in this life, they will later come back through the family.

I once had a client called Heather who lost a lovely little girl to cancer. When I got in contact with the spirit of the girl, she said she was coming back again because her mother was having another baby within two years. About a year later, Heather rang me and said she was pregnant. I told her when the baby is born, just look into its eyes and only you will know if this is the same soul. Within a year the lady had a healthy baby boy which was the same soul, but different sex. She was overjoyed.

How do I know that I am psychic and how do I develop it?

Most people have an inner knowing or sense about things because that is the way it was all intended to be. It is all about faith and trusting your inner knowing and wisdom. It is just that some people are more developed that others. Sitting in meditation groups can lift your vibration and can teach you many things but not everybody is meant to do the work professionally. I have met so many people who want to work as psychics and healers over the years, but never seem to make it perhaps because of their intention.

If they feel their life's plan or purpose is to help people, and they are sincere and compassionate, then the doors of success and prosperity will open as they will be driven to succeed. If they don't, perhaps they were meant to do other important things in their lives. Jealousy, resentment and deceit will never get you very far. The tall poppy syndrome is just a name some poor misguided soul just made up because they never made their lives what they wanted it to be.

I always am happy for people when they are successful as they are on the path they are meant to be. Perhaps their success comes from being passionate and excited about what they are doing. We are all given a great plan in life we are meant to work with from the divine or source before we are born, which is part of our spiritual contract. Once we are on this, our life becomes much easier and doors will open without much effort.

I always wanted to be an actor as I loved to dress up and pretend I was another person. No matter how hard I tried and how many doors I knocked on, none of the doors would open. I sadly realised after many years, this was not my path as in the end; it was just too hard. It may have been great in a past life, but not this one. It took me a long time to come to this thought but after I accepted my fate I never looked back.

Every morning when I open my eyes, I can't wait to start the day and just be part of life's never-ending journey, as whatever happens is just another exciting learning experience. I am so happy and humbled to be connected to the Great Spirit which reigns supreme in my heart.

Is there a devil and a hell?

Everybody can now relax because I am here to tell you that there is absolutely no devil or hell as this was just something invented by the church to control the masses. Sure, there are people around I would call dark souls and are not who they say they are. Their world is very dark and they will get their just desserts in the end, because what goes around come around. When you play with fire, you are always going to burn your hands.

Those wretched people that get involved with black magic, Satanism and the dark arts will always have problems with their emotional lives and their world will be very bleak and miserable, full of fear and angst.

Heaven is a beautiful name given to the place where we cross over when we die and leave our bodies. It is an incredible vast consciousness of light, lovely colours and space, just like the nature we have on earth but only brighter. It is just an arm's length away, but in another dimension. Once we get there we are met by our guide, the wise ones and other souls from our soul group. We don't eat or drink or do other earthly things as we are on another vibration and there is no longer the need. Heaven is connected to the source of all things which is pure love.

Why do you do this work?

My aim as a medium and energy worker is to work from my highest potential, as a channel for spirit, so that the client will receive the best possible healing and outcome. Most of the time, I do not even know what I am talking about because in reality I am just a channel of light, just passing on messages from guides and spirit people I don't usually know. It sometimes feels like I am at the other end of a telephone just listening to messages and watching pictures and images in my mind's eye.

On a personal level, I am indeed very passionate about my work as it is never dull and is a journey of spiritual learning and betterment for me as a person. It is also an honour and a privilege to work with team spirit, as life is never boring. The main thing for me is to just do the work, not worry about what other people may think of and just trust in the whole process. Perhaps this can be an inspiration to others on the path to enlightenment as we all do our best to make this world a better place. All we have to remember is that love is eternal and it never dies, it just keeps going.

Working for spirit is like an apprenticeship and not for the faint-hearted as it can be difficult. It takes years to fine-tune you with this work and is a continual journey of enlightenment. It also teaches you the ability to be humble and grateful for everything and everyone you meet in your life who remind you of who you are as an eternal soul. Remember, as souls we all chose to be here now to witness the earth's changes in its time of rapid growth. So why not make the most of this life? I dare you all to do so!

Kerrie Jean Erwin
Medium, clairvoyant and healer

Live Your Life To The Fullest

From an early age Kerrie was blessed with a special gift. Always concerned about the health and wellbeing of others, she began her working life in the health industry, and worked as a Registered Nurse in Australia and Norway. During this time, she witnessed the suffering of many whose loved ones had died and, as healing on every level has been her motivation in life, it was logical for Kerrie to assist others by using her gift of spiritual mediumship to help them connect with their loved ones on the other side.

Kerrie Erwin then became a professional psychic medium and now has many years of experience. She is currently performing around Sydney and Australia in the Rainbow Show, an educational program that teaches that spirit is always with us in our daily lives.

Connecting to our loved ones, who have passed over to the other side, our guides and angel helpers shows that we are never alone and that love is eternal. She also teaches metaphysics and is a trained hypnotherapist with the Michael Newton Institute in Life Between Lives and Dolores Cannon in past life regression.

Closely aligned to her healing work is a vibrant creative nature. Kerrie is trained in performing arts at the University of Wollongong, and has also worked professionally as an actor on stage, television and in the film industry for 22 years.

She also toured for Side Track theatre as an actor and musician all over NSW. She has played bass guitar in different bands, including a heavy metal band, in Australia and overseas. Kerrie shared her joy of the performing arts to teach others and has worked as a drama teacher in tertiary education.

Kerrie is also a highly sought-after writer and regularly contributes to publications. She has written several articles on the paranormal over the years for *Insight* magazine and *Woman's Day*. She also hosted a TV program, *Let's have a chat with Kerrie* on CTV-1 cable television.

Besides writing and performing, she also teaches metaphysics, vibrational medicine and is a trained hypnotherapist.

In writing this book, her second to date, Kerrie shares and gives us insight into what it is like to live her world and what it is like to work as a psychic medium.

"Being on the right path has brought me immense fulfilment and enlightenment. Healing on every level has been my key motivation in life. Hopefully, this book will give more insight into the life of an ordinary working suburban medium and the highs and lows of what it is really like in my world.

342

"May there be love, light and blessings to everyone on the planet. May we show gratitude and give a blessing to God every day for the little things that come our way, because they are all tiny bits and pieces, in the scheme of things."

www.pureview.com.au

Recommended reading

A World beyond Ruth Montgomery
Auras and Colours Paul Lambillion
Australian Bush Flower Essences Ian White
Creative Visualization Shakti Gawain
Custom Design your own Destiny Dr Bruce Goldberg
Destiny of Souls Dr Michael Newton
Edgar Cayce on Atlantis Edgar Cayce
Healing Lost Souls William J Baldwin, PHD
Life Between Lives Dr Michael Newton
My Life as a Medium Betty Shine
Shamanism Leo Rutherford
Soul Healing Dr Bruce Goldberg
Stephen Turoff: Psychic Surgeon Grant Solomon
The Australian Bush Flower Essences Ian White
The Twelve Healers Edward Bach
Vibrational Medicine Richard Gerber MD
Voices Doris Stokes